HOW TO FILE

AND

INDEX

By

BERTHA M. WEEKS

DIRECTOR, RECORD CONTROLS, INC., CHICAGO

REVISED EDITION

REVISED PRINTING

THE RONALD PRESS COMPANY ⟡ NEW YORK

Library of Congress Catalog Card Number: 51-13477

PRINTED IN THE UNITED STATES OF AMERICA

83369

PREFACE

The acceptance which the first edition of *How to File and Index* has everywhere received during the past fourteen years is a most gratifying evidence of success in the basic objective of the book—increasing filing efficiency by showing how to install and how to maintain a satisfactory filing system, and by explaining how the actual filing operations should be performed to meet the standards of the best practice.

This revised edition brings the working information in the book up to date in all respects. In addition the revision puts increased emphasis on problems of records management in the modern office. It should therefore be even more useful as a guide and working reference to those who plan and direct the clerical operations in offices, as well as the secretaries, stenographers, and other personnel interested in them, and to teachers and students of office methods and practice.

The author's presentation is a distillation of many years of varied experience in studying the records problems of all types of businesses, in reorganizing records systems, in giving courses of lectures planned for the training of file clerks, and in answering requests for information from firms needing aid in setting up their records so that they will operate smoothly. It is hoped that the results of this experience will continue to be of real benefit to those who do not have specialists available for consultation and must therefore work out solutions of their records difficulties for themselves.

The methods and procedures covered in the book are based on certain fundamental principles which have proved to be sound and which give the key to all filing problems. These principles are presented here definitely and simply. The value of a particular filing system in practice will depend

iii

upon how skilfully these principles are adapted to fit the service of all business departments and the requirements of efficient office management; every system must be tailor-made to the business if it is to function effectively. How to apply the principles to specific businesses is also covered in this book. It explains how to choose the most efficient labor-saving equipment, how to streamline operations, how to select and train the most competent personnel for filing. It shows how to analyze and reduce filing costs. And a profusion of illustrations and examples is given so as to show just how the various filing operations should be performed.

Grateful acknowledgment is made to the following, who have brought to this book a wealth of wisdom and familiarity with practical filing problems: the various equipment houses who have kindly furnished illustrations, specifications, and dimensions; Mr. A. R. Baar of Kixmiller, Baar and Morris; Miss Irene Warren, a pioneer in filing procedures; and Miss Dorothy Daggett and Mrs. Nina Riehle of the staff of Record Controls, Inc.

BERTHA M. WEEKS

Chicago, Illinois
July, 1951

CONTENTS

ILLUSTRATIONS

HOW TO FILE AND INDEX

Chapter 1

MODERN RECORDS ORGANIZED FOR USE

Filing is the systematic arrangement of records so that they may be quickly found again. Even the smallest office has files, whether they be comprised of correspondence, orders, bills, cards, catalogs, blueprints, clippings, bills of lading, tear sheets, electros, or checks. Government statistics show that the number of clerical and kindred workers has increased from 2,000 in 1870 to 7,600,000 in 1950. Since nearly every clerical worker is concerned with the making, processing, or handling of records, the foregoing figures give an indication of the growth in volume and kind of papers which are found in modern offices in recent years.

Modern Growth of Paper Work.—There are several reasons for this growth of paper work. One is mechanization. It is simple today to make many duplicate copies on modern office machinery. Other factors are also responsible, such as the requirements of the Government for detailed records in connection with tax matters. The research work which many large organizations are undertaking today in order to keep abreast of the times means the development of special types of files. It is contended that record-making and record-keeping are the most costly in office salaries, space, and equipment of all the service functions of an organization.

Filing can be a very simple problem, although in some offices it is a complex one. The size of the office is not always the determining factor. Usually large offices have many types of material and elaborate routines, whereas small offices may have few types and simple routines. Specialized files, requiring study to organize, are often the property of a small professional office.

3

Roughly, records may be divided into:

 A. Original Transactions (papers)
 B. Transcribed Transactions (cards)
 C. Printed Materials (sheets, pamphlets, even books)

Controls for Records.—The tremendous growth of records has brought in its wake a demand for adequate controls. Some of the ways in which organizations have been able to manage this are:

1. The elimination of unnecessary forms so that duplicate papers and those of temporary value do not get into the files. This control is exercised at the source rather than in the file room.

2. The maintenance of files in efficient locations so that information is readily available to all who need it. This eliminates duplicate individual files.

3. The installation of labor saving devices in the file room, such as modern, easily operated cabinets, mechanized equipment such as sorters, and photographing of records—all of which are to be discussed in future chapters.

4. A flow of work so that records move rapidly from the time they are made through the various processing steps to the files, out of the file department to the storage room as they become less useful, and final destruction.

5. Adequately trained personnel. The tendency today is toward putting one person in control of all records in an organization, from their inception to final destruction, in order to coordinate those which are in the various departments and to assure that valuable papers are accounted for and are not kept in desks. A records administrator may be either a man or a woman. A knowledge of the various methods of arranging papers, of modern short cuts, of the office machines and filing equipment available, of improved forms design, and of setting up schedules for regular disposal of valueless records is essential.

6. Standardization.

A. Standardized procedures for getting papers into file. The handling of certain forms, such as orders, can be so repetitious in nature that clerks can be trained to acquire considerable speed through using a few simple motions and eliminating unnecessary ones.

B. Standardized systems of filing. As the accounting systems in any office are based on the same fundamental principles of debit and credit, so the fundamental principles of filing systems are the same everywhere although their adaptation to different businesses may vary widely. There are only four ways to classify material:

(1) By name (of firm or individual)
(2) By location (of state, city, or street)
(3) By subject (content of paper)
(4) By date (when issued or when it is to be used)

When the classification has been determined, one of four arrangements is chosen:

(1) Alphabetic (whether by name, location, or subject)
(2) Numeric
(3) Date
(4) Color

Alphabetic and numeric are basic methods of filing; date and color, subsidiary methods.

These standardized filing systems will be described in detail in the following chapters.

C. Standardized sizes of papers, cards, and forms universally adopted. Standardization of sizes of papers is still in process. Letterheads uniformly 8½″ x 11″ in size, and the 5″ x 3″, 6″ x 4″, 8″ x 5″ card sizes are universally used, and because of their uniformity are easily handled. Other papers such as bills of lading, orders, credit memoranda are haphazard in size, suited to each firm's requirements. In the aggregate they affect the size of the cabinets into which they are filed, waste space, and increase filing time.

D. Standardized equipment manufactured and stocked. Filing equipment has been fairly well standardized but not altogether so. The height and width of a letter-sized drawer are practically the same no matter which manufacturer has made it, but it has been only very recently that these manufacturers have agreed upon a drawer 28″ in depth. In most offices cabinets still range from 25½″ to 30″ in depth. An average of 175 letters can be filed to an inch; therefore, the capacity of a 25½″ and 30″ drawer differs considerably. Again, filing cabinets come in wood or steel; the wood, in oak, mahogany, or walnut, the steel in gray, olive green, or imitation oak, mahogany, or walnut. But the olive greens and grays of the different manufacturers vary to such a marked degree that when placed side by side they constitute a poor-looking battery of files.

Control of purchases to permit interchange of filing equipment and supplies in various departments as a means of controlling records is frequently overlooked.

Value of Records.—Management is not interested in files as such, but only in the information which can be obtained from them. To give effective service, the filing systems must be simple and direct, consistent throughout, expansible for future growth, coordinated to eliminate duplications, and purged at regular intervals to eliminate useless papers. Records set up in this manner will provide management with the following:

1. Data too complicated to be trusted to memory.
2. Communication between departments.
3. A history of the company so as to provide a basis for future operations.
4. Information needed by those outside the company, such as the Government.

Information readily available through records results in

1. A saving of executive time.
2. Expeditious conduct of daily business.

3. A complete history of transactions so that decisions can be based on all facts.
4. Reduction of clerical time.

No matter how well the records are planned and kept, if they do not serve management they have no value to the business supporting them.

Cost of Records.—The rising cost of record keeping as well as the increase in volume of records since World War II are the reasons that management is giving more thought to its records than ever before. The estimated annual cost of maintaining one 4-drawer filing cabinet is about $320, varying with localities. This averages about $20 per M papers. Costs include salaries of clerical workers and supervision, amounting to about 80 per cent of the total cost; cabinet amortized over a period of ten years; supplies; overhead including rental, light, heat; and a 10-per-cent carrying charge.

Control of Departmental Files.—It is the practice in some companies to limit the number of current drawers of material to an average of two for every employee in the office. In the accounting department the average per employee will be much higher; in other departments there will be very few records. This limit makes it quite necessary for individual departments to keep their records on a current basis and also keeps to a minimum the purchase of new cabinets.

Chapter 2

HOW TO JUDGE A GOOD ALPHABETIC INDEX; ALPHABETIC CARD FILES

An alphabetic name file means an alphabetic arrangement of surnames as is found in the telephone directory. This arrangement is sometimes called the dictionary plan. Such an arrangement of material is found in 85% of all files.

Selection of Manufacturers' Guides.—Ready access to an alphabetic file, or indeed to any file, is by means of the guiding. The guides are the dividers, usually of stiff material with a tab on which is given the notation projecting above the body of the guide. A notation has been defined as a shorthand sign standing for the name of a term and forming a convenient means of reference. In the case of an alphabetic file this notation comprises the divisions of the alphabet, such as Am, Ar, At, etc. These divisions of the alphabet range from 25 (one for each letter except X and Y which are combined) to 10,000. In a 2000 division there may be over 200 guides for S, for example.

These guides should come at equal distances in the file and not too far apart in order that the clerk will not have to finger too many cards or papers to find the particular one in question. For cards, a half-inch spread is usually desirable.

Unfortunately the guides furnished by the different filing equipment manufacturers are not equally good in that they do not divide the file evenly. The making of an index is not to be undertaken haphazardly by amateurs as a good index requires a knowledge of names and of the values of letters. Seven letters of the alphabet, B, C, G, H, M, S, and W, take up 53% of a normal name file; X is practically negligible; and the remaining 18 letters have the rest of the 47% of the space. Therefore, in a 500 division of the alphabet, about 265 of the guides should be for the letters B, C, G, H, M, S, and W in order to be rightly apportioned. The A's and B's of a 120 division of the alphabet demonstrate this uneven value of letters:

1 A	5 B	10 Bo
2 Al	6 Bar	11 Br
3 An	7 Be	12 Bro
4 Ar	8 Ben	13 Bu
	9 Bi	14 Bus

When purchasing an index it is a good plan to secure in advance a list of the divisions of the alphabet, at least for the A's and B's, in order to try them out on the file which is under consideration.

Every manufacturer of filing systems has to remake his compilations occasionally, because names change. As certain nationalities settle in certain neighborhoods, names prominent to that nationality come to the fore. In Minnesota and Wisconsin the preponderance of names is Scandinavian, such as Johnson, Swanson, etc.; in Boston there are a great many Irish names; in New York, Jewish names. The letter L used to be considered the dividing line in the alphabet, and two drawers of correspondence would be divided A–L; M–Z. Especially in the case of given names there is a tendency today to concentrate in the first half of the alphabet. Some of the newer indexes now divide the alphabet as follows: A–I; J–Z. At any rate, the more enterprising manufacturers revise their indexes every few years.

Following is the value of each letter of the alphabet in percentages. This tabulation was compiled from a study of the telephone directories of the large cities.

A	4.08	H	6.60	O	1.47	V	1.02
B	8.53	I	.60	P	4.81	W	5.47
C	7.03	J	2.37	Q	.21	X	.001
D	4.40	K	4.72	R	5.18	Y	.42
E	2.07	L	5.05	S	10.87	Z	.71
F	4.10	M	9.06	T	3.00	Total	100.031%
G	5.51	N	2.18	U	.57		

Notations on Guides.—Guides come with single or double notations, sometimes called open and closed notations. Each has advantages and disadvantages. By a single or open notation is meant not that a single letter but that a single group of letters is given on each guide:

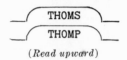

(Read upward)

Fig. 1.—Single Notations on Guides

In order to know where to stop filing behind such a guide, one is required to glance at the guide following. The Thompsons would be filed behind Thomp but in order to be sure whether the Thomsens belong back of the same guide, it is necessary to look at the next index tab. It is a nuisance when filing behind the last guide at the back of the drawer to have to refer to the first guide in the following drawer. On the other hand, the advantages of a single open notation are:

1. Simplicity. The mind has but three points to carry: name to be filed; nearest combination to that name; a quick glance at the following guide to be sure that the name to be filed falls between these two guides.
2. Lettering on the index can be large and thus easily legible.
3. Special guides can be inserted at will when expansion is necessary without throwing the file out of order. For instance, in the example given above, a special guide reading Thompson can readily be inserted between Thomp and Thoms.

Samples of the double and inclusive (closed) notation are:

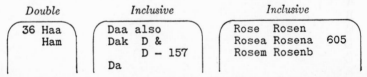

Fig. 2.—Double and Inclusive Notations on Guides

Because so many groups of letters are found on one guide tab, it means that the type must necessarily be small, and sometimes even hard to read. Another disadvantage of the closed notation is lack of opportunity to expand the file. By looking again at guide 605 given above, it will be observed that behind it would be filed such names as Rose, Rosehill, Roseland, Roseman, and Rosenbaum, which in the aggregate might reach such a volume that further indexing would be desirable. Since guide 605 is inclusive from Rose through Rosenb, an extra guide which one might wish to insert, such as Rosel, would have to be filed behind Rosenb, so that one guide would read Rose-Rosenb and the next one following, Rosel, which would thus be out of alphabetic order. Such a condition causes confusion and the filing and finding are slowed down considerably.

Special Name Guides.—Indexes have been manufactured to fit the normal file. Many files, however, are not normal in that there is a preponderance of certain names, depending on the locality or type of business, which makes necessary the addition of auxiliary guides. After the insertion of the main or primary guides it is a good plan to go through the file drawer by drawer, noting where the gaps occur in the indexing. These gaps are liable to come at the points where the common names are filed, such as General, United, American, United States, the name of the local city, and surnames as those listed below. A count of the commonest surnames made by the Social Security Administration in a study of their records illustrates this point:

Smith	1,119,404	Davis	484,213
Johnson	812,070	Wilson	363,797
Brown	745,872	Anderson	359,472
Williams	635,551	Thomas	314,252
Jones	605,322	Moore	314,133
Miller	536,537	Taylor	307,118

Special name guides can be printed or typed to fit into the gaps and those in turn broken down with A–Z guides, an alphabet within an alphabet:

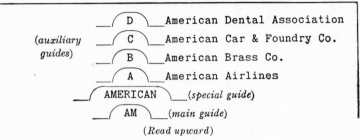

(*auxiliary guides*)

D   American Dental Association
C   American Car & Foundry Co.
B   American Brass Co.
A   American Airlines
AMERICAN   (*special guide*)
AM   (*main guide*)

(*Read upward*)

FIG. 3.—Special Name Guides

If the projections or tabs of the guides are of celluloid or metal, blank inserts which come in perforated strips can be typed and inserted at will, thus permitting the clerk to make

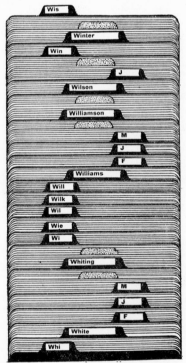

FIG. 4.—Auxiliary Guides

... *A-Z guides, breaking down White into given names*

... *special surname guides*

... *main guides*

(*Read upward*)

up new guides as needed. The insertion of auxiliary guiding is helpful even in a small file.

Standard Card Sizes.—Card sizes are well standardized as follows:

$$2\tfrac{1}{4}'' \times 3'', \quad 3'' \times 5'', \quad 4'' \times 6'', \quad 5'' \times 8'', \quad 6'' \times 9''$$

These dimensions are also given as $3'' \times 2\tfrac{1}{4}''$, $5'' \times 3''$, $6'' \times 4''$, $8'' \times 5''$, $9'' \times 6''$, and used interchangeably. This is due to the fact that manufacturers of wood equipment always give the height as the first dimension, while the steel manufacturers always give the width as the first dimension.

About 100 cards of average weight are filed to an inch. For the active file there should be a guide for every 25 to 50 cards. Where reference to the file is very heavy, such as bank signa-

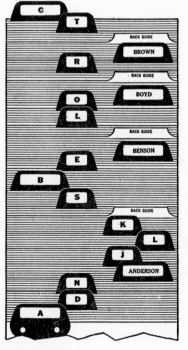

Fig. 5.—Expansion of an Alphabetic File

... *back or end guide*

... *auxiliary A-Z guides*

... *special surname guides*

... *Adler filed here*
... *main guides*

(*Read upward*)

ture cards, there are often not more than 8 or 10 cards behind a guide.

End Guides.—Where there are several names behind one index guide, it is sometimes advisable to use end, or terminal,

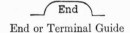

End or Terminal Guide

guides. These end guides merely indicate where one name ends and another begins. By referring again to guide tab 605 described previously, behind which are filed such names as Rose, Rosehill, Roseland, Roseman, etc., each one of these names can be separated from the others by means of such an end guide. This device is another means of eliminating the handling of ten or a dozen cards and enabling the clerk to go more directly to the name wanted.

Sorting the Cards.—It would be a waste of time and energy to take one new card at a time and file it in its proper place. A preliminary arrangement of cards before their final filing is called sorting. It is done seated at a table. A rubber tip for the thumb, forefinger, or middle finger is an aid in picking up the cards. The fingers should not be moistened in the mouth. The cards should not be thrown out in wabbly alphabetic groups on the table. A sorting tray with low sides is needed, which comes in all the standard card sizes, and a set of A–Z guides. The sorter should be one size larger than the card so that the cards can be thrown back of the guide readily.

A flat sorter with tabs bearing the divisions of the alphabet (see Chapter 18 on equipment) will save much time and confusion. A small group of cards should be fanned, then the proper sorter guide selected with the left hand and the cards thrown into the sorter with the right hand. The first sorting is by the initial letter of the name to be filed. If the cards are well typed, 100 cards can be handled in 3 minutes in this first sorting.

Where there is a volume of filing to be done, it may be necessary to have a second and even a third sort of the cards before the final filing. The cards for names beginning with A

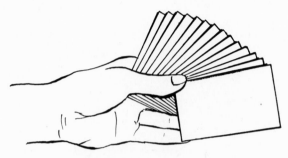

Fig. 6.—Fanning Cards for Sorting

should be sorted by the second letter in the name, using the same sorter after it has been emptied. In the second sort:

Aagard would be filed back of the A guide
Abbott back of the B guide
Ackland back of the C guide
Adams back of the D guide

Papers awaiting attachments, such as shipping data, may be accumulated for several days in the sorter before filing in permanent cabinets. The advantage is in saving energy in opening and shutting drawers, as 96% of the daily lookups will be found in the sorter. Such a routine will require a sorter with enough divisions of the alphabet so that there will be no more than 5 papers under each tab, instead of using the stock divisions of the alphabet. Many firms have sorters with tabs made to order—tabs for branches, principal customers, salesmen, etc.

In some file rooms where papers are kept in the sorter for a month or two until reference begins to die down, the sorter in effect replaces the filing cabinet. To house a large volume of papers even temporarily in this manner, elevator cabinets have been manufactured which have as many as twenty levels with any of them coming to the one working level where the file clerk, always from the same chair, can either file in or do lookups. The various levels are brought to the operator by means of a flick of a switch on the control panel.

Fig. 7.—Flat Sorters (SorterGraf Co.)

The secret of speed in sorting is working with rhythm of motion. The eyes should be held at the pile of cards or papers until the hand has been sent to the tab. By *thinking* the location of the tab, the hands will not need the eyes at the tab, except to determine the *exact* tab. The eyes should leave the tab as soon as the fingers touch it. The operator must read the next card or sheet and think location before the hands finish their part of the previous operation. If the eyes remain at the tab until the paper is thrown in and the tab dropped, the hands will be idle.

When cards or sheets are wider than they are long, they should be picked up by the lower corner farthest away with the thumb on top and fingers underneath. Sheets should be thrown end-in, instead of crosswise. If sheets or checks are to go in crosswise, pick up by the upper corner. If sheets are

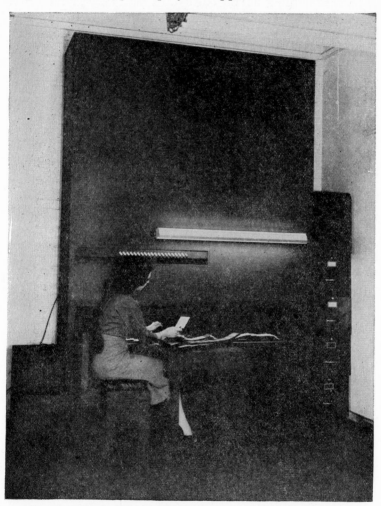

Fig. 8.—Elevator Cabinets with up to 20 Levels (SorterGraf Co.)

longer than they are wide, they should be picked up at the
far upper corner with thumb on top and fingers underneath.

Importance of Accuracy in the Typing of the Cards.
—Government offices, insurance companies, and large corporations sometimes have from five to ten million names in a
single alphabetic card file. If one is to find a given name instantly in so large a list, the order of filing must be very
exact. Moreover, the method of typing the card must be
exact: surname first, followed by given name with the typing
of the name in capital letters; name typed as close to the
upper edge of the card as possible, starting at the extreme left

```
SMITH   THOMAS & COMPANY
316 Arlington Street
Boston   Massachusetts
```

Fig. 9.—Details of Typing

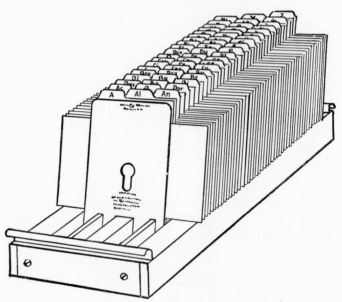

Fig. 10.—Sort-o-mat (Yawman & Erbe Co.)

edge; address on second and third lines in block or indented form. Modern usage favors the block form but the indented form is more easily read. Punctuation is omitted, two spaces being used instead of one space and comma or period. Use ampersand (&) instead of writing "and" in full.

Cross References.—It is obvious that a card or paper can be filed in one place only. When such a card or paper is called for under a variety of names or where the name may be subject to a variety of spellings, cross references are inserted in the file. A cross reference is a signpost referring the reader to another place for all or part of the material wanted.

Cross references may be used when firm names are changed:

> Barton, Durstine and Osborn (cross reference)
> SEE
> Batten, Barton, Durstine and Osborn (main card)

When names of the same sound have different spellings:

> Kane
> SEE
> Cain, Cane

When a firm is called by two different names:

> "Katy" (nickname)
> SEE
> Missouri, Kansas and Texas Railroad

When a filing name is confusing:

> Hancock Mutual Life Insurance Company
> SEE
> John Hancock Mutual Life Insurance Company

In a card file cross references are often typed on a card of a color different from that of the main card.

Chapter 3

HOW TO SET UP THE CORRESPONDENCE FILE; CODING

Correspondence Filing.—The method of handling papers is similar to that of handling cards except that cards are stiff and stand upright in the files quite easily, while the papers must be put into containers, called folders, to keep them upright. No matter what classification of correspondence is made, whether (*a*) alphabetic by name of individual or firm writing; (*b*) by the geographic location of the writer; (*c*) by the subject of the letter he writes; or (*d*) by the date of his letter as in follow-up work, the papers are grouped into folders properly labeled and filed behind index guides.

Folders.—A few points on paper filing, regardless of the alphabetic system used, are:

A. About ten folders are filed back of a guide. Adequate guiding saves human effort and insures accurate and speedy filing and finding.

B. Papers are placed within the folder in neat, orderly fashion, with the top and left edges even. The letterhead should be at the left-hand side of the drawer. Papers should never hang partially out of a folder. The paper should be folded if it is too large for the folder. If half sheets, they can be laid side by side so that the folder will not bulge at one end.

C. There are two kinds of folders: the regular and miscellaneous. The regular folder is for the correspondent for whom there are 3, 6, or 10 papers (each firm sets its own figure) and whose name is inscribed on the folder. Within the folder these papers ordinarily are arranged by date, with the latest date toward the front because the most recent paper is the one to which reference is most likely to be made and therefore it should be handy.

The miscellaneous folder is marked the same as its guide. In most systems it comes behind the regular correspondent folders. It contains the papers from those customers for whom there are less than 3, 6, or 10 papers, whichever figure has been decided upon. Within the miscellaneous folders papers are filed in strict alphabetic sequence (then within each group by date) in order that it may be easily determined when a sufficient number of papers have accumulated for one name to require a regular folder.

D. If the guides and folders are in a printed index system, they must be purchased of the same company or they will not match.

E. Folders should be kept upright and under compression at all times when the file is not in use to avoid sagging.

F. Folders should not bulge. Usually 75 papers per folder is the maximum. A single scoring in the bottom of the front flap allows a ⅜″ expansion of folder. Some folders carry 2, 3, or more scorings. The use of such scoring is to provide a base on which folder rests, which prevents buckling in file.

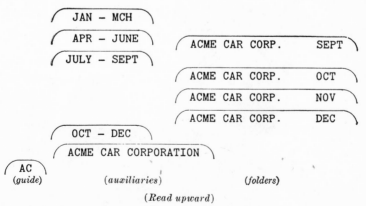

Fig. 11.—Correspondence File Guides and Folders

Guides.—An average of about 25 guides to a drawer is adequate. If it is estimated there are to be ten drawers of correspondence by the end of the year, 250 guides will not be too many. The type of correspondence determines whether these guides are to be only the main divisions of the alphabet or largely auxiliaries. If the correspondence is with many individuals or firms, with a comparatively small amount of correspondence with each, as in a retail business, 250 main guides with a corresponding number of miscellaneous folders will be needed.

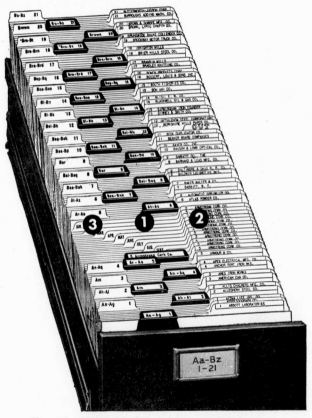

Fig. 12.—Alphabetic Filing (Yawman & Erbe Co.)

1. Primary guides; 2. regular customer folders; 3. miscellany.

Where there is a large amount of correspondence with each of a few customers, an entirely different arrangement of the index is desirable: a small division of the main guides, perhaps 100 or 150, with the balance of the 250 guides supplied by auxiliaries. These latter are of several kinds: special name, months, A – Z.

Assume one drawer to comprise correspondence with one firm: Ace Steel Company. A special guide for that name is followed by a set of monthly guides for the folders broken down biweekly or even weekly.

Again, there may be correspondence with a number of firms beginning with the word American. A special guide for American is followed by a set of A – Z guides for subdivision by second name, as American Aniline Dye Co., American Brass Co., etc.

Labels for Folder Tabs.—It is possible to type directly on the tab of a folder, in which case a typewriter with a large

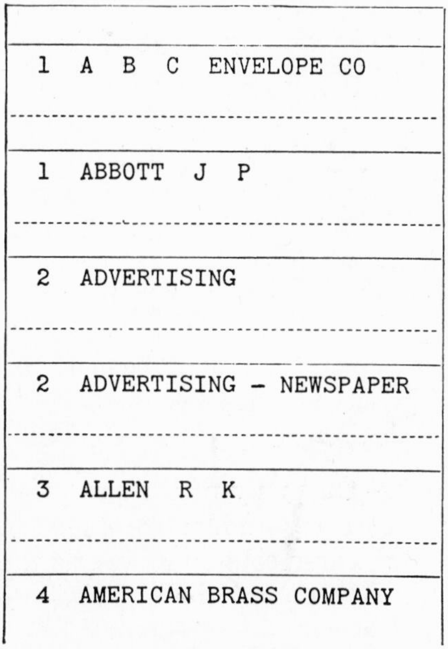

FIG. 13.—A Strip of Perforated Labels

roller, or better yet, a billing machine is used. Gummed labels, about 4 inches wide, may be purchased in manila or in several colors, or the label may be of manila with colored bands. There are usually ten labels in a perforated strip and 250 to 1000 labels in a package. Labels also come in continuous rolls for speed in typing. Care must be used to select colors pastel in shade so that the typing shows plainly. For further information about labels, see Chapter 18.

Fig. 14.—Gummed Labels in Rolls. Choice of nine colors: white, buff, blue, salmon, green, pink, yellow, orange, or manila. (Amberg File & Index Co.)

Rules for typing labels:

1. Start typewritten entry uniformly at the second space from the left edge, and just far enough below top edge to leave rim above lettering. Capitalize top line.
2. Omit punctuation and use two spaces where comma or period would ordinarily be placed.
3. If the entry needs more than one line, use block form or indentation.
4. If current year is placed on folders, it is advisable to stamp this date on the front of the folder, or to place it on the label in such position that it will not interfere with rapid alphabetizing.

Code Numbers.—On many of the printed guides it will be noticed that they carry numbers arranged in consecutive order from A to Z. These code numbers, as they are called, serve as symbols to represent the alphabetic combinations for the purpose of brevity. In a 5000 coded division of the alphabet, for example, the letter combination and its consecutive number are placed one each on 5000 guides. The number of divisions in the file can always be determined by consulting the last guide. In the illustration in Chapter 2 of the double notation guide Rose, 605 is the 605th guide in the entire index. This system of numbering or coding developed as the larger indexes were made up, and the value of these numbers is based on the fact that numbers are much more easily grasped than are combinations of letters.

Coding offers two advantages: speed in sorting and a check for accuracy. By constant usage, all the combinations and code numbers in even a 2000 or larger subdivision can be memorized so that the assignment of numbers to incoming mail can be done rapidly. Then the sorting by these numbers is also a speedy process. The code number provides a check against misfiling, because, as the material is actually inserted into its proper folders in the cabinets, the number on the paper is checked to assure its matching the number on the guide. It is rarely advisable to make use of coding under a 300 division of the alphabet because in a small division the time saved in sorting by number does not compensate for the time spent in affixing the code numbers. Flat sorters with large subdivisions of the alphabet permit material to be fine sorted with only one handling. As a result, coding is being used less and less in modern file departments.

Supplementary Letter Guides Rather Than Code Numbers.—Some manufacturers of filing systems have not accepted coding as a desirable adjunct to an alphabetic index. Indeed, because of the design of some filing systems, coding or consecutive numbering of guides is impossible. Such indexes start with the 26 letters of the alphabet on guides in first or second position at the left. As needed, supplementary guides are dropped in between these primary guides, not according to any prearranged plan but purely as the volume of material behind each guide warrants. For instance, there may be a good deal of material behind F. Dividing the F material in half, a supplementary guide of I is found necessary. These supplementary guides are placed in the second position from the left. Later the material behind FI grows heavy enough to require additional supplementary guides. An R may be inserted, also in the second position; or if there is a large amount of material beginning with the word FIRST, a supplementary guide R is placed in the third position. The illustration below brings out the point.

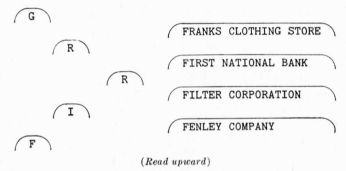

(Read upward)

FIG. 15.—Supplementary Guides According to Volume of Correspondence

Code numbers cannot be used where guides are added at will.

Inspection and Reading of Correspondence.—In preparing material for an alphabetic file it is necessary that the clerk glance over the contents of each paper in order to familiarize himself with them. He cannot service the files intelligently unless he knows what is in them. This does not mean a laborious reading of every word but merely a quick glance for the gist of the matter. Light reading can be accomplished at the rate of 5 words per second; heavier reading at the rate of 4 words per second. Without familiarizing himself with the contents of a paper the clerk is apt to misfile. For example, the signature on an order reads J. R. McIlvaine, the professional who is buying for the Meadow-

Fig. 16.—A Complete Alphabetic File Drawer (Globe-Wernicke Co.)

brook Golf Club. The signature is misleading in this case because the order should be filed under Meadowbrook.

Correspondence from salesmen must also be inspected with some care because, if the salesman writes about a customer's account, this paper should be placed in the customer's folder. In the salesman's own folder belongs only such correspondence as is personal: matters regarding his account, itineraries, etc.

Recent studies show that many adults cannot read rapidly nor can they grasp what they do read with comprehension. It is an accomplishment which can be developed with practice. This fact should be taken into consideration when selecting new employees for a records department.

Duplicate copies of orders or other papers can be destroyed unless (a) there are notations written on duplicates which need to be retained; (b) one copy is to be filed by name, another by number, etc.

Marking Mail for Filing.—A colored pencil is a convenience in marking mail for file. The following procedure should be observed:

1. The name under which the paper is to be filed is underscored.
2. An "X" (cross) is placed under any name which needs to be cross referenced in the file. Often the cross references are made on the spot.
3. The important word or words that indicate the content of the paper are encircled for quick reference in lookup work.
4. If coding is used the code number is put in the upper right corner of the correspondence. This code number is the same number that is on the guide back of which this letter is to be filed. The chart of alphabetic combinations with code numbers is furnished by the equipment house from which the index guides were purchased.
5. Letters are then roughly sorted by the initial letter of the name under which each is to be filed.

Cross References.—Cross references can be written on sheets of colored paper, 8½″ x 11″, and filed directly in the regular or miscellaneous folders. Where a cross reference is permanent in nature, the front half of an old folder can be torn off and the back half with the tab inserted in its proper place among the other folders in file. A distinctive colored label, such as a red one, should be used exclusively for cross references, so that they can be spotted instantly in the file.

> HUB
> SEE
> Vaughn John G Sons
> Sedalia Missouri

To staple general correspondence into a file is a time-consuming process not warranted in most cases where ordi-

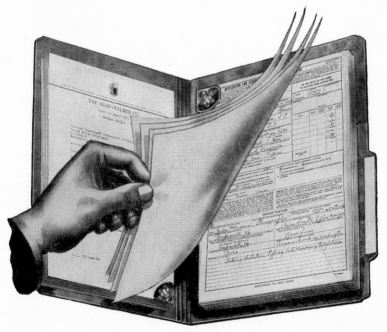

Fig. 17.—Corner Clip (Shaw-Walker Co.)

nary controls are in effect. Contracts, legal papers, matters pertaining to patents, are often considered important enough to fasten into folders as an added safety precaution.

When a paper is missing in an alphabetic file, it might be well to check the following:

1. Has the name been transposed?
2. Has every name mentioned in the lookup been searched?
3. Have the folders before and after the one involved been searched? Look between folders. Has the paper slipped to the bottom of the drawer?
4. Look under other vowels. For a name beginning with Ba, look also under Be, Bi, Bo, and Bu.

Chapter 4

ROUTINES IN PREPARING PAPERS FOR FILE

Flow of Work to Files.—Often the file department is blamed for not producing papers which have not yet reached the file. Therefore, if the files are to function promptly, the first routine which must be established is that of the even and straight-line flow of papers through the office. It is not unusual to find several days elapsing between the time the mail is received in the office and the time it reaches the files. This may be due to "bottlenecks" in the office where work is held too long at one desk, or it may be due to a poor arrangement of departments. The following diagrams illustrate how one medium-sized office cleared up its difficulties in the file room:

BEFORE REARRANGEMENT OF DEPARTMENTS

AFTER REARRANGEMENT OF DEPARTMENTS

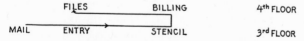

Fig. 18.—Flow of Papers (Before and After Rearrangement)

Usually no more than 24 to 48 hours should elapse between the time the mail is received in the office and the time it reaches the files. So far as possible forms should not be allowed to accumulate in a department and then be dumped upon the file room in a mass. Mail should be collected from departments at regular intervals—at least once a day in small organizations and hourly in larger firms. In good-sized firms a conveyor method of transporting papers or a continuously moving belt or messenger service is utilized; in small concerns the file clerk makes the rounds of the departments at stated intervals to pick up the material ready for file.

Preparation of Material for File.—Immediately after the arrival of the material in the file room it may be desirable to time-stamp it, which serves as a protection to the file department in case there is ever a question when the paper reached the files. Then the papers should be laid out into as many piles on the table as there are different files; for instance, the correspondence and orders in one group, vouchers in another. The fewer the groups, the less pre-arrangement of papers is necessary. A quick count can be taken of the material in each group by using rubber tips on the thumb and forefinger of the right hand. The total number of papers filed each day is recorded on a sheet which should be submitted to the office manager each week. Such a record of work accomplished not only acts as a check on the file clerk but gives an excellent picture of the peak loads during the year and in turn the slack periods when the clerk can be given added duties. A more detailed description of a production chart will be presented in a later chapter.

The routine of preparing material for file varies in different offices, but whatever it may be, two points should be borne in mind: the file clerk is responsible for checking, marking, and filing all material, and there should be as few handlings of each paper as possible. For correspondence the following is the usual procedure:

Segregate papers belonging in different files: vouchers, canceled checks, catalogs. Orders, correspondence, credit memos need not be segregated if filed under one index. In the segregation of papers they are often counted in order to secure a total of the day's work.

Read letters rapidly in order to get the gist of the matter.

Check for authorization to file. The file clerk is responsible if a paper gets into the file before it is ready to be placed there. He must notice whether every department indicated on the letter has been checked off and if not the letter must be returned for further action. In some firms a line is drawn through the body of the letter when it is ready for file; in others a rubber stamp marked File is used; in others papers are initialed by department heads.

Underscore with colored pencil the name or word under which the letter is to be filed. It must be remembered that a letterhead may be misleading. If a salesman is staying temporarily at the Washington Hotel and uses that hotel's stationery, the firm receiving his letter would not file it under Washington, but under the salesman's name if it is a personal matter, or under the name of the firm he represents if of a business nature.

Encircle important word or words in the letter so that quick reference may be made to the letter when it is called for later. The clerk may have 100 letters from the Jones Manufacturing Company in file. He is asked to find immediately the letter pertaining to a damaged shipment of goods written last spring to this firm. If the subject matter of each of these 100 letters has been high-lighted so that the eye catches the important word or words at once, the paper in question can be extracted much more quickly than if each letter has to be consulted at some length.

Place cross under names requiring cross reference unless this has already been done before the material was sent to file. The cross references often are made on the spot, or if there are many to be made in the course of the day, letters may be laid aside until the other material has been placed in the sorter so as not to slow up the work on the bulk of the correspondence.

Mend torn papers with transparent tape, straighten out crumpled ones, trim or fold papers too large for folders.

Remove all clips and pins. They catch on papers not intended to be fastened together and thus are a fertile source of misfiling. Moreover, they make a file lopsided and hard to handle. If letter and carbon of answer are to be attached, staple in upper left-hand corner. The paper bearing the latest date, whether carbon or letterhead, should be on top.

Check through every paper even if several come attached, because the grouping may be only a temporary one and the top paper may not be the one under which all should be filed.

Place code or file number in upper right-hand corner of paper.

Stamp every paper with name of file, as Credit File or Sales Department, to identify it instantly when it returns if more than one file is kept, for confusion may arise on return of borrowed papers.

Watch for ephemeral material such as letters of formal courtesy, such information as a temporary price list which may be used but once, memoranda of transmission, material in more permanent form elsewhere which may be destroyed or retained in a temporary file.

Coordination of Operations.—At this point the letter is ready to be put into the sorter. While the right hand has been doing the necessary marking, the left hand has been reaching for the proper sorter tab. Then while the right hand is inserting the paper, the eye is already reading the next sheet. Such coordination of hands and eyes will cut down the time necessary to prepare matter for file. Moreover, unnecessary steps have been eliminated. Each paper is read, marked, and sorted with one handling.

No department in an organization can benefit more from careful time and motion studies than the files. Where bonus systems have been installed in filing departments, job analyses are made of every task in the department by means of a stop watch or a motion picture camera (micrometer). Some filing departments have been broken down into 56 different duties; others into 33. Such studies are made at all times of day and on clerks of all degrees of efficiency. Then each task is studied by management engineers to determine the best and shortest method of accomplishment. In one mail-order house it was found that by teaching the best method and through a bonus system providing an incentive for further short cuts, the cost per hour of work was reduced in 28 weeks' time by one third, and the output increased by 65.7% to 141% in the same length of time. See Chapter 19 for details of bonus plans. Of course, the ordinary office does not need to make such exhaustive studies of its file department but the fact remains that, since all ways are not the best way, some thought given to this matter of routines in the file department will effect definite savings.

How Often Filing Should Be Done.—If the press of lookups is such that the filing cannot be done at this time, the material is in such order that it can be easily found. But nothing should interfere with the practice of getting papers into the sorter as soon as possible after they reach the file room. Some smaller firms follow a practice of filing only two or three times a week, thus eliminating drawer-opening. Instead of filing 10 or 12 papers in a drawer each day, 20 or 25 or even more are filed at less frequent intervals.

Even if the filing is done once a day, it is often left until afternoon; then the final pickup and sorting are handled in the last hour of the day. This leaves all material in order for the early morning rush of matching papers to first delivery mail. Some organizations permit no access to the files until about ten o'clock in the morning or until every piece of yesterday's mail is in the file. This, however, makes it hard for the rest of the office and is not unqualifiedly recommended. After all, the function of the files is to give service.

Filing from Sorter.—Before filing it is well to remove the papers from behind each sorter tab and arrange them in strict sequence, laying them face down on the table until the sorter is emptied. In very large departments or where large sorters are used, the material behind only a few tabs is prepared and filed at one time. Some file clerks prefer to start with Z and work backward, obviating the necessity of laying papers face down.

Filing Cabinets.—The contents of each drawer should be plainly marked on the outside on the label provided for that purpose. Printed or typewritten labels or gummed letters pasted on a background of contrasting color may be used. Not a second should be wasted in locating the right drawer.

Filing cabinets should be bolted together. There are apt to be accidents of cabinets falling forward upon the file clerk when he leaves two or three loaded drawers pulled out at one time. It is well to make a practice of shutting one drawer before opening another.

Rubber mats under cabinets hold the cabinets firmly so that it is not necessary to bolt them together or to nail down a quarter round to keep them from shifting on smooth floors. The mats may be cut in strips four inches wide of a length to correspond with the depth of each file cabinet. They are laid under the edges of the cabinets.

A filing shelf, hitched over the handle of an adjoining drawer and provided with a clamp to prevent papers lying thereon from being blown away, is a big help in saving energy while filing. A file stool on casters is an aid for filing in a bottom drawer.

Putting Papers in File Drawer.—The file clerk should never grasp the tab of the guide behind which he wishes to file in order to pull it forward. Not even the strongest tab will stand such treatment. The best method is to stand in front of the drawer and with both hands grasp either side of the guide in order to push the contents of the drawer forward.

Always file *behind* the guide.

It is a good practice to pull up any folder in which papers are to be filed. Otherwise papers are apt to slip between folders and fall to the bottom of the drawer where they are lost. An experienced clerk pushes up the folder with a rubber tip on the fore or middle finger of the right hand and then lifts up the papers therein, in order to find the proper spot for the paper to be filed. Papers should be jogged evenly before being replaced to give a neat appearance to the drawer.

The drawers must not be crowded to the point where material cannot be put in and taken from the files easily. Three inches in a drawer is needed for handling papers.

Miscellaneous Folders.—While filing in the miscellaneous folders the clerk should extract the groups of papers which have reached the required number under one name, whether three, six, or ten and lay them aside until the filing is completed. Then, in a less crowded hour, folders for new regular correspondents should be prepared. If this is not done regularly the miscellaneous folders will become too crowded for quick filing and finding.

Folder Labels.—The typing of labels has been described in the previous chapter. It takes practice to paste labels on folders so that they are uniformly placed and firmly attached. The best way is as follows: Lay on the table a package of folders with edges even. Place a ruler upright against the extreme left edge of top of tab. Run a pencil along the ruler so as to leave a mark across the thickness of the tabs. This gives at the upper left-hand corner of all tabs a uniform point at which to paste the label. This point for the label is as near the left edge as possible without any part of the label overhanging the curve of the tab.

49 SMITH JOHN COMPANY
419 Main St
Kent Ohio   19 -

FIG. 19.—Label on Folder Tab

Each label has a front and a back half with a crease between. The front on which the typing is done should cover the front side of the folder tab. Press down the crease with the thumbnail, but avoid cracking the label. Wet the gummed side of the label, but not too much, or the glue will be washed off. A dry spot, however, will leave a "bubble" which later causes the label to pop off. Smooth the back half of the label to the back of the folder tab. The crease should come exactly to the top of the tab. Then fold over the front part of the label from the middle to the outer edges with a blotter, or the front half of the folder between the fingers and the label, because thumbs rubbed over the typewritten matter will cause blurring. Not a wrinkle should remain or the label will soon fall off.

Other Duties of File Clerks.—There is a growing tendency, as has been previously stated, to place records, from their inception to final dispositon, under the supervision of one person. Such supervision may include other service departments, such as communications and the mail room. The obvious advantage of this latter combination in a small organization is that the file clerk is familiar with the contents of the incoming mail and is able to identify a certain paper when it is asked for even before it reaches the file room.

The file personnel is sometimes expected to write follow-up letters comprised of form paragraphs. If catalogs for the use of the purchasing or engineering departments or pamphlets or bulletins used by the executives are kept in the file room, it is often the duty of a file clerk to check their date of publication from time to time and, when they are obsolete, write for more recent editions.

Short Cuts.—One of the ways by which the routine part of filing work can be made palatable is to give each clerk an incentive for working out short cuts in his daily routines. Effective saving of time can often be accomplished by arousing his initiative. Where, however, a condition of "made work" is suspected, it may be necessary to have the file clerks write out step by step their daily procedures.

Lookups Received by Telephone in a File Room

Pick up telephone
Pick up pencil
Reach for requisition pad

Write information on requisition form
Replace telephone

Lookups Received by Telephone in a File Room (*Cont'd.*)

Tear sheet from pad

Stand up

Walk to proper cabinet

Inspect labels on drawers

Pull out proper drawer

Inspect labels on folders

Open proper folder

Inspect correspondence

Remove proper letter

Walk back to table

Pick up out-card

Walk to cabinet

Insert requisition in pocket of card

Insert out-card in folder

Shut drawer

Walk to tube

Reach for "to & from" pad

Address "to & from" form

Tear sheet from pad

Pick up pin

Pin "to & from" form to letter

Hand to tube attendant

Walk to desk

Sit down

(Operations 21, Distance 64, Inspections 3, Moves 5)

Proposed new method: Move telephone to filing cabinets so that the distance traveled would be reduced by approximately 25 feet. Also, eliminate trip to table for out-card by placing cards on cabinets or in some more convenient spot.

Transfer of Records.—Just as important as getting papers into file promptly is their removal from the current file to semi-active storage and then to dead storage as soon as the usefulness of the papers is past. Chapter 8 is devoted to this portion of the records program.

Chapter 5

RULES FOR ALPHABETING; PHONETIC FILING

The great majority of files are arranged according to the alphabet but they are not all equally accessible because of the liberties which are taken with the alphabet. The rules given below are simple and have proved satisfactory in the largest files.

When a file is arranged alphabetically, pronunciation is not a factor; that is, Cain is filed under C and Kane under K. When the clerk is not familiar with all the names in the file he may be forced to look in both places if the card is called for orally. There is such a system as phonetic filing but its usage is not as common as are the files arranged in strictly alphabetical sequence.

Individual Names.—1. File each name in the exact sequence of its letters. To file to the second or third letter only will cause confusion and delays:

2d letter	*3d letter*	*4th letter*	*7th letter*
Aaron	Czajka	Scharf	Schille
Abbott	Cziczo	Scheck	Schillhahn
Acme	Czop	Schilling	Schillinger
Adalman	Czrynski	Schmidt	Schillmoeller

2. Simplify filing and finding by dividing a name mentally into units. The surname being the most important name is the first unit, the given name or initial the second unit, the middle name or initial the third unit. Complete each unit before going on to the next one:

1st unit	*2d unit*	*3d unit*
Clark	George	
Clark	Samuel	N.
Clark	Samuel	W.

3. File *nothing before something*. This odd little rule has been borrowed from the librarians. It has helped many a file clerk in difficult situations.

File *Brown* A, then Brown B, and so on through Brown Z
Follow with *Browne* A, then Browne B, through Browne Z
Continue with *Brownell* A, then Brownell B, through Brownell Z

Brown with nothing after the "n" precedes Browne spelled with an "e" which in turn precedes Brownell. The following list is correctly filed:

1st unit	2d unit	3d unit
Clark	R	
Clark	Ralph	
Clark	Ralph	J
Clark	S	
Clark	S	H
Clark	S	Harry
Clark	Sidney	
Clark	Sidney	W
Clark	Sidney	William

To put it in a different way, initials are always filed before names beginning with the *same* initial.

This same rule applies to subjects as well as to names. The general subject of

Gas
precedes Gas—bottled (a subdivision of the main subject)

4. Disregard diacritical markings used with foreign names as they do not change the spelling of a name but only its pronunciation:

Cabaña Höhler DePré

Hohler without the umlaut and Höhler with the umlaut are spelled identically even though pronounced differently. Occasionally a name such as Müller has been anglicized to Mueller and may require a cross reference.

5. File after the given name titles important enough to be retained. A married woman may be Mrs. John Adams so-

cially, but for business purposes she is Mrs. Jane Adams (Mrs. John) and must so sign her name on legal documents. Banks do not permit man and wife to sign a joint account as Mr. and Mrs. John Adams because of the confusion which is apt to arise in filing; they require the signature to read John and Jane Adams. When the names come to file as Mr. and Mrs. John Adams and there is no further identification, file as follows:

Adams   John   (no title)
Adams   John   (Mrs)

When names are identical titles may give the necessary distinction:

Williams   A   A   Jr
Williams   A   A   Sr

Exception: Titles are considered the first unit in filing where the title and one name are given or where the surname is omitted:

Father Dolan
Dr. Pepper Bottling Company
Mother Superior

6. Write out abbreviations to prevent errors in filing:

Wm. should be written William
Jno. should be written John

7. Treat compound names as one word:

deVere should be filed as though written	Devere
Van Gelder should be filed as though written	Vangelder
von Der Linden should be filed as though written	Vonderlinden
Mac Laren should be filed as though written	Maclaren
McDonald should be filed as though written	Mcdonald
M'Lean should be filed as though written	Mlean
Abd El Nour should be filed as though written	Abdelnour
P'Pool should be filed as though written	Ppool
Daniel Int-Hout should be filed as though written	Inthout Daniel
David Lloyd George should be filed as though written	Lloydgeorge David

Van is a Dutch prefix meaning "of"; von is a German prefix originally meaning "of the family of"; and Mac and Mc originally meant "son of," Mac being Scotch, Mc Irish.

NOTE: There is no 27th letter Mc. Names beginning with the prefixes Mac or Mc should not be taken out of their alphabetic order but filed exactly as spelled:

Maas	Mallard	Mears	M'Lean
MacLaren	McLean	Miller	Morris

Some manufacturers make provision for a Mc guide before the M's, but it is best to remove or ignore it.

Company, Institution, Government Names.—A company is always more important than an individual or department in a company. A letter signed by John Gates, manager of the Shoe Department of the Star Department Store, should not be filed under Gates, nor under Shoe, but under Star, providing of course that the letter is about company business.

Large companies having subsidiaries or divisions may be filed either by name of parent organization or the subsidiary. The method adopted should be followed consistently.

> General Motors Corporation
> A C Spark Plug Division
> Allison Division
> Delco Remy Division

can be filed under General Motors or under the subdivision.

1. When an individual forms a company named after himself, invert the name:

	1st unit	2d unit	3d unit	4th unit
G S Crane & Company is filed	Crane	G	S &	Company
Andrew Barnes & Sons is filed	Barnes	Andrew &	Sons	
William Smith & Nephews is filed	Smith	William &	Nephews	
Jane Andrus & Cora Jones Shop is filed	Andrus	Jane &	Jones	Cora

Note that the name, surname and given, is kept together even though inverted.

2. File coined or trade names as written:

Aunt Jemima Pancake Flour Company   is filed under Aunt
Bit of Sweden (restaurant)   is filed under Bit
Ye Olde Chocolate Shop   is filed under Ye
Committee of Fifteen   is filed under Committee

3. When initials comprise a firm name treat each initial as a unit:

		1st unit	2d unit	3d unit	4th unit
A A A Export					
Company	is filed	A	A	A	Export
A-1 Cleaners	is filed	A	One	Cleaners	
A P W Paper					
Company	is filed	A	P	W	Paper
Aagaard, Hanson					
Company	is filed	Aagaard	Hanson	Company	
B & O					
Restaurant	is filed	B	O	Restaurant	
B Square					
Market	is filed	B	Square	Market	
Elizabeth Baab	is filed	Baab	Elizabeth		

Note that the list given above is in alphabetic order, observing the rule of "nothing before something."

Radio stations are filed under their initials, each initial being considered a unit: W T M J; K Y W; W J K S.

4. When two people with the same surname form a company, repeat the surname to avoid confusion:

		1st unit	2d unit	3d unit	4th unit	5th unit	6th unit
G. T. & R. L.							
Black	is filed	Black	G	T	Black	R	L
Harold & Minnie							
Stevens	is filed	Stevens	Harold	Stevens	Minnie		

If the surname is not repeated there is apt to be an appearance of an omission.

5. Disregard the word "and" as a unit in filing. It does not add to the identification of a name. Whether one says Clark Company or Clark and Company is immaterial for identification:

1st unit		2d unit
Clark	&	Company

The sign for "and" (&) is called the ampersand, a word of Anglo-Saxon and middle English origin. "Ampersand" is a contraction of "and per se and." The ampersand should always be used in place of the word "and" when typing entries.

6. Disregard A, An, and The in filing and when typing entries. Certain states have laws requiring corporations to carry the word "the" in order that they may be readily distinguished from partnerships or privately owned concerns. The Martin Paper Company would mean a corporation; Martin Paper Company a privately owned concern. Thereby the word "the" carries no significance as a name.

> The Illinois Steel Company should be typed Illinois Steel Company on the label.

Prepositions, such as *of, in, for,* in a name are not considered in alphabeting.

Examples:

	1st unit	2d unit	3d unit
House of Rothschild	House (of)	Rothschild	
Commission for the Advancement of Science	Commission (for the)	Advancement (of)	Science

Exception 1: When a name cannot be distinguished as belonging to an individual or an institution, "The" typed in parentheses after the name indicates an institution.

> Burlington may mean an individual, but when written Burlington (The) it is evident that a corporation is meant—a railroad in this instance.

Exception 2: Towns whose names begin with the word "The" retain "The" as an integral part of the name. This will be discussed more thoroughly under the alphabeting of geographic names.

7. Treat names composed of or containing numerals as if spelled in full:

	1st unit	2d unit	3d unit
3d Presbyterian Church	Third	Presbyterian	Church
Thomas Thirsk	Thirsk	Thomas	
1345 Jarvis Avenue Apartments	Thirteen	Forty	Five

For numbers over 1000 there is a choice of One thousand three hundred and five, or Thirteen hundred and five. The latter is given preference.

	1st unit	2d unit	3d unit
200,000 Strong Committee	Two	Hundred	Thousand
5¢ Souvenir Company	Five	cent	Souvenir

8. Disregard the " 's" in filing. Its purpose is to denote possession but it does not alter the name. In the name Albert's Drug Store, Albert is the first unit. The following names are correctly filed:

1st unit	2d Unit	3d unit
Johnson	Andrew	
Johnson's	Book	Store
Johnson	Company	

9. Write out abbreviations to prevent errors in filing. Y M C A should be spelled in full: Young Men's Christian Association. A hasty glance at the two following entries might give rise to the thought that they were incorrectly filed:

N. Y.	Coal	Company
N. C.	Tar	Corporation

If spelled out even momentary confusion is avoided:

New York	Coal	Company
North Carolina	Tar	Corporation

10. Treat compound words as one unit:

1st unit		2d unit	3d unit
Chapman-Catt		Harriet	
Ten Eyck		Glass	Company
DeCoppet	&	Doremus	
Co-operative		Book	Stores
Inter-State		Bus	Lines
Mid West		Utilities	Company

Non Pareil	Drug	Corporation
Air-Sea-Land	Aircraft	Company
Full-o-Pep	Heaters	Corporation
New Orleans	Picayune	
All American	Ball	Team
Saint Regis	Apartments	
Dan-dee	Pretzel	Company

Experience favors filing Saint under Sa rather than St.

11. Watch signatures when names are hyphenated as the hyphen is occasionally used instead of a comma.

A Hall-Marx Company letterhead may bear the signature of H. M. Hall showing that two men, Hall and Marx, are members of the firm. In this instance the name Hall-Marx Company is comprised of three units instead of being a compound name. In the absence of a letterhead or other means of identification, treat Hall-Marx Company or Long-Bell Company as three units, since in the majority of cases the name actually comprises two units with a hyphen used instead of a comma.

12. File, as written, Bureau of, Commission for, etc.:

> *Board* of Foreign Missions
> *Bureau* of Works
> *Commission* for the Advancement of Science

13. File as written the names of private institutions or corporations which include City, State, etc., as initial word:

> *City* Realty Company
> *State* Auto Repair Shop
> *Town* of Lake Bakery

14. File hotels, schools, hospitals, libraries, etc., under their distinctive titles if they have them; otherwise under locations:

> Hotel *Astor*
> City of New York *Bellevue* and Allied Hospitals
> *Blackstone* Library
> University of *Chicago*
> District School No. 1, *Lincoln*, Nebraska
> *Yale* University
> *Starrett* School

Trustees of *Cornell* University
Thomas J. Ward, Trustee for Alice *Oakes*, minor,
　　with a cross reference under the name of Ward,
　　the trustee.

15. Guardians, receivers, trustees, etc. considered as agents for an individual or an organization are indexed under the name of the individual or organization for whom they act. A cross reference should be made under the name of the guardian, receiver, or trustee.

Example: Thomas J. Ward, trustee for Alice Oakes, a minor, should be filed under Oakes and cross referenced under Ward.

16. Where people or names are identical file by city:

Sears, Roebuck & Company	Chicago
Sears, Roebuck & Company	Philadelphia
Sears, Roebuck & Company	San Francisco

Exception: Banks file their correspondence with other banks first under the name of the city because of the preponderance of First Nationals:

Aurora First National Bank
Bloomington First National Bank
Champaign First National Bank

17. Enter material received from departments of the federal government, states, or cities under the official name of the governing body. Thus correspondence from the Post Office should be filed under United States Government (or United States of America) Post Office Department; U. S. Coast Guard under United States Government Coast Guard. Under the primary term subdivide by name of department:

United States Government	Agriculture Department
United States Government	Post Office Department
United States Government	War Department

filed thus:

	United States Government—Navy Department
Senior Medical Officer	
Submarine Base	
Pearl Harbor, T. H.	Pearl Harbor T H—Submarine
Commanding Officer, S. S. Panay	Base—Steamship Panay
(location)	

Name	1st unit	2d unit	3d unit	4th unit	5th unit
A B C Uniform Company	A	B	C	Uniform	Company
A Better Key Shop	A	Better	Key	Shop	
A & C Auto Parts	A (&)	C	Auto	Parts	
A G M Optical Co.	A	G	M	Optical	Company
A & J Electric Co	A (&)	J	Electric	Company	
A J Food Mart	A	J	Food	Mart	
A 1 Appliance Service	A	One	Appliance	Service	
Aagaar Insurance Agency	Aagaar	Insurance	Agency		
Acco Fastener Co	Acco	Fastener	Company		
Ace Rent-a-Car Co.	Ace	Rentacar	Company		
Ace-Hi Fuel Service	Acehi	Fuel	Service		
Aceweld Co	Aceweld	Company			
Acro-Sol-Tex Corp	Acrosoltex	Corporation			
Across-the-Line Transport Co	Acrosstheline	Transport	Company		
Lite's Pharmacy	Lite ('s)	Pharmacy			
Lite-Rite Light Mfg Co	Literite	Light	Manufacturing	Company	
Lit-L-Tyke Apparel Shop	Litltyke	Apparel	Shop		
Lit-O-Products Co	Litoproducts	Company			
Little Boy Blue Play School	Little	Boy	Blue	Play	School
Little Company of Mary Hospital	Little	Company (of)	Mary	Hospital	
Little Fur Shop	Little	Fur	Shop		
Little Jack's Restaurant	Little	Jack ('s)	Restaurant		
Little Margaret	Little	Margaret			
Littleford John R	Littleford	John	R		
Sain Edward	Sain	Edward			
Sainsbury Club	Sainsbury	Club			
St. Adrian's Cemetery	Saintadrian ('s)	Cemetery			
Ste. Elizabeth High School	Saintelizabeth	High	School (e of feminine form of Sainte omitted)		
St. John the Divine Evangelical Lutheran Church	Saintjohn (the)	Divine	Evangelical	Lutheran	Church
St. Lo Lodge	Saintlo	Lodge			
St. Louis Academy	Saintlouis	Academy			
Sanitary Board of St. Louis	Saintlouis	Sanitary	Board		
Sak Peter	Sak	Peter			
Saks-Fifth Avenue	Saks	Fifth	Avenue		
Sak-Son Paint Co	Sakson	Paint	Company		
Star City Laundry	Starcity	Laundry			
Starrett George	Starrett	George			

NOTE: File U. S. Government before commercial titles. Treat state and city offices in the same manner:

> Ohio (state of) Highway Department
> Ohio Acceptance Corporation
> Columbus (city of) Police Department

18. Frequently a firm whose name is that of its founder becomes so widely known that with the passing of years there is a question as to whether the name should be filed under given or surname. In such cases it is permissible to file the name as written. For example, the John Hancock Mutual Life Insurance Company may be filed under John, although filing under the surname Hancock is still technically correct. It is wise in such cases to use a cross reference.

1st unit	2d unit	3d unit	4th unit
Marshall	Field &	Company	

(File under Marshall, cross reference under Field, or vice versa.)

Robert	Burns	Hospital	
Betty	Wales	Dress	Shop
Johns	Hopkins	University	
Montgomery	Ward &	Company	

The names listed in the three groups on page 49 are shown correctly filed.

Geographic and Foreign Names.—1. Do not give the state when the name of a city is part of the name:

> Indianapolis Law Institute

2. Telephone directories almost invariably treat compound geographic names as two units, although opinion varies:

One-unit arrangement	*Two-unit arrangement*
Port Arthur, Texas (filed Portarthur)	Port Arthur, Texas
Porterville, California	Port Huron, Michigan
Port Huron, Michigan	Port Lavaca, Texas
Portland, Maine	Port Washington, Wisconsin
Port Lavaca, Texas	Porterville, California
Portsmouth, Ohio	Portland, Maine
Port Washington, Wisconsin	Portsmouth, Ohio

3. File Mt. as Mount, Pt. as Point, Ft. as Fort, St. as Saint, and similar abbreviations used for cities as if spelled in full.

Mount Vernon, Indiana
Mount Vernon, Virginia
Mount Vernon, Washington
Point Fermin, California
Pointville, New Jersey

Fort Wingate, New Mexico
Saint Anthony Park, Minnesota
Saint Paul, Minnesota
Sanborn, Minnesota

NOTE: All but a few cities have dropped the final "e" of the feminine form of Saint and in those cases the "e" is disregarded:

Sainte Genevieve, Missouri filed as though written Saintgenevieve
Sainte Marie, Illinois filed as though written Saintmarie

4. When points of a compass are part of the name, index as written:

North Chicago Coal Co.

5. Include The in the alphabeting of those few towns in the United States where the article is part of the name:

The Plains, Ohio
The Hollow, Virginia
The Rock, Georgia

6. Use the English spelling of foreign countries, provinces, and cities:

Bruxelles, Belgium	filed as	Brussels
Firenze, Italy	filed as	Florence
Helsinki, Finland	filed as	Helsingfors
Kjobenhaven, Denmark	filed as	Copenhagen
Iasi, Romania	filed as	Jassy
Moskva, Russia	filed as	Moscow
Habana, Cuba	filed as	Havana

Cross references to the native spelling should be made when needed.

7. File foreign governments under the name of the country:

Dominion of *Canada*
Republic of *France*

8. If there are only a few foreign names in the file arrange in exact letter sequence as written:

> *Sun* Yat Sen
> *Moy* Sam
> *Arrendondo* Perez Y Ca
> *Banco* de Londres Y Mexico S. A.
> *Beraud* Y Comu (Mexico)
> *Cia* De Machinas Keystone S. A.
> *Giovanni* Conti & Nipoti (Italy)
> *T*. Fukuhara Shoten (Japan)
> *Kay,* Grandjean & Cia (Argentine)
> *Maquinaria* Textil, S. A. (Mexico)
> *Compania* Molinera de Herran (So. America)
> *Stache* & Troncoso, Sur (Mexico)
> *Renato* Zapata & Cia
> *Talleres* Perez Zozaya

If there is much foreign correspondence with a large number of countries definite rules for filing foreign names should be established, and plenty of cross references should be made to other forms under which users of the file may call for a given paper.

A few difficulties in filing foreign names:

A. The articles in firm names are included in the alphabetic arrangement since some languages use different forms for articles modifying singular and plural words and also different forms for the masculine, feminine, and neuter genders:

> *LaBanque* Provinciale du Canada

B. Spanish surnames are composed of mother's surname before marriage and father's surname. A son often uses only father's surname. Portuguese surnames are formed in reverse order to Spanish, giving the father's name first.

C. In certain countries, as in Russia, the masculine and feminine form of the same family name vary:

Masculine	*Feminine*
Karinin	Karinina
Meltzoff	Meltzova

D. Chinese names present complications since so many of the Chinese in America have taken Christian given names:

> Charlie *Wun*
> Frank *Yong*

In such cases it is customary to alphabetize under the surname given in Chinese as is done in English.

Reference Books: For use with geographic files it is advisable to have at hand the following books: United States Official Postal Guide, published annually by the United States Post Office Department with eleven monthly supplements, which should be used as authority in case of question as to the spelling of the name of any town in the United States; a good atlas; an almanac.

Phonetic Filing.—Mention has been made of phonetic filing or filing by sound. There are several systems on the market.

A phonetic method which is perhaps the simplest one is an alphabetic arrangement of surnames identical or similar in pronunciation but different in spelling. Included also in this system are names which offer little possibility of confusion phonetically, but which advise cross reference because of marked similarity in spelling.

Sample:	BAEHR	Bare	Beher	*Try also:*
	Baer	Bayer	Behr	Baier
	Baeyer	Bear	Behre	Bayers
	Bair	Beare	Ber	Bir
	Baire	Behar	Bere	Boyer

These different spellings of the same name, not including those referred to by the "Try also," are filed together, and are broken down by given name or initial. In the place where the alternative spellings would be alphabetically filed, cross reference cards are inserted to indicate the removal of a name group to the group heading; i.e., a card filed under Bere would refer the user to Baehr. The group headings used are usually the first alphabetic spelling of the name; i.e., Baehr, rather than Baer, or Bear, even though the latter may be the more common spelling.

The purpose of this system is to facilitate the process of distinguishing names of like sound and variant spelling; to reduce the possibility of overlooking in the file unusual names with spellings similar to those of greater frequency; (i.e., Bergdall, try also Bergdolt, or Burckdall). In the case of the three names just listed, each would remain in its own alphabetical position in the file, but would be given a cross reference card to the other possibilities. Unusual spellings of names with familiar pronunciations would also be easily found; i.e., Bacar and Baker would, under this system, be brought together.

Another system known as the Soundex is based on a number scheme.

Rules

File by initial letter but do *not* code it

Code remaining consonants to 3 figures only

Code double consonants or equivalents as one letter. Double or equivalent of and initial letter are disregarded

Disregard *VOWELS* a e i o u & y except as separators of like or equivalent consonants

Disregard *H* and *W* entirely except as initial letters

Code

1 represents b f p v
2 represents c g j k q s x z
3 represents d t
4 represents l
5 represents m n
6 represents r

For example, Sheppard is coded 163

S   not coded because it is the initial letter
h   disregarded
e   disregarded
p = 1
p   disregarded because it is a double consonant
a   disregarded
r = 6
d = 3

Examples

Bird	B 630	Simms	S 520
Byrd	B 630	Dickson	D 250
Earhard	E 663	Lloyd	L 300
Ashcroft	A 261	Hughgill	H 240
Shea	S 000	Schworer	S 660

Arrangement is alphabetic by given name in each Soundex numeric group.

Such systems are valuable where information comes over the telephone, where spelling is not known, or where handwriting is illegible. It has been useful in insurance companies, utilities, charitable organizations, and credit bureaus.

Chapter 6

GEOGRAPHIC METHODS OF FILING

Reasons for Geographic Filing.—A number of businesses are not interested in information by name, but rather by location. For a variety of different reasons files are set up geographically:

1. Sales organizations must keep track of their branches; or, if they deal directly with their customers by means of salesmen who travel the road, they need to know how much business they are getting from such localities as a whole state or a part of the state. Many sales organizations have put on advertising campaigns over the radio the past few years. These have brought an onrush of replies. Usually the geographic method of filing them has been found best.

2. Mailing lists including addressograph plates are arranged geographically by those houses which carry on mail campaigns. The United States Post Office does not accept second-class mail except when it is separated by state and town, so that when addressing of envelopes is done from lists arranged geographically they are in order for delivery to the post office. Mail-order firms and publishers particularly come under this category.

3. Businesses may be licensed in some states and not in others. For example, insurance laws differ in various states, and an insurance firm operating in one state may not find it worth while to operate in another one because of its very different regulations. Or, if it wishes to operate in the latter state, it must have printed special policies for use in that state. Such forms are filed geographically.

4. A public utility may operate over a wide territory, in which case its records are filed by the names of the towns in

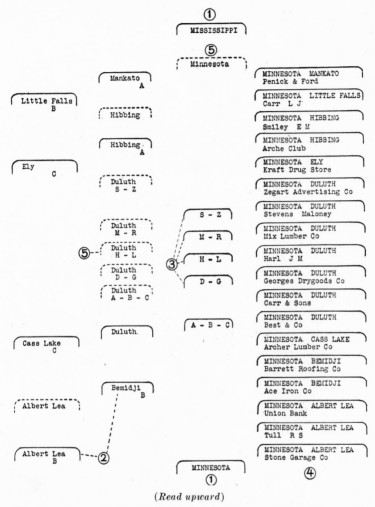

(Read upward)

Fig. 20.—Geographic State File. 1. State guides centered. 2. Town guides at left. Letters represent population: A, 10,000 and over. B, 5,000–10,000. C, 2,000–5,000. 3. Auxiliary guides for subdividing correspondence in important cities. 4. Regular correspondent folders. Note labels: state first, then town, then firm. 5. Miscellaneous folders (broken lines) for every state behind all the town guides for that state, and for such towns as require it; if preferable, a miscellaneous folder may be set up for each town.

which it does business. Again, a utility may operate in but one town (municipal ownership), or a branch of a large utility may retain its own files covering one town. In such cases the card records on each gas, electric, or water meter are filed by street, which is one form of geographic filing.

5. Real estate houses may arrange their material by town, or if they operate within one town, by street and lot number.

6. A great many government files are set up geographically: at Washington by states, and in each individual state capital by counties in that state.

Supplies for Geographic Files.—Supplies for geographic files are not as well standardized as are supplies for name files, first because the latter are so much more widely used and also because geographic files in different firms vary greatly, defying standardization. Some require miscellany for states only, others require miscellany for a few important towns in each state; some companies desire state guides in the center positions of the drawer, while others like the state tab on the left-hand side of the drawer. Fortunately, the supplies devised for name files can be adapted to geographic files with few exceptions but it does take some ingenuity to set up guides and folders for a geographic file best suited to the needs of a particular firm.

Types of Geographic Filing Systems.—There are four types of geographic filing: state, town, and name; town, state and name; group of states, such as New England States, town, and name; salesmen's routes, usually numbered, then by town and name. The latter two are not sufficiently important to warrant special description.

State Arrangement.—The state file is arranged alphabetically by states, then alphabetically by towns in that state, then alphabetically by names of firms in that town. (It still is not possible to get away from the name, but it has now become a secondary consideration.)

ALABAMA	BIRMINGHAM	Smith & Company
ALABAMA	MONTGOMERY	Jones & White Hardware Corp.
ARIZONA	PHOENIX	Addison Sam
CALIFORNIA	LOS ANGELES	Cates A K
CALIFORNIA	SACRAMENTO	Brooks Corporation
CALIFORNIA	SACRAMENTO	Dee & Ames

This state arrangement is the most common geographic file even though it is rather cumbersome with three classifications.

Guides with insert tabs are the most desirable sort because one can build up a file to fit his own needs. One company may do much business in Illinois and none in Alabama, or vice versa. The two companies would need entirely different state and town guides. The state guides come in one position, usually centered, and of a special color. Most state guides include the 48 states, District of Columbia, Canada, Alaska, Cuba, Hawaii, Guam, Mexico, Philippine Islands, Puerto Rico—57 guides in all. Tabs for town guides are usually staggered on the left side of the drawer in two or three positions. Inserts for guides can be purchased with the name of the town or county printed thereon. These are compiled from the latest United States Bureau of Census report and are carried in sets for towns and cities of a population of 500 and over, 1000 and over, 2000 and over—each town bearing a key figure or letter. Towns having a population of 1000 or more, for example, are indicated by a key showing the number of thousands of inhabitants, as:

Bovey   Minnesota   D   (D   1000-2000   pop.)

FIG. 21.—Printed Tab for Town Guide

If the miscellany is small in volume, one miscellaneous folder for each state and one for the principal cities in each state may be all that are required. They should be distinguished from the regular correspondent folders by means of a differently colored label. The tabs for the regular correspondent folders usually come at the right of the drawer.

Their labels should be typed with the state and town on the top line in capital letters; the name on the second line in upper and lower case.

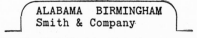

ALABAMA BIRMINGHAM
Smith & Company

FIG. 22.—Tab Used for State Arrangement

Not as tailormade as the system described above but still in common usage is the plan of buying printed state guides and then 48 sets of A – Z guides for the towns. Unimportant states with correspondence filling one drawer or less would use a 25 division of the alphabet; states with as much as 10 drawers of correspondence would use a 250 division of the alphabet. Miscellaneous folders under such a system would match the divisions of the alphabet under each state.

Town Arrangement.—The second geographic arrangement is alphabetically by names of towns (regardless of the state unless there are two or more towns of the same name in different states) and then alphabetically by firm name:

ABERDEEN	(SOUTH DAKOTA)	Smith Brothers
ABERDEEN	(WASHINGTON)	Parr & Dobbs
ABILENE	(KANSAS)	Koons L F
ADAMS	(MASSACHUSETTS)	Regal Sport Shop
ADRIAN	(MICHIGAN)	Haskins & Sells
AKRON	(OHIO)	First National Bank
ALAMEDA	(TEXAS)	Chase J I
ALBANY	(NEW YORK)	Central Railroad Company

Two setups of guides and folders are possible: a regular subdivision of the alphabet, as large or small as needed, with miscellaneous folders to match, may be found satisfactory. In the Ab miscellaneous folder would be filed material from firms or individuals in Aberdeen and Abilene. Should the correspondence with an Aberdeen firm become heavy, a special folder is set up with label typed as described above. The size of the division required depends upon the amount of material in file. Guides should average about 25 to a drawer. At best this setup is never entirely satisfactory because the subdivision of the alphabet as worked out for surnames does not fit town names.

The second possible arrangement for a town file is to use guides with insert tabs, one for every town in which the firm does business, or for the principal cities only. These guides are tabbed at the left of the drawer, as they take the place of regular guides with alphabetic combinations. Printed names of the principal cities may be obtained; others will have to be typed on blank inserts. When correspondence for any one firm is heavy, special name guides may be inserted exactly as is done in the alphabetic name file. Each town that has a guide should have a miscellany folder made for that town as soon as there is need for it. If there are odds and ends of correspondence for towns not important enough to have guides, some special arrangement such as an A miscellaneous folder at the end of all the A town folders will be required. The regular correspondent folders tabbed at right of drawer should have labels typed, with the name of the town first and then the state on the top line in capital letters, the name of the firm on the second line in upper and lower case.

Combining Geographical and Name Filing.—In a small file it is possible to combine without confusion under one index information filed geographically and material filed by name. The various department papers of a State Department of Education have been very satisfactorily combined in this manner, making use of color to distinguish one type of paper from another:

> Rural education matter filed by name of *County* designated by a salmon label.
>
> Secondary education (high school) material filed by name of *City* designated by a blue label.
>
> General correspondence with outside firms filed by name of *Person* addressed and designated by a white label.
>
> Legal correspondence on rural schools filed by name of *County*, salmon label.

Certification material including applications for positions and credentials filed by name of *Teacher,* buff label.

Cross references in geographic files are made out on colored sheets and placed in the proper folders in the same way as in the alphabetic name file except that the town and state (or county, or route number) must be added:

Idaho Rockford Bay Carr White & Co SEE Idaho Rockford Bay Board of Education	Three Oaks Michigan Cruver Company SEE Detroit Michigan Cruver Company
(*Misleading letterhead*)	(*Firm moved and cross reference left under old address when folder is retyped.*)

Fig. 23.—Cross Reference Sheets

Procedure for Geographic Filing.—The method of procedure in filing geographically is to inspect papers as they come to file to see that they are actually ready for file; make necessary cross references; underscore firm name (it is not necessary to underscore state or town name); encircle important subject matter; sort by main division—state, group of states, town, route numbers, or counties—according to the plan of file; then sort by second division such as town under a state arrangement; in a large file sort by third division, as individual or firm name.

For a state arrangement the sorter should contain a guide for every state. If the file is fairly good-sized, a second sorter equipped with A – Z guides is helpful in sorting the towns under each state. For a town arrangement the sorter need be equipped only with A – Z guides.

Not only is every geographic file less simple to set up than a name file, but it also requires considerably more time to get papers in and out of the file. It is the difference between handling papers three times (state, town, firm name) as against *once* in the name file, or *twice* in a town and name arrangement. Firms are beginning to realize the saving of time of this town method over that of a state, town, firm arrangement, and in analyzing the uses to which their records are put, a number of organizations have been shifting to this less cumbersome method where it has been necessary to keep a geographic file. Often a geographic file has been maintained over a period of years as a habit despite the fact that the firm's ledgers give the information needed by territory, and a name file would be more adequate. Those firms which have changed from a state to a name arrangement have estimated a saving of at least 33% and often more in filing labor. Recent years have seen a decided growth in the appreciation of filing with a subsequent study of filing costs. The result has been a simplification of many files.

When a change seems desirable from a state arrangement to a town or name setup, one drawer or one state should be changed at a time. The regular correspondence folders and then the miscellany from that drawer or state should be thrown into the sorter under the new arrangement. No confusion is necessary. Every paper should be in one of three places so as to be readily accessible: untouched as yet under the old arrangement; in the new file by town or firm name; or in the sorter in process of change.

Foreign Correspondence.—A certain portion of the correspondence of many firms is with foreign countries. Such correspondence may be voluminous as in large sales organizations or in banks, or, in the case of small organizations, very limited indeed, comprising a few folders only. Foreign correspondence is usually filed under the name of the country, followed by the name of the city, and then the name of firm or individual. This foreign material is placed at the end of, or entirely separate from, the regular (domestic) file. A guide with large tab indicates the "FOREIGN" division, and country guides take the place of state guides in the United States file. Some firms prefer to file Canada, West Indies, Alaska in alphabetic order by name among the states, while others group them alphabetically at the end of the main file. A separate filing cabinet is not necessary for foreign correspondence, unless volume requires it. The distinguishing guide "FOREIGN" marks it clearly enough within the drawer and the label on the outside of the drawer indicates the drawer contents.

Street Filing.—Street filing is not geographic location filing, although it seems to fit better into the discussion of geographic filing than anywhere else. This method of filing is used largely by two types of organizations: those which deal with public utilities such as gas, electric light, telephone, the water works, and other departments of a city; real estate and mortgage firms.

For example, gas companies keep a record of every meter installed. This is often called the history card, because it gives information as to the date of installation, dates of repair service on the meter, and other pertinent data. The name of the tenant occupying the building where a particular meter is located is not essential to this particular record, because there may be many tenants in one apartment during the life of a building, all using the same meter. This file is set up alphabetically by the names of the streets, and under each street by building number. A guide should separate each street and under each street should be subdivision guides for its 100's.

Rules for Street Filing.—

1. Named streets are filed alphabetically by name and then by house number.
2. Numbered streets may be filed in one of two ways:
   a) Spell out the number and file alphabetically:

> Tenth Avenue
> Tuthill Street
> Twentieth Place
> Twenty-eighth Street
> Twenty-fourth Street
> Twenty-sixth Street

This method is confusing to most people who think of numbers in their normal sequence and who prefer to:

b) Group all numbers together in consecutive order at the end of the named street file:

> Urbana Street
> Vliet Street
> Washington Avenue
> Ziegler Street
> 1st Street
> 2d Street
> 3d Place
> 3d Street

3. North is filed before South; East before West:

> Adams, E.
> Adams, W.
> Ashland, N.
> Ashland, S.

Treat Adams, East and Adams, West as two separate streets with a guide for each.

4. Corners where street numbers are not given:
   a) In the case of named streets, the name which comes first in alphabetic order is used for filing:

   Yates and Ashland Streets, filed under Ashland

   b) In the case of numbered streets, the number which comes first in alphabetic order is used:

   Twenty-first Street and Sixth Avenue, filed under Sixth

   c) In the case of named and numbered streets, the name which comes first in alphabetic order is used:

   Adams at 59th Street, filed under Adams
   Yates Street and Tenth Avenue, filed under Tenth

   d) In the case of corner locations, where names of streets only are given and the numbered location is

not obtainable, the named streets should precede
the numbered address on the same street:

Ashland and Yates
9 Ashland
100 Ashland

Maps as Aid.—It is often desirable to use maps in connection with geographic files. They are one of the oldest forms of graphic presentation. These maps may be hung on the wall, laid flat in shallow drawers, or tacked to a swing-wing displayer. Because of their volume, the filing of maps constitutes a real problem in several types of offices. In real estate firms they are in constant use, so require systematic care. In fire insurance companies they are filed in sections in large bound books, a special colored crayon being used to indicate the buildings on the various streets covered by fire insurance as distinguished from those not so covered. They are valuable in planning campaigns, such as national drives for membership put on by clubs, or campaigns for increasing business put on by sales organizations.

One special kind of map occasionally needed in business is a topographical map made by government surveyors. They are usually filed alphabetically by state and then by section.

Often a printed map in itself is not sufficient. Facts which appear in correspondence or in reports and are translated onto a map make the map valuable. This is done by means of map tacks which make visible at a glance on maps or charts important information desired by every businessman, such as salesmen's routes, sold or unsold territory, agencies, work of municipal departments, etc. These map tacks are made in several sizes with spherical or flat heads brilliantly colored and with sharp points of tempered steel. They come in solid colors of all hues, in combinations of colors, with numbers or letters—a total of more than one thousand symbols being available.

A sales organization might decide to have a map for every state in which it does business. Every prospect requesting a catalog could be designated by a green tack on the town where he lives. A customer might be designated by a red tack. Cities having ten or more prospects might be marked by an especially large green tack. A shifting of business can thus be readily detected by the sales manager who accordingly plans new routes for the salesmen.

Chapter 7

LENDING AND SAFEGUARDING RECORDS; CHARGE-OUTS

Recording Charge-Outs.—The most beautifully kept file avails no one if it is not used. Such a file is analogous to a library of valuable books carefully indexed which no one ever reads. The purpose of a file room, like that of a library, is to give service. Part of the service a file room renders is to find instantly any information required from the records and to maintain adequate methods of lending papers for temporary use. It is obvious that if the file room personnel is to be held responsible for material which is in its care, some record must be kept of those papers which are loaned. In a very small department file, memory rather than a written record might be adequate if nothing happened to the clerk, but a scientifically planned filing department never depends upon memory. And should the file clerk be absent there would be no memory to depend upon. It has been argued that the time it takes to record a loan could better be used in other directions. Five or ten minutes, and sometimes even hours, can be expended in frantic search for a lost paper, while it takes only five or ten seconds to make a charge-out. Such hunting is not at all unusual, even in small organizations, where there is no record of loans. But there is another psychological reason for the written record of a loan in that the borrower is much more conscientious about returning papers which are charged against his name than he is apt to be if no such information is kept.

The points to be noted about the paper lent are as follows:

Item (kind of paper)
Who wrote it

Date
Subject
   (address for geographic files)
Borrower's name and department
Date borrowed

This can be written in telegraphic form as: Let. of 3/3/5-, Barret Bros., Atlanta, re credit on chairs. DFE Acctg dept. 4/10/5-. The card on which the charge is penciled is put in the folder from which the paper is removed and remains there until it is returned.

Rules for Use of Files.—Every file department should have definite regulations for the use of the files. Included might be the following, which are adhered to by a great many firms:

1. No one except the file department is permitted access to the files during working hours.
2. Requisitions for material in file must be in writing on blanks provided for the purpose.
3. Papers charged to one person may not be lent to another without recharging.
4. File clerks will not be held responsible for running down material not in file.
5. Papers may be retained for ten days. If required for a longer period of time a second charge will be made for the same length of time.
6. Whole folders should not be requested when two or three papers therefrom will suffice.

Access to Files.—Permitting no one in the file department except the clerks often involves the arrangement of the files in a special room or in some compact fashion that physically bars all but the file clerks. It often means also that the file cases are kept locked at night. When the work in the file room is heavier than the personnel can manage advantageously, it is sometimes expedient to limit the time during which calls can be made upon the file room, as from 10 to

12 and from 2 to 4 (excepting in emergencies) so that the clerks can have uninterrupted periods for collecting, sorting, and filing. Or again, firms may allow employees other than the file clerks access to the files for finding only. These employees will then charge papers borrowed to themselves. When finished with the papers in question they put them in baskets on top of the cabinets. They should never be allowed to refile anything.

If files are locked at night, access to them is then impossible. This is a hardship for departments working overtime and does not give the service the file room should render. As stated above, employees can be trained to make out their own charge-out cards. Wherever possible, however, those needing papers after working hours should ask ahead of time for what they will need—a practice followed by many organizations.

How Material Can Be Borrowed.—Methods of borrowing include interdepartment telephone, messenger, requisition slips, and calls in person. Telephone, messenger, and calls in person are "word of mouth" calls and require the trained ear. The requisition slip challenges the eye. When each borrower writes out his own requisition for papers wanted, signing his name to it, the file clerk has at once an accurate description of the material required and also has the person's own signature as a receipt to prove that he took the material out of the file room. Where mail is collected several times daily for the file room, requisitions for material which is not needed immediately are placed in the file baskets on department desks and picked up with the correspondence. These are then filled and delivered by the file department.

Time Material May Be Held.—The length of time a paper may be loaned depends on the business. The usual length of time is from a week or ten days to two weeks. Where material is very confidential the rule is that everything has to be in file every night. On the other hand, if a certain department has occasion to use a paper over a period of time and no other department calls for that paper, there need be no hard and fast rule recalling it. A good method is to ask for the paper in ten days' time, then recharge it for another ten days. The file clerk should set aside a definite time of the week to go through the charge-outs and to trace the papers which have been out of file longer than the stipulated period. Unless this is done, overdue charges may remain in the file for months and even years and it may not be possible to find the material when needed.

Recharging of File Material.—It is a question how best to handle material charged to one person who in turn passes

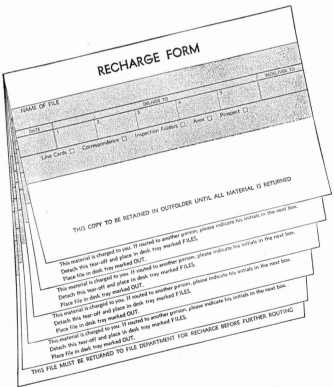

Fig. 24.—Blank for Recharging of File Material

it on to some one else. Theoretically, the person charged with the paper should be held responsible for it. Actually the file clerk usually does the tracing. Some firms require that correspondence be sent back to the file room and be recharged before it can be handed to some one else. This causes unnecessary delay where records must go the rounds of several departments. One method, which has been found successful to a varying degree, is to provide each department with pads of blank slips, similar to the illustration. As the person to whom the paper is charged passes it on, he fills out one of the blanks and puts it in the file basket to be collected with his other papers. When it reaches the file room it is substituted for the present charge in the out-card. Such a recharge system can be used an indefinite number of times for the same paper.

The scheme is only as good as the cooperation granted to the file room by the various departments. If any one is un-

Correspondence of		Date
Address		
Reference to		
Signed	Department	Date

CORRESPONDENCE REQUISITION

Correspondence will be sent from Files, and charged to the person signing this requisition.

If it is necessary to give all, or any part of the correspondence, to any other person or Department before it is returned to the File Room, see that a requisition for the same is signed by the person to whom the correspondence is given, then send that requisition to File Room.

Be very careful to keep all correspondence together, and return to files as soon as possible.

FIG. 25.—Correspondence Requisition

willing to fill out the recharge slip it remains a scrap of paper and the whole system breaks down. However, those who have suffered the inconvenience of waiting for papers which have to be traced are usually willing to cooperate.

Supplies for Charging.—There are a variety of supplies available for charging: an out-guide of pressboard, letter size, with celluloid tab reading OUT which protrudes above the folder in which it is placed, has a pocket or clamps for holding a 3 x 5″ charge-out card. The out-guide is put in the folder from which the paper is taken and when the paper is returned the charge card is taken out (not destroyed), the empty out-guide being placed in front of the drawer to be used over and over again as needed.

A letter-sized out-guide less expensive than that described above is made of heavy card stock with proper captions and wide ruling to accommodate 30 or 40 entries written directly on the card. As a borrowed paper is returned, the entry is

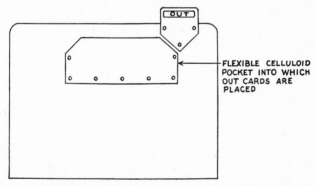

FIG. 26.—Out-Guide. The Whole Guide Replaces in the File the Papers Which Are on Loan.

scratched off and the next line used for the next charge. This type of out-card is apt to look untidy, and as the card fills up, new ones are required. As a matter of fact, any colored card stock high enough to extend above the folder, even if only four inches wide and without captions, can be made to do in a pinch.

If a whole folder has to be sent out of the department, it is wise to use an out-folder in its place so that any incoming mail for that name which is being filed while the regular folder is out will not by mistake get into the miscellaneous folder. This habit of filing material in the miscellany when

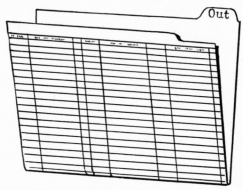

FIG. 27.—Out-Folder

the regular folder is charged is a common error. The folder has printed on the front flap the same wide rulings as described in the paragraph above so that it is used both as a folder and a charge-out.

Unless the papers are fastened, lending out a whole folder involves the possibility of return with papers missing. Since the file clerk cannot count each paper in a folder before sending it out, there is no way to check the return of all of them; thus papers are apt to become lost. Moreover, lending a whole folder where two or three papers will suffice means that some one else is delayed in receiving papers he needs from the same folder.

Many firms do not wish the pockets to go out of the file room as they become badly worn through handling. If the full contents of a folder must be lent, special folders, often of a brilliant color to call attention to the fact that the material is on a loan only, are furnished with the loan, and the regular folder is kept in its place in the drawer.

One coming to the file room merely to consult, say, a newspaper for a stock market over-the-counter quotation for a previous date, and not expecting to take the file back to his desk, is not charged with this material.

Lost Papers.—Despite the utmost precaution, papers do occasionally get lost. Salesmen take quotations with them on their trips and forget to bring them back; substantiating information is sent out to branch offices and is never returned; papers get lost even in executive desks. As soon as the loss is discovered, as much of the contents of the paper as can be remembered or such information as there is concerning the paper should be typed, together with the exact time of its disappearance as reported and the first request made for it after its disappearance. Some firms place this information in a bright red folder provided for that purpose and file it with the other folders. Other organizations mark one of their regular correspondent folders with large letters "LOST" or use a special colored label on a folder and file as previously described.

Tests which have been taken with an ordinary file show that about one paper in ten sent to file is ever called out again. Yet it always seems to be the paper most needed which is gone. There is a logical explanation: the important paper has been called for and lent time and again. The correspondence which is never taken out of the cabinet is rarely missing.

Division of Work.—Where there are two or more file clerks, the "lookups" may be divided among them, or the person most familiar with the files and the routines of the office may be designated as the "lookup" clerk. A good lookup clerk must have imagination in order to ferret out the hiding place of a needed paper if it is not where it belongs, and persistence in never giving up even if the paper is gone for weeks. The lookup clerk is often the best paid member of the file staff. If the practice is followed of giving all the "lookups" to one clerk his desk should be located near the entrance to the file room so that he can serve immediately those who come with special requests. This also holds true of the file department with one clerk.

As has been said, a charge-out card removed when its paper is returned should not be destroyed. In some file rooms these cards are counted daily and the totals recorded on a statistical sheet provided for that purpose; in others the clerk keeps a daily count of the lookups as he gives them out. These counts may be classified so as to show the activity in the various files. They also, together with the record of the number of papers filed daily, show the "load" which the file clerk carries. Wherever executives hazard a guess as to the activity of their files, they are apt to err on the side of underestimating. Such figures, therefore, prove illuminating. In addition to totals for the day, they are also kept by the week, month, and year for purposes of comparison. It should be noted that such checks are maintained in file rooms with one clerk.

A bonus system applied to lookups has sometimes proved successful. A minimum salary with an incentive, perhaps 5¢ per lookup, stimulates the alacrity with which requests are serviced.

If every one who came to the files had the sense of *borrowing* material and therefore of returning it, much of the irritation resulting from papers not being quickly located would be eliminated.

Chapter 8

TRANSFER AND FINAL DISPOSITION
OF RECORDS

Annual Transfer.—The average concern transfers once a year and sets up a new file for the current year. This is usually done on a specified date, often the last day of the calendar year. If midwinter is the busy season another date such as the last day of the fiscal year is preferable. It is never advisable to transfer merely because the folders are full. In such cases it is a simple matter to add another folder for the same name, dividing the material by dates or by departments and marking the folders accordingly. Then at the end of the year the records for the full year in their folders are removed. Some organizations, cramped for file space, transfer semi-annually or even quarterly, while others transfer only once in two years.

Supplies Needed for Transfer.—Several weeks before transfer season, supplies are requisitioned: blank tabbed folders for regular correspondence with a matching number of labels, a set of miscellaneous folders carrying the same division of the alphabet as that already in file, and whatever containers may be required for the transferred material. The file clerk goes through the file drawers one by one, jotting on paper the names of those with whom the firm is certain to have communication during the coming period. A common and wasteful fault is to make up new folders for all customers who had folders the past year. Often that means that empty folders clog the files all year. The names selected for new folders should be written exactly as they are to appear on the labels of the new folders. If a color scheme is used the color should be indicated after each name listed. This list is given to a typist who copies it exactly. The guides remain in file from year to year.

It is not always necessary to use new folders; those already used, if in fair shape, may be salvaged. When it is time to destroy the papers within the folders, a scalpel or a razor blade is used to remove the labels from the folder tabs and the folders are then reused instead of being discarded. This requires, of course, high grade folders. This method has proved cheaper in some instances than buying new, poor grade folders annually. Another saving is to type one's own miscellaneous folders, copying exactly the notation on the guide behind which it is to be filed and using a distinguishing label.

Methods of Transfer.—There are three methods of transfer:

A. The bodily method is to remove all material for the period, whether one year or half a year, to a storeroom or less accessible space. This means that with the beginning of the new period the file drawers are empty, with inevitable reference to the old files, especially during the first part of the new period, requiring a great deal of running to the storeroom. Therefore it is advisable to keep last year's transfer in the current file room whenever possible in one of the two methods described below.

B. The double capacity method uses the bottom row of drawers in a battery, or even the two lowest drawers, for last year's material. The upper two drawers are kept for current material. Sometimes, when space is at a premium, transfer cabinets in units four drawers high are placed on the tops of the current files. Occasionally units eight or twelve high are stacked in a store room near the files with a "shoestore" or a platform ladder used to reach the contents.

C. The perpetual or continuous method permits material to be assembled for fifteen months (or eighteen months or even two years) in the current files. Toward the end of the year new folders are prepared as in the two preceding methods. With the beginning of the new year each new folder is placed in front of its matching folder in file. The year must be very clearly stamped on both folders. Material of the new year is put in the new folders while the old folders are easily accessible for reference. At the end of the fifteenth month the first twelve months of material are removed. In this way the current files are never empty, carrying as a minimum three months of material, and as a maximum fifteen months of material.

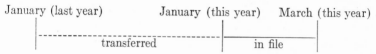

This last method of transferring is not so well known as the other two but it has proved very satisfactory where used and when space permits.

Weeding Out Current Records.—The time to begin thinking about the retention and final destruction of records is when they are current. Much material of a temporary nature gets into cabinets, which might better not have been filed in the first place. For example, letters of acknowledgment, letters of transmittal, temporary price lists, forms and reports which are in more permanent form elsewhere, and requests for catalogs and information could go into a temporary file to be weeded out every 90 days.

A number of firms have worked out satisfactorily the imprinting of the destruction date on the papers as they go to file; that is, some papers are stamped 30 days, some 60 days, some Permanent. Clerks go through the drawers systematically every month, pulling those records which have reached the obsolescence date; or the pulling is undertaken a little each day at the time the regular filing is being done.

The Department of Labor of the United States Employment Service suggests that the following records be retained six months only:

1. Letters and memoranda of transmittal without attachments.
2. Requests for comment without attachments.
3. Letters, notes, and memoranda of simple acknowledgment.
4. Requests for information and replies requiring no administrative action, no new decisions, and no original development of special data.
5. Minor items of reference data sent to field offices solely for their information and not requiring any specific administrative action. (This is not intended to cover any orders, directives, instructions, or statements of policy.)
6. Correspondence regarding plans for meetings or conferences (e.g., invitations to attend and acceptances or regrets, notices, arrangements for space and facilities, arrangements for chairmen, arrangements for speakers), not including finally approved agenda or programs, minutes, transcripts of proceedings, speeches delivered, and comments made at or after the meetings or conferences.
7. Memoranda and correspondence regarding changes or correction in mailing lists and directories, but not including directories themselves.
8. Mailing lists.
9. Correspondence and internal memoranda regarding details of office management (e.g., preparation and forwarding of checks; arrangements for leave, for travel, for courteous reception and general cooperation).
10. Correspondence regarding progress in publication of completed studies.
11. Issuances, notices, reports, releases, tabulations, and publications of other federal or state agencies and private organizations requiring no administrative action and submitted for general information only.
12. Records pertaining to the approval of forms.
13. Internal memoranda making arrangements for duplicating, for photographing, for the preparation of graphs or charts, and for stenographic or clerical service.
14. Statistical information supplied to other agencies on the basis of data elsewhere compiled by the agency.

15. Records pertaining to charity drives, bond campaigns, and other voluntary activities not part of the regularly assigned functions of the agency.

16. Applications for positions and notes and memoranda regarding qualifications of unsuccessful candidates for positions, including notes on interviews.

17. Records pertaining to the deferment of officers and employees, other than those placed in official personnel folders.

18. Letters consisting primarily of excerpts or quotations from documents that are retained elsewhere in complete form.

19. Correspondence referring inquirers to field offices of the agency or to other government agencies.

20. Follow-up requests for delayed reports from field offices.

21. Gratuitous suggestions and stereotyped replies or non-stereotyped replies requiring no administrative action, no new decision, and no original development of special data.

22. Requests for and offers of forms or publications, replies to such requests, or offers and summaries of requests.

Storage of Obsolescent Papers.—When the transfer season arrives, the oldest material in the file room may be packed and sent to the warehouse. The drawers with contents from succeeding years are moved into their place in proper order. The new folders, regular and miscellaneous, should have been sorted into alphabetic order so that they can be slipped into their scheduled places immediately as the old regular and miscellaneous folders are removed. The guides remain in the current file and should, with proper handling, last from five to ten years. In the transferred file the miscellaneous folders act as guides.

Binding is one method of keeping old records. It means putting papers in book form with cloth covers and descriptions stenciled on the back. A special machine forms and shapes the steel back to proper size, drills holes through the two covers, the back, and the sheet body. Lock pins are then inserted. Without taking the book from the shelf the caption can be read. There is a permanence and neatness obtained through binding which can be secured in no other way. Records once bound into a neat volume remain there indefinitely, always instantly accessible. Regardless of the number of times they are referred to, they never become

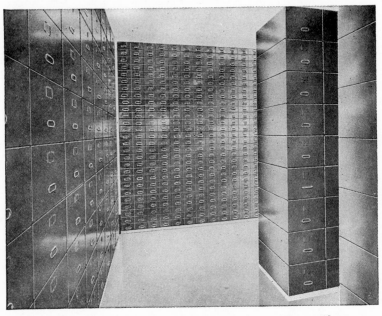

Fig. 28.—Storage Cabinets, Legal, Tabulating, and Letter Sizes.
(Record Files, Inc.)

lost or misplaced. These bound volumes can be placed on shelving built above the filing cabinets, thus utilizing space which is ordinarily wasted. Sometimes it is considered a disadvantage to handle and carry an entire book instead of just the one paper needed. Papers should not be bound for a year after being removed from the current file. If binding is done too soon, papers may be out at the time binding is done. Supplementary volumes are then invariably neces-sary to pick up the loaned papers. Expense is also a factor if the work is done outside. However, since binding machines can be rented, the work can be performed in the filing department in spare time. This lowers the expense of the process considerably. The machines are simple to operate so that one complete binding operation takes but a few minutes.

Fig. 29.—Binding Machine (McBee Co).

Microphotography.—In the past few years an entirely new process of photographing records called microphotography has been developed. Microphotography is the taking of pictures of business documents at a high rate of speed on narrow width motion picture film (16 or 35 millimeters), at a level of reduction so high that the image produced cannot be read with the naked eye. Readability is secured through a projector which brings the image back to normal or larger size. By means of this filming technique a volume of reproduction can be accomplished at a reasonable rate and there is considerable condensation of space in addition. Seventy mm. film, which does not require enlargement to be read, is also available.

The life of the film is a factor which recommends this method of reproduction, particularly in view of the short duration of present-day sulphite paper. This point has been thoroughly studied by the National Bureau of Standards. Their preliminary announcements state that the safety film used exclusively in microphotography under ordinary conditions has a life equal to that of 100% rag paper; i.e., 100 years. If the film is found to be deteriorating it is a simple matter to run it through the printing machine to reproduce a new copy. The film should be kept free from dust and in normal room temperature.

Generally speaking, the 16 mm. film is used for copying checks and other loose papers, while the 35 mm. film is used in copying current newspapers and in the reproduction of large sheets. Seventy mm. film is useful in the recording of engineering data, maps, land records, and bound volumes. Papers to be copied can be arranged in alphabetic order, in numeric order, or according to any of the standard methods of filing, before being put through the machine which houses the camera. Thus the film will be self-indexing. The photographing machine may also be equipped with certain indexing devices which can be changed as required. These indexes which can be compared to guides and folders are set at any desired point and the notation shown by the indexing device will be photographed continuously along the edge of the film. Indexing can also be done by inserting targets at regular intervals.

The amount of condensation possible from microfilm reproduction is shown in the following figures (these vary of course with different companies): one roll of 16 mm. film which occupies space about 4 inches square by ¾ inch thick (4″ x 4″ x ¾″) is sufficient to photograph.

13,000 bank checks
5,800 4″ x 6″ cards
3,000 letters

On one roll of 35 mm. film can be obtained the equivalent of 6000 8½″ x 11″ letters, or on one 200-foot roll of 16 mm.

film 20,000 normal-sized bank checks. The cost of film includes developing and is calculated by three separate methods: per thousand documents, per running foot of negative, per frame or single exposure. Special cabinets are now manufactured which house 600 of these rolls of film.

There are several concerns which manufacture cameras for microphotography purposes and the cabinets which house the cameras. These may be purchased outright or rented on a lease operational basis. Papers can be fed into the hopper of the machine at the rate of 70–80 statements per minute, or 60–70 checks per minute. The process is so simple that the office boy can quickly learn to operate it. As the papers pass a certain point in the machine the photograph is taken. Two cameras may be used if it is desired to have a duplicate. The papers come to rest at the bottom of the machine in the same order in which they were inserted. Feeding into the machine can also be done automatically.

Film-reading machines which are self-contained projectors can be operated either manually or electrically. The reader shows the documents in their original size or larger so they are easily read.

The microcard is a very new development. This is a card 3″ x 5″ in size on which a whole 8½″ x 11″ letter is reproduced. All information is easily read with average eyesight and there is no need for readers, projectors, or magnifiers. Adequate space permits indexing and cross referencing. Thus a whole folder or even a drawer of letters can be reduced to a 3″ x 5″ size, occupying a fraction of the space needed by the originals. Drawings as large as 38″ x 50″ can be efficiently reduced to microcard form.

Colored prints are also now available in card sizes. Illustrations of fabrics or of a machine taken on film in color are useful to salesmen.

The earliest use of microphotography was in banks for the reproduction of checks. When a canceled check has been paid and returned to the depositor the bank can protect itself from fraud only by its own records. The application of microphotography is becoming fairly widespread in the simplification of accounting techniques. Department stores are using it for their accounts receivable. As the invoices are ready to be mailed to the charge customers the first of

FIG. 30.—Projector (Recordak Corp.)

each month, they are put in alphabetic arrangement and photographed that way. The film is filed by months.

Many organizations are using microphotography to make a small file of their important records which can be stored away from the original location to protect against fire, loss, and theft. Insurance companies are using it more and more for their inactive records because of the great condensation of space involved.

The advantages of microphotography may be summed up as follows: a saving in cost because the film occupies a small fraction of the space occupied by the original material; equipment is eliminated; labor is reduced. There is no necessity of going to a warehouse for the consultation of old records. If the papers are filmed in sequence, as alphabetically by name or numerically, they cannot be lost. The film

Fig. 31.—Feeding Cards into the Hopper of a Microfilmer.
(Recordak Corp.)

in a safe deposit box acts as a protection in case the original records are destroyed.

There are still some difficulties to be overcome. Reductions can be made at such a high rate that they are not easily read. The indexing of miscellaneous matter presents another problem. When a film runs in a certain sequence, such as alphabetically by name or numerically, it is simple to locate the particular item wanted, but when miscellaneous data are being copied it is difficult to index the material for rapid reference.

Where a saving in the cost of storing records is the only objective of microfilming, the desirability of the project is normally based on the difference between microfilming costs and the costs of storing the records in paper form. In general, records to be retained ten years or less are not approved for filming.

Storage costs may range from $1.00 to $2.00 a square foot. At 6 square feet per cabinet,

```
$ 6.00 would be the annual cost of space renting at $1.00 a sq. ft.
  9.00    "    "    "    "      "    "    "        "    "  1.50 "  "  "
 12.00    "    "    "    "      "    "    "        "    "  2.00 "  "  "
```

Figure $40.00 for the cost of the storage cabinet, and the microfilming cost of one 4-drawer cabinet at $100.00. The cost of storage exceeds the cost of microfilming when records are

```
11    years old for space renting at $1.00 a sq. ft. ($40.00 plus $66.00)
 7      "    "    "    "        "    "  1.50 "  "  "
 5½     "    "    "    "        "    "  2.00 "  "  "
```

The rate of operation depends partly on the uniformity of the papers as to size and type and condition of media, and partly on the industry and dexterity of the operator. A good operator can microfilm 20,000 to 30,000 index cards per working day. Letter-sized sheets of uniform quality may be microfilmed at the rate of 12,000 per day. Production rates of only 7000 or 8000 images per day are common when both sides of many of the papers must be photographed. Because of the difficulty of correcting mistakes made in microfilming, the quality of the product is more important than the rate of production. In terms of drawers of letter-sized records, production will vary from one to three drawers per camera day. A fair average would be about one and one-half drawers, normally filled. Upon completion, every film should be viewed for legibility and then labeled and logged before being stored.

The most difficult types of records to photograph are green tissue carbon copies, faint hectograph and mimeograph material, negative photostats, deep shades of colored papers, and blurred carbon copies on white paper. It is of paramount importance that all film be proofed for assurance that every image is clearly legible. If not, it may be necessary to rerun the film.

The legal aspect of microphotography is of vital importance to any firm. If the original records have been destroyed, will a film shown in court stand as evidence? Before secondary evidence (including films) is admitted, the cause or motive of destruction is closely scrutinized. Where circumstances establish that destruction was free from suspicion or intended fraud and that the papers were destroyed in the natural course of business, secondary evidence is admitted. Targets inserted at the beginning and end of each film verifying their authenticity and signed by an officer of the company are of value in establishing their authenticity. The Bureau of Internal Revenue states that it is undesirable and impracticable to attempt to make tax determinations on the basis of microfilm reproductions of general books of account, such as cash books, journals, voucher registers, ledgers, etc. However, no objection will be interposed to the retention by taxpayers of only microfilm reproductions of supporting records of details, such as payroll records, canceled checks, invoices, vouchers, etc., provided the following conditions are met: (1) the taxpayer will retain microfilmed copies so long as the contents thereof may become material in the administration of any internal revenue law; (2) the taxpayer will provide appropriate facilities for preservation of the films and for the ready inspection and location of the particular records, including a projector for viewing the records, in the event inspection is necessary for tax purposes; and (3) the taxpayer will be ready to make any transcriptions of the information contained on the micro-film which may be required. According to a recent ruling, Social Security quarterly reports and supporting data may be filmed, the originals of which are filed with the collector under the Federal Insurance Contributions Act.

Factors Affecting Retention of Records.—A retention schedule is a planned life span of every group of records. Mail order houses with their eye on a small margin of profit circumvent the problems of storing old records by not re-taining files. They return the customer's order with the goods, leaving only bookkeeping records for reference.

Usage requires most companies to keep their records for a varying number of years. Most companies keep their rec-ords far too long. It is estimated that 35% of all existing records should be destroyed. Those records important enough to be retained should be put on suitable paper. The National Bureau of Standards has specifications for the strength of paper, which is measured by folding endurance, tearing resistance, and tensile strength. Inks must also be carefully selected where permanency is desired. Highly acid inks fade and also weaken the paper. The dye base developed for fountain pens also fades. India ink, however, does not fade and causes no damage to paper. This should be borne in mind when making entries in ledgers and journals, and when writing contracts.

The purpose of the retention of records is not merely to yield information in case of a lawsuit or request from the government. It should also serve as a history of the com-pany. In selecting records for preservation, therefore, care should be taken to retain papers covering all fields of the business, not only sales and accounting, but production, management, personnel, and plant. At the beginning of World War II, many organizations felt themselves in great need of information about their policies in World War I. Most management records had not been retained and the memory of some of the old-time employees had to be relied on. A sampling from the file may give enough information in future years to indicate important trends; for example, saving all papers for one letter of the alphabet, such as "A," discarding the balance; or leaving all material for certain key days of the year, eliminating the others.

The prime factors affecting the retention of records are the law and usage. Certain types of business, such as the public utilities and railroads, have their schedule for retention of records laid down for them by government agencies without too much opportunity for discretion. In private business the retention of certain types of records is governed by law, but there is considerable latitude permitted in disposing of other records not so governed. The type of business also is a factor in the retention of records. Some sales offices have little use for their records after six months, while others may refer back to orders placed 20 years ago. The location of a record, whether difficult of access or close at hand, determines to some extent its period of retention. Original records and duplicate copies may be handled in different ways.

The usage which a record receives can be accurately determined by keeping a check on all requests for old material. It is not uncommon to find a department head wishing to retain certain records a long period of time because "we refer to it so frequently." By having the file clerk tabulate all requests for material which has been transferred out of the file room through listing the nature of the paper desired, date of paper, and borrowers' names, a very accurate check can be made on frequency of reference to old records. One concern found, upon completing such a tabulation over a period of several months, that 91% of the requests were for material less than six months old, 1% for material over a year old. The statutes of limitation govern the time during which suit may be brought to collect an account. When an account is outlawed, there is no need to retain the supporting papers. Most firms, therefore, take into account the statute of limitation in their particular state in deciding when to destroy records. The following table indicates the number of years in which suits may be brought on simple contracts:

	Years		Years		Years
Alabama	6	Maine	6	Oklahoma	5
Arizona	6	Maryland	3	Oregon	6
Arkansas	5	Massachusetts	6	Pennsylvania	6
California	4	Michigan	6	Rhode Island	6
Colorado	6	Minnesota	6	South Carolina	6
Connecticut	6	Mississippi	6	South Dakota	6
Delaware	3	Missouri	10	Tennessee	5
Dist. of Col.	3	Montana	8	Texas	4
Florida	5	Nebraska	5	Utah	6
Georgia	6	Nevada	6	Vermont	6
Idaho	5	New Hampshire	6	Virginia	5
Illinois	5–10	New Jersey	6	Washington	6
Indiana	10	New Mexico	20	West Virginia	10
Iowa	10	New York	6	Wisconsin	6
Kansas	5	North Carolina	3	Wyoming	10
Kentucky	15	North Dakota	6		
Louisiana	10	Ohio	15		

Other records covered by law include matters of interest to the federal government, such as data on income tax, unemployment insurance, and wage stabilization. See pages 96–102.

It is on the records not covered by law that there is the greatest divergence of opinion. Each firm must work out its own schedule, because its usage of records will be different from that of any other concern.

Preparing a Schedule of Retention.—To undertake a study of the retention of records, most firms have found it wise to appoint a committee. Counsel and the comptroller are almost invariably found on such a committee. The office manager or executive in charge of office operations will be included. Department heads may or may not be included.

To go about making such a schedule for the retention of records a form might be prepared as shown in Figure 32. Each department head is given as many blank forms as he has different kinds of records. These reports are turned in and tabulated, and then the committee studies each record

FINANCIAL DIV. OFFICE MGT. DEPT.	RECORD RETENTION			NO. DATE PAGE
ITEM NUMBER				
DEPARTMENT				
DESCRIPTION AND PURPOSE				
ORIGIN				
CLASSIFICATION	☐ VITAL ☐ ESSENTIAL	☐ IMPORTANT		☐ USEFUL
REASON FOR RETENTION				
HOW FILED				
LOCATION–ACTIVE				
LOCATION–INACTIVE				
RETENTION PERIOD				
APPROVALS			DEPT. MGR.	DIV. HEAD

Fig. 32.—Schedule for Retention of Records

from the angle of law and usage in order to establish its retention period. It must be borne in mind that certain records in one department may be duplicates of those in another; for example, the master copy of the order filed by name of customer may be kept seven years, while a copy filed by number need be kept only two years.

If records are worth preserving at all they should be preserved in such a manner as to be properly protected and easily accessible. Insuring records is becoming increasingly popular, but many records are irreplaceable at any cost. There are two basic methods of protection:

a) Combustible surroundings may be eliminated so that the exposure of records to fire may be very slight.
b) Duplicate records may be kept at different points.

The Store Room.—Vaults, safes, and steel files are commonly used to house inflammable records. Some business concerns have provided a detached building of fire-resistive construction where infrequently used but important records may be kept. Open shelving and bins, even within fireproof

Fig. 33.—Mobile Storage Units. In front of rows of fixed units where ordinarily space is reserved for an aisle, pairs of steel rails are installed level in the floor. Mobile storage units are placed on the rails. By rolling them to appropriate positions, any unit becomes immediately accessible. Existing storage capacity can be increased up to 50%. (Acrow, Inc.)

buildings, are not satisfactory because the contents are exposed to the air so that the paper becomes soiled and brittle. Under these conditions steel filing cabinets are the ideal solution. In some instances business houses have steel filing cabinets in their warehouses where the drawers are interchangeable with those in the current records. This saves a great amount of time in the transfer period in shifting from one drawer to another because the entire drawer is taken out of the shell without removing the papers.

The aisles of the storage room should be lettered or numbered, each type of record should be listed, and an index card should be prepared giving the name of the record, its department, date, form number if any, retention schedule, and location. The label on the front of each drawer should give the contents of that drawer so that reference to the files should be a very simple matter. One person should be in charge of the storage room and all requests for material should come to him in requisition form. This requisition can be made out in duplicate, one copy to go back with the papers requested and the other to remain in the storage department until they are returned. In other words, a record should be kept of the papers out of file in the store room, just as in the current file department.

Final Destruction.—The final destruction of records is usually supervised by an officer of the company. Burning is preferable to other methods and is much better than selling papers as junk, for instance. One method of destroying records is to have the papers cut into very narrow strips by means of a paper shredder. The paper thus shredded can then be used for packing purposes. It has been found effective to keep a permanent notebook giving a brief description of the items disposed of, periods covered by these items, date of destruction, and signature of officer authorizing destruction.

Laws and Government Regulations on Record Preservation by Business.—The laws and regulations that are pertinent to record preservation fall into two general classes. The first class consists of rules definitely prescribing the periods of time various records must be preserved. After any such period has passed, other things being equal, it is proper to destroy such related records. The second mentioned class consists of various statutes of limitation. After the passage of the applicable period of time so specified, the businessman having a defense as to such possible liability may, other things being equal, destroy his related records.

It may be added that, with the present trend toward governmental regulation, the subject of business record preservation becomes increasingly important.

Income Tax, Federal. Books of account and records that establish gross income and other matters required to be shown in any federal income tax return should be retained by the taxpayer for as long as the contents thereof may become material in the administration of any Internal Revenue law. It is ordinarily advisable to preserve for federal income tax purposes books of account and records that establish gross income deduction, credits, and other pertinent items for at least SIX years after the filing of the related federal income tax return.

It should be noted that it may be advantageous for the taxpayer to preserve certain books of account and records for LONGER than the indicated five-year period where such books and records help establish a cost basis for capital gain or loss purposes or other items of long-term tax importance. It is advisable to preserve INDEFINITELY copies of all federal income tax returns. Such continuous preservation of old tax returns may help the taxpayer establish the filing of a particular return that the Bureau of Internal Revenue may claim was not filed.

Labor. Fair Labor Standards Act of 1938 as amended, effective June 19, 1950 (Federal Wage-Hour Act). Each employer subject to sections 6 and 7(a) of the Fair Labor Standards Act shall maintain and preserve the following payroll account:

1. Employee's name in full
2. Home address
3. Date of birth if under 19
4. Occupation in which employed
5. Time and date on which employee's work week begins
6. Regular hourly rate of pay and basis on which wages are paid
7. Hours worked each work day and total hours worked each work week
8. Total daily or weekly straight-time earnings or wages
9. Total weekly overtime excess compensation
10. Total additions to or deductions from wages, for each pay period
11. Total wages paid each pay period
12. Date of payment and pay period covered by payment

Somewhat similar provisions for payroll records are made under sections 516.11 to 516.24, inclusive, and section 516.3, covering the following:

Section 516.11—Employees under certain union agreements who are partially exempt from overtime.

Section 516.12—Employees employed in industries "of a seasonal nature" who are partially exempt from overtime pay requirements.

Section 516.13—Employees exempt from overtime pay requirements during 14 work weeks.

Section 516.14—Employees totally exempt from overtime pay requirements.

Section 516.15—Employees exempt from both the minimum wage and overtime pay requirements.

Section 516.16—Employees employed pursuant to a bona fide individual contract or a collective bargaining agreement, and compensated in accordance with sections 6 and 7(a) of the Act.

Section 516.17—Employees compensated for overtime work on the basis of the "applicable" piece rates or hourly rates.

Section 516.18—Employees compensated for overtime hours at a "basic" rate which is substantially equivalent to the employee's average hourly earnings.

Section 516.19—"Red Caps" and other employees dependent on tips as part of wages.

Section 516.20—Learners, apprentices, messengers, or handicapped workers under special certificates.

Section 516.21–Industrial homeworkers.

Section 516.22—Additional records required when additions or deductions are made to or from wages for "board, lodging, or other facilities" customarily furnished to employees.

Section 516.23—Employees under more than one minimum hourly rate (applicable only in Puerto Rico and the Virgin Islands).

Section 516.24—Minors employed in agriculture.

Section 516.3—Bona fide executive, administrative, professional, and sales employees. Employers shall maintain records containing all the data required in section 516.2, except items 6 through 10, and in addition the basis on which wages are paid.

The length of time records must be kept under the Fair Labor Standards Act follows:

Section 516.5—Records to be preserved THREE years.

(a) Each employer shall preserve for at least THREE years:

    (1) Payroll Records. From the last date of entry, all those payroll or other records containing the employee information and data required under any of the applicable sections of these regulations.

    (2) Certificates, Agreements, Plans, Notices, Etc. From their last effective date, all written

      (i) Union agreements, under sections 7(b)(1) or 7(b)(2) of the Act, and any amendments or additions thereto,

     (ii) Plans, trusts, employment contracts, and collective bargaining agreements under section 7(d) of the Act.

    (iii) Individual contracts or collective bargaining agreements under section 7(e) of the Act. Where such contracts or agreements are not in writing, a written memorandum summarizing the terms of each such contract or agreement,

    (iv) Agreements under section 7(f) of the Act, and

    (v) Certificates and notices listed or named in any applicable section of these regulations.

Section 516.6—Records to be preserved TWO years.

(a) Supplementary Basic Records. Each employer required to maintain records under these regulations shall preserve for a period of at least TWO years:

    (1) Basic Employment and Earnings Records. From the date of last entry, all basic time and earning cards or sheets of the employer on which are entered the daily starting and stopping time of individual employees, or of separate work forces, or the individual employee's daily, weekly, or pay period amounts of work accomplished (for example, units produced) when those amounts determine in whole or in part the pay period earnings or wages of those employees.

(2) Wage Rate Tables. From their last effective date, all tables or schedules of the employer which provide the piece rates or other rates used in computing straight-time earnings, wages or salary, or overtime excess compensation, and

(3) Work Time Schedules. From their last effective date, all schedules or tables of the employer which establish the hours and days of employment of individual employees or of separate workforces.

(b) Order, Shipping, and Billing Records. Each employer shall also preserve for at least TWO years from the last date of entry the originals or true copies of any and all customer orders or invoices received, incoming or outgoing shipping or delivery records, as well as all bills of lading and all billings to customers (other than "cash") which the employer retains or makes in the course of his business or operations.

(c) Records of Additions to or Deductions from Wages Paid. Each employer who makes additions to or deductions from wages paid shall preserve for at least TWO years from the date of last entry:

(1) Those records of individual employee accounts referred to in section 516.2 (10),

(2) All employee purchase orders, or assignments made by employees, all copies of addition or deduction statements furnished employees, and

(3) All records used by the employer in determining the original cost, operating and maintenance cost, and depreciation and interest charges, if such costs and charges are involved in the additions to or deductions from wages paid.

Section 516.7—Place for Keeping Records and Their Availability for Inspection.

(a) Place of Records. Each employer shall keep the records required by these regulations safe and accessible at the place or places of employment, or at one or more established central record-keeping offices where such records are customarily maintained. Where the records are maintained at a central record-keeping office, other than in the place or places of employment, such records shall be made available within 72 hours following notice from the Administrator or his duly authorized and designated representative.

(b) Inspection of Records. All records shall be open at any time to inspection and transcription by the Administrator or his duly authorized and designated representative.

Section 516.8—Computations and Reports.

(a) Each employer required to maintain records under these regulations shall make such extension, recomputation, or transcription of his records and shall submit to the Wage and Hour Division such reports concerning persons employed and the wages, hours, and other conditions and practices of employment set forth in his records as the Administrator or his duly authorized and designated representative may request in writing.

Since the statutes of limitations of the various states vary as to employees' suits based on the time-and-a-half provisions of the Fair Labor Standards Act, it also is advisable for an employer to consider such statute in his jurisdiction before destroying any records pertaining to his employees. The statute of limitations bars such employees' suits.

Microfilm retained for the periods specified will satisfy the requirements provided that their inspection is made possible and that the employer will make any extensions, computations, or transcriptions which may be requested.

Walsh-Healey Act. (Also known as *Public Contracts Act.*) Official Regulations 504, Series A, provide that there shall be kept on file for at least FOUR years from the last date of entry the following records of employment:

1. The name, address, sex, and occupation of each employee covered by the contract stipulations.
2. Date of birth of each employee under 19 years of age.
3. Wage and hour records for each such employee, including the rate of wages and the amount paid each pay period, the hours worked each day and each week, and the period during which each such employee was engaged on a government contract, together with the number of such contract. (Section 201.501 of Regulations 504)

Under the Walsh-Healey Act, every person who is a party to a government contract, and subject to the provisions of the Act, is required to keep a record of injury frequency rates on a quarterly calendar basis. These must be kept on file for at least FOUR years after the date of entry thereof.

Social Security (Old Age and Survivors Benefits.) Section 408.609 of Treasury Regulation 106 requires each employer, regardless of the number of his employees, to keep for at least FOUR years after the date the tax to which they relate becomes due or the date the tax is paid, whichever is later, the following records as to each employee:

1. Name, address, and social security number
2. Total remuneration, date of payment, and period covered
3. Wages subject to tax
4. Amount of employee's tax withheld

as well as copies of pertinent returns, schedules, statements, and other documents required by the Regulations.

Employers are also required to maintain records pertaining to claimed refunds, credits, or abatements of any tax, penalty, or interest for at least FOUR years after the date the claim is filed.

Social Security—Unemployment Insurance. Treasury Regulation 107, Section 403.511 requires employers to keep the following records for at least FOUR years after the date that the tax to which they relate becomes due or the date the tax is paid, whichever is later.

1. Total amount of remuneration paid during the calendar year
2. Amount of remuneration that constitutes taxable wages
3. Amount of contributions paid to each state unemployment fund, showing separately (a) payments made and not deducted from employees' compensation, (b) payments made and deducted from employees' compensation.

Persons who employ, but consider themselves not subject to the Federal Unemployment Tax, must, under the same subsection, keep supporting records for at least FOUR years after the due date of the tax for the calendar year to which they relate.

Employers are also required to maintain records relating to claimed refunds, credits, or abatements of any tax, penalty, or interest for at least FOUR years after the date the claim is filed.

In addition to the four-year period required by the Federal Act, it should be noted that the state in which the employer is located has requirements as to the length of time records should be preserved. The periods required by the states vary from a minimum of FIVE years to SEVEN years. Also, the period may begin at different times; for example, in Alabama the period begins after the calendar year in which the remuneration with respect to reported services was paid. In Illinois the period begins after the date of filing returns; in Indiana, after the current calendar year; and in Massachusetts, after the date on which the report was filed. Reference should be made to the individual state for requirements. In general, however, the following states require records to be kept longer than the four-year period required by the Federal Act.

FIVE YEARS: Alabama, Arkansas, Colorado, District of Columbia, Florida, Georgia, Idaho, Illinois, Iowa, Kansas, Louisiana, Maryland, Missouri, Montana, North Carolina, North Dakota, Ohio, South Carolina, Texas. Hawaii, five years also.

SIX YEARS: Connecticut, Kentucky, Michigan, New York.

SEVEN YEARS: Tennessee.

War Contracts, Terminated.—The Office of Contract Settlement, General Services Administration, has ruled that the records of any *completed* or terminated World War II contract may be destroyed.

Records of war contracts, either prime or subcontract, unsettled on Dec. 31, 1950, may be disposed of (1) THREE years after disposition of terminal inventory, or (2) THREE years after the final payment or settlement of such war contract. (18 U.S.C.A. Sec. 443)

Any records which can be reproduced through photography without loss of their primary usefulness may be destroyed, provided that clearly legible photographs thereof are made and preserved. Records which contain features that would not be clearly shown in the photograph must be marked before being photographed to show the existence of such a feature. A certificate of authenticity executed by a person having a personal knowledge of the facts must be attached. The photographs shall be indexed in such manner as will render them readily accessible. (Reg. 11, Part 2011.6, Office of Contract Settlement)

Renegotiation.—The Renegotiation Act and regulations thereunder contain no specific record-keeping requirements. The type of records which should be kept for renegotiation should be determined more from the nature of the substantive matters which have to be proved and depend in each case on the specific nature of the business. In general, however, a complete and reliable set of records should prove of great aid in proving the businessman's side of the various factors on which renegotiation is based.

With reference to the time which these records are to be kept, it should be noted that the Renegotiation Act of 1951 provides that no proceedings to determine the amount of excessive profits for any fiscal year shall be commenced more than one year after the statement required to be filed by the contractor. The statements referred to are to be filed on or before the first day of the fourth calendar month following the close of the fiscal year. The Act further provides that if an agreement or audit determining the amount of excessive profits is not made within two years following the commencement of the renegotiation proceedings, all liabilities of the contractor for excessive profits with respect to which the proceedings was commenced shall be discharged except as specifically provided in the Act. (Sec. 105(c))

Price Stabilization.—The Ceiling Price Regulation issued on January 26, 1951, has been rescinded. However, records on base period (December 19, 1950 to January 25, 1951) prices of commodities must be retained for TWO years after the Defense Production Act expires, or until June 30, 1955. Records on sales made after an item has been decontrolled need not be maintained. This does not apply where compliance action has been instituted.

TABULATION OF OVER 250 COMMON PAPERS FOUND IN A NORMAL BUSINESS OFFICE
WITH LENGTH OF TIME RETAINED

Record	Number Firms Reporting	% 2 Yrs. or Less	% 15 Yrs. or More	Median Retention	Remarks
Accounting					
Acc. Payable Ledgers	50	2	62	P	
Acc. Rec. Ledgers	66	3	50	P	
Appropriations	51	3.9	48	P	
Audit Reports	87	0	87	P	
Balance Sheets	74	0	91.9	P	
Balance Statements	9	22	77	P	
Field Cashiers	23	8.8	39	10	
Managers & Agents	24	4	29	10	
Treasurers.	36	11	63.9	P	
Bills, Receipted	48	2	18.7	7	
Capital Assets Ledger Cards	43	0	86	P	
Cash Books	76	0	78.9	P	
Cash Payroll	37	10.8	45.9	10	
Cash Receipts	70	7	4	15	
Cash Requisitions	47	14.8	29	9	
Check Register	68	4	51	10	
Check Stubs	28	0	39	8	
Checks, Canceled	6	0	33	7	
Dividend	68	1.4	25	7	
General	86	4	24	10	
Payroll	84	4	19	7	
Petty Cash	74	12	16	7	
Correspondence	51	13	11	5	
Cost Acctg. Recaps	57	3	24	10	
Cost Statements	52	1.9	53	21	
Depreciation Sched.	61	0	81.9	P	
Draft Register	24	4	45	10	
Drafts Paid	29	6.9	34	7	
Expense Records	69	1.4	46	25	
Journals & Ledgers					
General	95	0	96	P	Microfilming not acceptable.
Subsidiary	83	0	92	P	Microfilming not acceptable.
Note Register	42	0	78	P	
Notes Paid	38	0	55	15	
P & L Statements	75	0	93	P	
Payroll Register	49	2	63	P	
Property Acc. Ledgers	46	0	93	P	
Trial Balance & Work Sheets	74	6.7	67	P	
Voucher Accounting					
Authority for Cash	49	6	55	10	
Distr. of Charges	53	13	47	10	
Index	42	4.7	57	P	
Requisitions	39	13	36	8	
Vouchers — Cap. Exp.	71	2.6	73	P	
Vouchers — Cash	78	3.8	32	10	
Vouchers — Journal	70	4	69	P	
Advertising					
Contracts	44	6.8	43	10	
Correspondence	52	13	9.6	5	
Drawings & Art Work	43	11.6	46	10	
Estimates	29	41	6.8	3	
House Organs	43	13.9	76	P	
Market Data & Surveys	39	17	25	10	
Polls	19	10	31	5	
Service Reports	20	20	25	5	
Tear Sheets	32	31	15.5	5	

Record	Number Firms Reporting	% 2 Yrs. or Less	% 15 Yrs. or More	Median Retention	Remarks
Bank Deposit					
Bank Statements	83	30	13	6	
Deposit Books	48	31	75	7	
Deposit Slips	70	35.7	14	4	
Reconcilements	73	35	19	4	
Budget					
Authorizations	40	17	37	5	
Departmental Summaries . . .	46	15	45	10	
Statistical Analysis of					
Expense	49	12	42	10	
Buidling/Property					
Appraisals	54	1.8	92	P	
Bids & Estimates	44	11	54	P	
Charges & Credits for					
Constr. & Repairs	50	6	56	P	
Inventories	46	4	78	P	
Maintenance & Repairs	18	11	50	P	
Plans & Specifications	50	8	92	P	
Corporate Papers					
Articles of Incorporation . . .	64	0	100	P	
Charter	64	0	100	P	
Constitution and By-laws . . .	64	0	100	P	
Documents with Register . . .	37	0	100	P	
Listing Issuances of Securi-					
ties	39	0	100	P	
Lists of Voting Stockholders .	57	5	77	P	
Minute Books	12	0	100	P	
Directors	69	0	98	P	
Executive	61	0	96	P	
Stockholders	65	0	98	P	
Proxies	60	10	58	P	Since some firms find a two year retention acceptable this should be given further study.
Correspondence — Gen.	63	4.7	12.7	6	
Credit Department					
Applications for Credit	32	25	15	5	
Authorizations for Credit . . .	36	19	19	5	
Correspondence	46	26	6.5	4	
Credit Reports & Ratings . . .	59	28	23	5	
Time Payment Charges	24	12.5	16	7	
Uncollectible Accounts	44	9	36	7	
Engineering & Technical					
Correspondence	51	3.9	45	15	
Drawings & Estimates	60	0	88	P	
Formulas	39	0	89	P	
Photographs	45	0	82	P	
Projects Abandoned	40	2.5	65	P	
Projects Completed	45	2	80	P	
Reports & Memos	47	0	74	P	
Product Development &					
Research	9	0	66	P	
Specifications	52	0	71	P	
Financing					
Bond Register	29	0	86	P	
Bonds Canceled	29	6.8	75	P	
Bonds, Sales or Transfers . .	29	3.4	82	P	
Capital Stock	3	0	66	P	
Applications for Issuances .	42	0	92	P	
Certificates Canceled	52	0	82	P	
Sales or Transfers	51	0	90	P	
Transfer Books or Ledgers .	54	0	92	P	
Coupons, Paid Interest	25	8	72	P	

Record	Number Firms Reporting	% 2 Yrs. or Less	% 15 Yrs. or More	Median Retention	Remarks
Dividend Records	45	0	91	P	
nsurance (After Expiration)					
Accident	63	8	31.7	10	
Fidelity...............	58	10	31	10	
Fire	63	14	23.8	7	
Group	64	7.8	32	7	
Hospital	43	9	39	7	
Inspection Certificates.....	54	11	29	7	
Liability	62	11	32	10	
Life	51	9	35	10	
Marine	51	11.7	25	7	
Property..............	58	12	22	8	
Surety................	51	11.7	43	10	
Workmen's Compensation...	59	6.7	40	10	
Inventory					
Inventory Control	42	4	38	7	
Plant & Fixtures.........	68	2.9	60	P	
Other	56	7	30	7	
Legal					
Claims	27	3	51	20	
Automobile	31	0	38	10	
Group, Life & Hospital Ins.	34	0	38	10	
Loss & Damage in Transit	31	3	32	10	
Occupation (Workmen's Comp.)	37	0	48	15	
Plant	27	0	51	10	
Compensation Cases	40	0	80	P	
Contracts	7	0	71	P	
Customers — Government .	58	1.7	70	P	Walsh-Healey Act, Regulation 504, Series A Provides retention for 4 years of name, ad-dress, sex, occupa-tion, date of birth, wage & hour rec-ords, and rate of wages for each em-ployee engaged on a government con-tract. Microfilm permitted War contracts un-settled on Dec. 31, 1950 may be dis-posed of 3 years after (a) disposition of terminal inven-tory, or (b) final settlement — Reg. 11, part 2011 of Office of Contract Settlement.
Customers — Non-govern-ment..............	56	5	51	20	
Employees	52	1.9	63	P	
Labor Unions	56	3	73	P	
Vendors	61	4.9	50	20	
Deeds	50	0	94	P	
Easements.............	44	0	93	P	
Franchises	43	0	93	P	
Leases	63	3	65	P	
Licenses	53	7	73	P	
Mortgages	45	2	86	P	

Record	Number Firms Reporting	% 2 Yrs. or Less	% 15 Yrs. or More	Median Retention	Remarks
Options	40	0	80	P	
Patents & Trademarks	64	1.5	93	P	
Royalties	55	3	83	P	
Water Rights	35	0	94	P	
Personnel	7	0	71	P	
Absence — Seniority	32	21	40	7	
Accident Reports	62	6	54	15	
Applications — Non Employees.	62	67	1.6	1	
Correspondence — General. .	55	30	12	5	
Credit Union Records	15	6.6	60	P	
Employees, Active	4	0	100	P	
Applications	62	3	80	P	
Bond Purchases	63	7.9	54	20	
Commissions or Bonuses .	45	2	60	P	
Correspondence	54	14	38	7	
Earning Records	80	2.5	62.5	P	Fair Labor Standards Act, Sec. 516.5 says each employer shall preserve for at least 3 years payroll records, certificates, agreements, plans & notices. Microfilming acceptable.
Payroll Analysis	56	5	44	10	
Payroll Rate Authorizations	41	2.4	53	P	
Payroll Summaries.	64	4	39	7	
Payroll Tabulating Cards .	57	29	14	5	
Suggestions	16	18	56	P	
Time Cards					
Government Contracts . .	58	1.7	8	5	
Overtime	72	5	5	5	
Part time	71	7	4	5	
Regular	83	8	4.8	5	
Temporary	69	5	5	5	
Employees — Separated	7	0	71	20	
Applications	45	4	48	10	
Employment Releases	59	8	47	20	
Fingerprints	42	4	45	10	
Garnishments	56	3	35	7	
Medical Histories	61	4.9	49	40	
Military Service.	53	3	50	20	
Bond or Stock Purchases . . .	46	6	41	10	
Commissions or Bonuses . . .	39	2.5	43	10	
Correspondence	50	14	28	7	
Earning Summaries	62	6	56	P	
Employee Suggestions	33	18	36	6	
Insurance, Hospitalization, etc.	48	8	39	8	
Pensions	48	0	70	P	
Retirements	39	0	92	P	
Service Records	57	5	70	P	
Indentification Badges, Passes	33	30	24	3	
Job Descriptions	43	4	67	P	
Messenger Logs, Routes . . .	19	57	5.7	1-1/2	
Wage Rate Changes	6	16	83	P	
Production Department					
Bills of Material	34	8.8	35	7	
Correspondence	49	8	16	5	
Distribution	34	14	38	6	

Record	Number Firms Reporting	% 2 Yrs. or Less	% 15 Yrs. or More	Median Retention	Remarks
Inspection Reports	39	23	20	5	
Machinery Repair & Maintenance	23	8	26	5	
Power Reports	19	21	26	5	
Quality Control	24	16	20	5	
Summaries	43	16	32	7	
Tests	37	13	43	6	
Time & Motion Studies	45	11	64	P	
Tool Reports	14	7	21	6	
Work Orders	37	13	29	6	
Public Relations					
Annual Reports	27	0	95	P	
Purchase Department					
Acknowledgments to Vendors	45	28	4	5	
Correspondence	64	9	14	5	
Credit Memos	56	7	14	7	
Debit Memos	58	6.8	13	7	
Invoices, Incoming	84	4	17	7	
Price Quotations	61	21	4.9	5	
Price Sheets and Catalogs . .	45	37	8	3	
Purchase Orders	4	0	0	6-1/2	
General	88	14	8	6	
Capital Expenditure	68	5.8	45	10	
Purchase Requisitions	81	40	6	3	
Receiving Reports	73	23	13	6	
Requests for Bids	48	25	4	5	
Shipping Tickets	43	30	2	5	
Safety or Injury Frequency Reports	46	6	52	20	Walsh-Healey Act, Sec. 201.502 of Reg. 504 provides that injury frequency rate records must be kept 4 years. Microfilming acceptable.
Sales Department					
Accounts Receivable Register	50	2	44	10	
Acknowledgment of Orders . .	42	23	2.3	5-1/2	
Adjustments, Complaint Reports	47	21	6	6	
Correspondence	71	9	9	6	
Credit Distribution, Summary of	19	5.2	26	7	
Credit Memos	71	4	11	7	
Customers' Orders	7	28	0	5-1/2	
Original	72	11	9	6	Fair Labor Standards Act, Sec. 516.6 (b) says each employer shall preserve at least 2 years from last date of entry originals or true copies of customer orders or invoices received, incoming or outgoing shipping or delivery records, bills of lading and all billings to customers. Microfilming acceptable.
Billing Copy	42	14	2	6	
Customers' Specifications . .	47	4	23	7	

Record	Number Firms Reporting	% 2 Yrs. or Less	% 15 Yrs. or More	Median Retention	Remarks
Debit Memos	62	4.8	12	7	
Export Sales	3	0	33	7	
Invoices	82	4.7	18	7	
Order Register.	46	23	28	7	
Price Estimates	42	19	19	7	Records on base period prices of commodities must be retained until June 30, 1955.
Price Exceptions and Adjustments	42	19	26	7	
Price Quotations.	50	22	16	6	
Price Sheets.	39	7	64	P	
Remittance Statements	54	42	3	3	
Sales Slips.	32	15	6	5	
Salesmen's Commission	37	5	18	6	
Sales Expenses	70	10	14	6	
Service Charges	26	7	7	5	
Service Reports	31	1.9	12.9	5	
Summaries of Expense	32	0	28	7	
Securities					
Ledgers	51	0	96	P	
Purchase & Sales	45	0	91	P	
Signatures, Authorized	34	2.9	82	P	
Stores/Warehousing					
Correspondence	34	20	8.8	5	
Issuances	33	39	6	4	
Receipts	37	35	5	4	
Recoveries to Stock	29	34	3.4	5	
Requisitions/Orders	37	40	5	4	
Returns for Credit	31	32	6	5	
Sold	37	35	0	5	
Stock Orders	30	36	3	4	
Transferred.	9	33	0	5	
Taxes					
Income — Federal.	88	0	92	P	Internal Rev. Code 26 U.S.C.A. 276 (a) says it is advisable to preserve indefinitely copies of all federal income tax returns. Filming not acceptable.
Income — State	83	1.2	85	P	
Property	80	0	85	P	
Sales & Use	82	2.4	62	P	
Social Security	80	0	75	P	Treasury Reg. 106, Sec. 402.609 (Social Security) requires each employer to keep for 4 years total remuneration, wages subject to tax, amount withheld, returns, schedules, refunds, and credits of each employee. Treasury Reg. 107, Sec. 403.511 (Unemployment Compensation) also requires a 4 year retention. Check the state law.

Record	Number Firms Reporting	% 2 Yrs. or Less	% 15 Yrs. or More	Median Retention	Remarks
Unemployment Insurance Returns.	11	0	54	P	
Withholding Certificates. . . .	74	1.3	29	P	
Traffic Department					See Remarks under Sales.
Bills of Lading	87	31	0	4	
Correspondence	55	18	9	5	
Freight Bills	76	21.	7	5	
Freight Claims	66	27	4.5	4-1/2	
Freight Claims Register. . . .	43	20	6.9	5	
Freight Drafts	35	25.7	5.7	3	
Inspection Reports	39	20	7	5	
Manifests.	40	37.5	2.5	3	
Packing Instructions	34	10	11.7	3	
Receipts, Delivery	56	35	1.7	3	
Shipping Instructions	50	26	16	5	
Shipping Tickets	45	15	6	5	
Tariffs	38	15	86	6	
Vehicle Operations and Maintenance.	45	20	15	5	

An executive order of President Truman on September 9, 1950, provides that all persons who sold or delivered goods or services or offered to sell or deliver goods or services from May 24, 1950, to June 24, 1950, inclusive, should preserve all records for such period relating to the price received or asked and the costs incurred in connection with the goods or services for which the price was received or asked. This order does not apply to wages or salaries, to agricultural commodities for individual producers, to rents or income from real estate, professional services, to prices or rentals in connection with certain items in the publishing, radio, advertising, or theatrical business, to insurance rates, rates for carriers, or to margin requirements on a commodity exchange.

The order does not indicate how long the records must be preserved, so presumably they should be preserved until change is made either by an executive order or the repeal or expiration of the Defense Production Act of 1950.

BIBLIOGRAPHY

Protection of Records, pamphlet published by the National Fire Protection Association, Boston.

Preservation of Public Records, published by the Business Historical Society, Inc., Boston, 1941.

Disposition of Inactive Records, published by the Policy Holders Service Bureau, Metropolitan Life Insurance Co., New York.

The Repair and Preservation of Records, Bulletin #5, National Archives, Washington, D. C., September, 1943.

Diebold, Inc., Flofilm Division data, Chicago.

Industrial Microfilming Company data, New York.

Recordak Company data, New York.

War Department Technical Manual TM 12–257, March, 1946.

E. J. Leahy, National Records Management Council, New York.

Chapter 9

FOLLOW-UP SYSTEMS

Use of Follow-ups.—In the rush of modern times, the personnel of an office is apt to forget what is not brought to its attention at regular intervals, so the follow-up was instituted as a reminder of matters not yet closed. Good prospects must be followed up every 10, 20, or 30 days; a director's meeting must be called to the executive's attention; a note at the bank is to be met the first of the month; a claim is to be traced; overdue accounts must be written regularly; magazines and other continuations are to be ordered on certain dates. At definite periods action must be taken on insurance expirations, advices of shipment of grain, confirmations of vessel clearings, railroad car arrivals, dividend payments, rentals. All such matters are cared for by a mechanical memory known as the follow-up system. Synonymous terms for the follow-up are the "tickler" (tickling the memory), bringup, comeup, hold for attention file, pending file, suspense file.

To secure the best results, the follow-up system should be handled as a whole and should be the responsibility of the filing department rather than that of the individual secretaries. The operation of such a system comprises a very important part of the file clerk's daily routine. It involves the daily rounding up of all material which needs future attention, instead of allowing it to be stored away in any individual's desk; and then of pulling all material requiring action on that day either during the first hours in the morning or even late in the afternoon before, so that it is on the dictator's desk without fail each day when he reaches the office.

Date filing is usually a secondary method of filing; that is, first in importance is the general file arranged alphabetically with the follow-up as a subsidiary file.

There are two different ways of setting up a follow-up system: (1) by date with an alphabetic control, or (2) by alphabet with signals to indicate the future date the material is wanted.

1. Follow-up Arranged by Dates.—The dictator notifies his stenographer that the matter in question is to receive future attention and she indicates the date on the paper before sending it to file. When this material reaches the file room, a charge-out card is prepared giving the name of the dictator, the date he wants the papers, and a description of the papers themselves (name of correspondent and address if necessary).

Example:

Jones Manufacturing Co., Boston   wanted by DRL   5-15

A separate file drawer has been fitted with a letter-sized set of monthly guides and one or two sets of 1–31 guides representing the days of the month. Where the follow-up is comparatively light, one set of 1–31 guides will serve. These daily guides are set up behind the current month and the charge-out card is filed behind 5–15. The papers, in the meantime, go to regular file. Late on the afternoon of the 14th, the follow-ups for the next day are pulled. The charge-out cards indicate what is wanted and by whom. The material is taken from the regular file and the charge-out card, which up to this point has served as the follow-up, now acts as the charge for the papers out of file and is inserted in the place from which the papers are withdrawn. The papers are sent to the dictator's desk so as to be ready for attention the first hour of the morning.

In the follow-up drawer, the daily guide for the current day is removed and inserted behind next month's guide. This is done each day so that at the end of the current month next month's follow-ups are already in order. Under such an arrangement, matter requiring attention several months hence is filed behind the month guide until the daily guides begin to be inserted. Under the system described

Fig. 34.—Follow-up System (Remington Rand, Inc.)

above, the material on follow-up is available at all times, even before the date indicated.

There are two variations to the plan described above.

a) The use of a 3″ x 5″ card instead of a charge-out card. As material to be followed up comes to file, the 3″ x 5″ card giving necessary information is prepared and filed behind month and daily guides 3″ x 5″ in size arranged in a small box on the file clerk's desk. The balance of the procedure is the same as described above except that as the material is pulled from file a charge-out card must be made. The 3″ x 5″ card can then be attached to the outgoing material to indicate to the dictator that he is receiving the matter on which he had put a future date.

b) Another variation of follow-up file arranged by date is handled through a second carbon of the outgoing letter. The stenographer is told by the dictator that the matter in hand is to be followed up on a particular date. She prepares two carbons of the dictated letter indicating the future date on each before she sends them to file. The incoming letter and one carbon of the reply go to the regular place in file, while the second carbon is put in a drawer set up by months and days. Each afternoon the records department pulls the second carbon, matches it with the papers in regular file, then pulls the whole file and lays it on the dictator's desk. A charge slip is prepared and inserted in the proper folder. If it is necessary to reply to a paper before the date set for the follow-up or to destroy the follow-up copy because further action is no longer necessary, the clerk consults the follow-up date penciled on the carbon placed in the main file; then goes to the follow-up file, and back of the proper date is found the second carbon which can now be destroyed.

Occasionally the dictator finds that the second carbon pulled from the follow-up file gives him sufficient information upon which to act so that it is not necessary to pull all past papers on the transaction from regular file. No charge is required for the duplicate copy pulled from the follow-up drawer.

2. Combination Alphabetic and Date Follow-up.—Because of the devious methods necessary to control a follow-up in date form, a combination alphabetic and date file has sometimes been found advisable, especially when it is necessary to keep together papers pertaining to one transaction. A set of A–Z guides, 25 divisions or larger, with miscellaneous folders to match, is arranged in the usual manner in a separate drawer or drawers. The follow-up material is filed by name even though the future date is clearly indicated on each group of papers in the special drawer described above. Within the *Am* folder, for example, or any folder, each group of papers is arranged according to date so that today's material is on top, tomorrow's next, etc. On a given day, say the 10th, it is necessary for the clerk to glance at the top group of papers in each folder to find those needing attention on that day.

Metal Signals.—A refinement of this scheme is to use folders bearing on the top edge printed range of dates from 1 to 31. Metal signals are slipped over the edge of the folder and cover the date on which the paper within is to be followed.

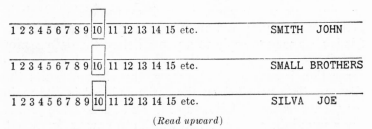

1 2 3 4 5 6 7 8 9 |10| 11 12 13 14 15 etc.   SMITH   JOHN

1 2 3 4 5 6 7 8 9 |10| 11 12 13 14 15 etc.   SMALL   BROTHERS

1 2 3 4 5 6 7 8 9 |10| 11 12 13 14 15 etc.   SILVA   JOE

(*Read upward*)

Fig. 35.—Folders with Metal Signals for Follow-ups

Each morning the clerk glances at every folder in the follow-up file to see if today's date is covered with a signal. If not, it is ignored; if it is so covered, the paper within must come out. This procedure is somewhat easier than it sounds as all folders bearing a tab for the 10th are in alignment, one directly back of the other, and so are quickly identified; the same is true for all folders to be pulled on the 15th, or on the 21st, or on any particular date. The problem in connection with this method of handling the follow-up is that the signals are apt to be brushed off the top of the folders and then the material within to be followed up is forgotten.

Occasionally straight-edge cards with the days of the month printed across the top are filed alphabetically. Metal or celluloid signals indicate the follow-up date. Such a system is often used to regulate the calls which salesmen make on their customers or prospects. Here again trouble is apt to arise from the fact that signals will fall off despite the greatest care, although within the past few years these signals have been made so they grip the card tightly and fewer casualties occur than formerly.

Fig. 36.—Follow-up File Using Signals (Remington Rand, Inc.)

Because it is such a prevalent practice, albeit a bad one, mention must be made of the fact that some firms still file original incoming papers and the only carbon reply in the tickler file. This means that when the folder is called for from regular file, the story is not complete, the most recent and often most important papers being in the tickler. Also, when the clerk is called upon for certain papers which are not to be found in the main file, it necessitates a hunt through the tickler. Where this method of follow-up has been a long-established custom, the executives are often loath to change.

Under such conditions a compromise can be effected by having two carbon copies made of all outgoing letters requiring future attention. Although the incoming letter and the first carbon are put in the tickler, the second carbon may be placed in the regular file so that any one calling for the folder will see at a glance that some papers are missing.

A pending file, strictly speaking, is not the same as a follow-up system, although the two terms are used synonymously. Ofttimes folders or papers are held in suspense awaiting further information. These may be kept in front of the sorter or in front of the A drawer where they cannot fail to be seen each day. Occasionally a change of some sort comes to file before the original papers arrive or while the original papers are out of the department on a charge. A case in point is information on change of beneficiary on an insurance policy which is not in file. The data are put in a temporary or pending folder in front of the regular folder for the transaction so that when the papers come to file the additional data can be attached thereto by the filing staff. This saves sending the whole file back to the general office.

Chapter 10

NUMERIC FILES

Key to Classification.—When it is possible to go directly to the files for material desired, the file is self-indexing. But there are methods of filing where papers are arranged in such fashion that there must be a key, in the form of an alphabetic index, usually on cards, in order to find what is wanted. The numeric arrangement is an example of indirect filing.

Advantages and Disadvantages of Numeric System.— As all reference to a numeric file set up for ordinary correspondence is indirectly through the index, the complete process of filing and finding is a slow and cumbersome one. If the number is not noted on the incoming mail it must be sorted alphabetically in order to check against the index, then re-sorted numerically for filing. Its use for correspondence has been almost entirely abandoned in the past few years with the advent of excellent alphabetic systems of indexing and guiding and efficient methods of sorting in the alphabetic systems as are now on the market. The numeric file was used almost exclusively in the preceding century for all papers and there is still to be found an occasional ultra-conservative office which clings to this method with which it started business fifty or more years ago. For the most part, however, direct alphabetic systems are time savers and have been found less costly to operate.

The "pink sheet" or second copy or an order is usually filed by number in book form and acts as a cross index to the copy filed by name of customer in the regular file. This copy is for the use of those who are concerned with processing the order and not with customer name, and for those who work with the order solely by its number (such as the accounting department). Vouchers are usually filed by number. The sender retains a carbon copy to which are attached supporting papers, such as bills, receiving reports, and correspondence pertaining to the bill. Vouchers are best filed in correspondence cabinets so that all attached papers may lie flat. Unfortunately, the common practice is to fold all papers to document size and file them on the short end in consecutive order.

The numeric system of filing still fills a definite need in certain other instances, as in "case" filing. A lawsuit, a hospital record, an insurance application are examples. It will be noted that these differ from the usual correspondence in a sales office in that they cannot be transferred at the end of the year but must remain intact until closed. In other words, a law firm, a hospital, and an insurance home office maintain an open and a closed file instead of annual files. A case may remain in the open file for a period as short as two weeks or as long as ten years. Transferring goes on all through the year. When a case is closed, the index card is so marked, but not transferred. Another point of difference in filing cases by number in contrast to filing correspondence is that there is no miscellany for the former. Every case is given a number although it may be opened with but one or two papers.

Conoco Oil Company	65
vs. John R. Jones	65 – 1
re Ralph Conway Estate	65 – 2
vs. Magnus Oil Company	65 – 3

Fig. 37.—Reference Card of Law Firm Where Client Is Involved in More Than One Case

When handling more than one case for a particular client, a law firm modifies the original number by a secondary number (Figure 37); then cross reference cards are made out for Jones, Conway, and Magnus as shown in Figure 38.

The need for secrecy sometimes justifies a numeric system. For instance, in dealing with patents or secret formulae it is often desirable to conceal names or titles from those handling the files. The index is not made available so that the file number alone on the correspondence gives no clue as to name.

Magnus Oil Company	65 – 3

FIG. 38.—Cross Reference Card Showing Secondary Number

The home offices of insurance companies usually file copies of the application in numeric sequence. Insurance companies have undertaken an extensive educational campaign to have their assureds always give the policy number when writing and they always type the number on correspondence and premium notices so as to eliminate the necessity of going to an alphabetical index.

Folders and Guides Used in Numeric Files.—Since usually only the numbers appear on the folders, it is unnecessary to have them tabbed. Straight-edged, guide-height folders serve the purpose and are inexpensive. The number should be clearly indicated on both front and back flap at the extreme right edge. The affixing of the number can be done with a stamping machine. In a legal office large expansion envelopes are often used because of the volume of papers pertaining to any one case. Where single sheets are numbered consecutively, from 50 to 100 may be assembled in one folder, with guides staggered across the drawer from left to right by 20's or even by 100's. If the papers to be filed are stiff enough, folders are sometimes dispensed with entirely.

Charge-Outs. Charge-outs should always carry the number and may carry a name and address in addition.

Sorting. If a 100-division sorter is used with each tab numbered consecutively, material being prepared for file can be sorted by the first two digits, taken out of the sorter, resorted by the next two digits, etc.

Methods of Filing Other Than by Consecutive Numbers.—There are methods of numeric filing other than consecutive. In large numeric files where the series run into six or seven digits, the filing is sometimes done by the final three digits. This means a setup of 999 divisions in the file ranging from 000 to 999. Further refinement can be provided through using the fourth, fifth, and sixth digits from the right. For example, if the final three digits are 919 the papers would be arranged from the lowest number to the highest.

635 – 919
234 – 919
1 – 919
(Read upward)

The value of this arrangement is that current work is spread into the various sections so that each is equally active. This terminal digit method of numeric filing is in contrast to a consecutive file where the cabinet containing the most recent material is the one where most of the filing and lookup work is being done. Firms which file insurance dailies, checks, requisitions, etc., by final digits find that it saves from 25% to 50% of the time required to file consecutively.

Rate cards for fire insurance companies are filed first alphabetically by name of street and then numerically by house number, all the odd numbers on the street being filed first, as:

Adams Street
19, 21, 25, 29, 33, etc.

Then follow all the even numbers on Adams Street. From long experience the clerks filing these rate cards find that they work much more rapidly and accurately under the above scheme than they do by filing the numbers consecutively under the street name.

One word of caution: although numeric filing is one of the simplest of all methods, requiring little experience to maintain, it is extremely easy to transpose numbers mentally; that is, 269–341 as 296–341. Such a number erroneously filed is difficult to find. A transposed figure does not appear as an error whereas a misspelled word or name is usually obvious. The best way to safeguard against errors is to have numeric files audited regularly. In some companies the auditing is made a part of the daily routine, so that certain portions of the file are audited each day and the entire file is covered several times a year.

Chapter 11

HOW TO SET UP A SUBJECT FILE

What Subject Filing Is.—Subject filing is the arranging of material by a given subject; it is filing by descriptive features instead of by name or location. This involves choosing a word or phrase to stand for each paper or to bring out some one phase of it. It is one of the most confusing methods of filing for both records clerk and the user of the files because no two persons think exactly alike about any one topic. Whereas the name "Jones" would not be confused with the name "Smith" in a name file, two persons can easily be thinking of the same topic under synonymous terms, so that an article filed under Export Trade, for instance, might be called for under the heading of Foreign Trade.

Subject or topical or data files, as they are often called, are found in executive offices where interest lies not so much in a particular customer but in an over-all picture, as Sales Forecasts; not in one particular insurance company, but in Insurance, Fire. Research files are also classified by the subject of the study being made, as Glass Blowing. Trade organizations anticipating new developments for a group of businesses engaged in similar activities, such as Baking, must arrange material by subject, as

Safety
Salt
Sanitation
Shortenings

The various types of material which are found in a subject file are as follows:

abstracts
accident reports
association material
bills of sale
blueprints
bond applications
bonds
brochures
charters
charts
clippings
Commerce Commission applications
contracts
dissolution papers
financial statements
government publications
house organs
incorporation papers
insurance policies
laws
leaflets
leases
merchandising data
minutes of meetings
mortgages
ordinances
pamphlets
pending legislation
periodicals
photostats
price lists
releases
reports—annual
reprints
speeches
state licenses
statistics
suits
surveys
tracings
trade association proceedings of meetings
trade catalogs
withdrawals from doing business

The sources of material for subject files are federal, state, city, and county governments in all their bureaus, trade and commercial organizations, financial houses.

There are organizations where the main files are arranged by subject, but in the business office subject matter is usually found in executive departments, for interoffice memos, and as a subsidiary arrangement in a name file.

Kinds of Subject Files.—The standard types of subject files are:

1. Alphabetic, with no logical connection between subjects filed next to each other.
2. Numeric, often called Duplex Numeric. Numbers are assigned to principal subjects which are subdivided as the subject grows.
3. Decimal, based on the Dewey Decimal System used in public libraries and highly specialized businesses.

The alphabetic subject file is the most common of the three in a business office. It may be expanded indefinitely. It is intelligible to the person who may want to use it when the clerk is absent.

There are two types of alphabetic subject files, as follows:

1. Dictionary method of many detailed subjects. Example:

Alphabetic systems	filed under A
Date systems	filed under D
Numeric systems	filed under N

2. Encyclopedic or classed method of a few main headings with many subdivisions. Example:

Systems—filing
  Alphabetic
  Date   } all filed under   S
  Numeric

The first method of many small subjects has been found to be the most satisfactory in those offices where no trained librarian is in attendance.

No matter which type of arrangement is used, it must in order to be a good file be simple to understand, have its divisions and subdivisions well defined, be as inexpensive as possible to operate in time, labor, and equipment, and be flexible in allowing for expansion. These results can be obtained by choosing the subject headings carefully, using plenty of cross references, and making an index.

Choice of Subject Headings.—A good subject heading must express the topic as exactly and concisely as possible. A single word is best chosen to describe the contents of the paper and that word a noun. Plural forms should be used unless usage calls for singular. In a letter discussing business morals the moral side is the dominant one, so that the heading would read: Morals—Business. Titles are often misleading and should ordinarily be avoided. *A Bulletin on Fire Escapes* should be filed under Fire Escapes (or Fire Protection) because that word is the gist of the content of

the material. Bulletin is simply the form in which the information comes; it might just as well have been a letter on
Fire Escapes. In the *Manufacture of Wire Ropes,* rope is
the important word. If the selected heading appears in the
title of the article, underscore in pencil. In case the heading
is supplied, use red pencil in the upper right-hand corner.
Temporary material permits of a more catchy heading than
permanent material. The name of an association can be
used as a subject heading. To sum up, subject headings
should be specific, technically correct, and composed of
terms in common usage. The term chosen as a heading
should be used thereafter for like material.

When the subject is extensive it may be subdivided by
place, time, item, function, or person. For example:

Branch offices	Advertising	Desks
Atlanta	Magazines	Mahogany
Boston	Newspapers	Oak
Chicago	Radio	Walnut

Subdivisions must be kept consistent. It is incorrect to
subdivide desks as follows:

Desks
  Mahogany   Because the viewpoint has changed in each sub-
  Rolltop   division. It is entirely possible for one desk to
  Office   be all three: mahogany in finish, rolltop in type,
              usable in an office.

Proper subdivisions would read:

Desks
  Office   Dividing Desks into office and school; office
    Flattop   desks into flattop and rolltop, each of those in
      Mahogany   turn divided into mahogany, oak, walnut.
      Oak
      Walnut
    Rolltop
      Mahogany
      Oak
      Walnut
  School

Printed Aids in Choosing Subject Headings.—

American Library Association List of Subject Headings, Chicago.

Library of Congress List of Subject Headings, Washington, D. C.

Agricultural Index, published by H. W. Wilson, New York.

Industrial Arts Index, published by H. W. Wilson, New York.

Public Library List of Subject Headings for information files, Newark, N. J.

Engineering Index (Decimal) University of Illinois, Urbana.

Readers Guide, H. W. Wilson, New York.

Harvard Classification for Business Literature, H. W. Wilson, New York.

Banking & Financial Subject Headings, Special Libraries Association, 1940, New York.

Accounting, American Institute of Accountants, New York.

Architecture (Decimal), University of Illinois, Urbana.

Business (Advertising, Selling, Management, Banking) Fremont Rider, Cumulative Digest Association, New York.

Electricity, General Electric Catalog, Schenectady, New York.

Medicine, Bellevue Classification, Bellevue Hospital, New York.

Government publications are extremely useful. The Superintendent of Documents, Washington, D. C., issues lists of government publications. The Library of Congress has a card service covering additions to the Library. Several of the federal departments publish their own lists. Lists of state publications are made up by the Library of Congress. The Brookings Institution has recently published *Government Publications and Their Use* by Schmeckebier.

The final decision in the matter of choosing subject headings should rest with the records clerk. Seldom do all persons in business look at the contents of a paper from the same angle. If the indexer uses the headings assigned by a given department it will soon be found that the same type of material is filed under two or more synonymous terms and the file will then be inaccessible. The indexer must be the person to see the "whole problem" and unify the headings.

A file department is indeed fortunate if it can find a printed list which can be checked into and adapted to the firm's needs. No two subject files are exactly alike, any more than the list of customers of two different firms are the same. If a published list is used, it should be interpaged for special subjects added or changes made.

Cross References.—Cross references are used where there is a choice of terms. There are three forms: a colored sheet filed in the folder; the tabbed half of a regular correspondence folder for a permanent cross reference; cards, usually 3″ x 5″ in size, used when cross references are heavy or a cumulative reference must be kept. There are two kinds of cross references used in subject files: the "See" reference already described, where nothing is to be found under the heading given:

Automobiles   See   Buses (nothing under Automobiles)
                            Passenger Cars
                            Trucks

The "See also" reference found only in subject filing is a reference to one or more places where allied material thought valuable in connection with this same subject may be found:

Claims   See also   Accidents
                    See also   Insurance
                (allied material under all three terms)

If an article to be filed contains more than one subject of importance, the paper is filed under the most important heading and cross reference made for the other headings. There is no limit to the number of cross references which may be made—six, ten, or twenty are not unusual for one pamphlet. Meaningless entries should be avoided.

It should be borne in mind that cross references should refer from a general subject to a narrower phase, never as a rule from the specific to the general:

Punishment   See also   Crime

If the article to be indexed contains several important subjects and is not too voluminous, the practice is sometimes followed of typing as many copies of the article as there are subjects and then filing each one of the copies under a different heading, thus eliminating cross references.

Index to Subject File.—The index is the subject heading control list. It is an alphabetically arranged list of subject headings and subdivisions under the main headings plus the cross references. Every subject file, no matter how small, should have an index. This applies even to alphabetic subject files to which reference may be made directly. The value of an index lies in the fact that it gives a quick review of the contents of a subject file when choosing new headings and that it acts as an aid in identifying material asked for under unusual headings.

There are no two indexes alike even in similar businesses because the viewpoint of every business is unique and the files must follow the business. Another's index then can be of value only in giving ideas. There are certain requirements for any good index: it should be standardized in that specific headings under which material shall be filed should be drawn up before the file is started; it must be flexible enough to allow for the absorption of entirely new material; it must be understandable to others than the indexer.

The index may be made up in bound book form; on loose-leaf sheets in a binder, alphabetically typed; or on 3″ x 5″ cards, alphabetically arranged. The use of cards is the most common of the three and allows for expansion without re-typing.

An entry is the act of recording information under subject headings made in an index. The total of the entries is the index. With a straight alphabetic subject file only the briefest entries are made. There should be an entry for each main heading, for each division, for each subdivision, for each cross reference—particularly from all synonymous terms.

        Personnel   (entry)
          Salaries   (entry) this is a subdivision of Personnel
        Also entry under Employees: See Personnel

Author and Title entries may also be included if the author is an important one or apt to be remembered, and the title of the material a catchy one. There is usually only one entry to a card, although for economy of time and space additional entries are often put on the same card. Series cards may be helpful in an index. These give a list of all bulletins received from any one government bureau. One card should always be regarded as the main card and all cross references and other references should be listed on this main card either at the lower left-hand corner on the face, or on the back. When the file is weeded out these cards must either be pulled or marked withdrawn, otherwise there will be a great many meaningless cards in the index.

As stated above, all entries (whether subject headings, corporate names, titles, or authors) should be filed together under one alphabetic index. Occasionally, however, it is found advantageous to make one exception by putting a card in the index with the author and title of an important pamphlet directly behind the subject card under which the pamphlet is filed:

> Subject heading: "Electric Power, rural applications." Directly behind this card is another reading: "Oklahoma Agricultural and Mechanical College—rural electrification in Oklahoma, Experimental Station Bulletin #207, Dec. 19—."

Color in an index leads to quick identifications: one color of card for headings, another for cross references, another for the special cards behind the subject cards mentioned above.

Sometimes all cross references made on a subject are listed on the reverse side of the main subject card, for ease in retracing steps at any time, for the purpose of reclassifying, transferring, or marking "discarded" when material is destroyed.

So important is the index that it is practically impossible for a subject file to function satisfactorily without one.

Guides and Folders.—The setup of guides and folders for a subject file must be determined by the kind of file: with the dictionary arrangement of many small headings an alphabetic set of guides as in name filing may be used, with auxiliary guides by months or special classifications.

With an encyclopedic arrangement of a few large subjects divided and subdivided, the better plan is to use one guide for each main subject, typing one's own inserts. The guide and folder tabs may be in various positions. One satisfactory arrangement is to have the main guides in first position at the left, with subdivision guides in second or second and

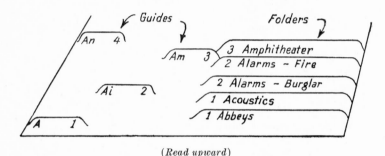

(*Read upward*)

Fig. 39.—Arrangement of Guides and Folders in Dictionary Subject Index

third positions in a different color from that of main guides. The folder tabs at the extreme right follow the same color scheme as the guides. At times so much information is required on the folder tab that folders with half cut tabs may be necessary. Again, material on any one subject may be bulky, requiring expansion folders of pressboard with metal tabs, the subject heading typed on a colored insert. The main headings may be typed in capital letters, with subdivision in lower case. The main heading, with subdivision, and subdivision of secondary division should appear in full on the folder tab. Example:

Taxes and Taxation—Illinois—Five million dollar road tax.

As every paper is written about a given subject, there is *no miscellany* in the sense heretofore described.

Note that there is in Figure 40 a general Advertising folder which carries material on all kinds of advertising other than that specifically signaled as magazine, newspaper, or radio: such advertising as billboards, signs, etc. This general folder of Advertising also carries material which discusses *all* kinds of advertising in one article, whether radio, billboard, or newspaper.

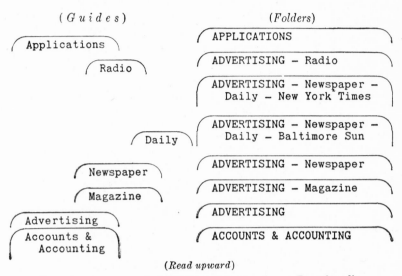

(*Read upward*)

Fɪɢ. 40.—Arrangement of Guides and Folders for an Encyclopedic Subject Index.

Discarding of Material.—A subject file is not transferred at regular intervals. Material on a subject becomes more valuable as it accumulates over a period of years. Old material that has been superseded should be discarded. The file should be gone through every two or three years in order to keep the number of pieces of material in file fairly permanent. The kind of material weeded out includes pamphlets of ephemeral service, clippings from popular magazines which appear later in books, advance sheets. From the index should be removed all cards, main entry and cross reference, which refer to the material discarded.

Charge-Outs.—To charge material from a subject file a card in the out guide should be used as has been described in previous chapters. It should show an exact description of the item loaned with the subject as the main item on the top line of the card followed by the borrower's name and department, also the date borrowed.

Sorting.—When as simple a classification has been worked out as is consistent with the nature of the material to be filed, and the list of subject headings is in form to be consulted easily, the daily routine should be worked out. Before the heading is definitely selected it is wise to check the list of subject headings already utilized. If not listed care should be exercised that no synonymous term has been used before assigning a new subject. An ordinary A–Z sorter is usually adequate.

Advantages and Disadvantages of a Subject File.—Subject files are the most costly of all files to maintain because they require experienced workers to choose the headings which describe the contents. Moreover, it always takes longer to prepare material for subject files than for any other method of arrangement. Perhaps it is because a subject file requires infinite care and thought to set up and maintain that it has been neglected more than any other type of file. Moreover, the content of every paper to be put in a subject file requires detailed perusal. When a subject file does function, it is a source of great satisfaction, especially to the executives who are its prime users.

As indicated above, subject material is found in the executive offices of a business house and in its research departments. In the purchasing department the stock and quotation records are filed by *name* of article; cabinets, oils, etc., which in this instance may be considered subject headings. The secondary arrangement in a name file may be by subject as in public utility company files, where the primary arrangement is by the name of the property, such as Akron, Atlanta, Auburn, etc. Because of the amount of material under each main heading a secondary arrangement is essential for quick filing and finding, as

Accidents
Advertising
Assessed Valuation   See Taxes
Benches
Boilers
Budgets
Calodorants
Claims
Coal and Coke
Construction
Compressors

Another example of subjects as a secondary arrangement may be found in the legal department. Large cases filed by number, as

Smith John vs. Chicago Coal Co. 432

may need further subdivision into:

Correspondence
Exhibits
Memos of Fact
Memos of Law
Pleadings

There is often considerable correspondence between department heads, between the home office and the branches, and between the various branches of a business. To file such material by name is begging the question. In the first place, under which name shall the memo be filed: the name of the writer or the receiver? Some firms follow one method, some the other, and some do both with constant confusion as a result. In the second place, the personnel changes but the memo may be just as important months hence when the name under which the memo was filed is forgotten. So such material is much more accessible when filed by subject, as

Accounting Procedure   Building Maintenance
Advertising   Conventions
Bonus   Donations
Budgets

Subject Headings for Interdepartment Correspondence and Executive Files

Accidents & Accident Prevention
Accounting
Addresses *See* Speeches
Advertising
Agreements *See* Contracts
Applications (Employment)
Appraisals
Bonus *See* Wages
Budgets *See* Accounting
Claims *See also* Insurance
Commissions *See* Wages
Commodities
Compensation—Workmen's *See* Insurance
Competition
Complaints
Conferences *See* Conventions
Constitutions & Bylaws *See* Corporation Data
Construction
Contracts
Conventions
Copyrights
Corporation Data
Decentralization
Donations
Dues *See* Memberships
Employees *See* Personnel
Equipment & Supplies
Expenses & Expense Accounts
Financial Statements *See* Reports
Financing
Foreign
Forms
Group Insurance *See* Insurance
Hotels, Reservations, etc.
Industrial Relations
Insurance
Inventories

Investments
Itineraries
Job Descriptions
Laws & Legislation
Leases *See* Contracts
Legal Matters
Licenses & Permits
Memberships
Minutes of Meetings
Mortgages *See* Financing
Motor Vehicles
Office Maintenance
Organization & Management
Patents & Trademarks
Payrolls *See* Accounting
Pension Plans
Personnel
Prices & Price Lists
Publications
Publicity
Purchasing
Real Estate
Reports
Research & Development
Rules & Regulations, Employees
Salaries *See* Wages
Sales
Sales Promotion
Service
Speeches
Stock
Storage
Taxes
Telegraph & Telephone
Testimonial Letters
Trademarks *See* Patents & Trademarks
Traffic
Trucks *See* Motor Vehicles
Wages

Automobile Subject File

ACCIDENTS
  Causes
    Alcohol
    Auto fatigue
  Death corners
  Investigations
  Rural intersections
  Statistics
ASSOCIATIONS & CLUBS
BEAUTIFICATION—Highway
BICYCLES
BOND ISSUE—Roads
BRAKES
BRIDGES
CAMPAIGNS—Safety
  Better driver groups
  Brake testing and car inspection
  I will drive safely
COMMUNITY SAFETY WORK
CONSTRUCTION
  Asphalt
  Bituminous surfaces
  Concrete
  Designs
  Estimates and costs
  Expansion joints
  Labor
  Resurfacing
  Secondary roads
  Steel reinforcements
CONTESTS—Safety
  Inter-Fleet Drivers
  Police
DAYLIGHT SAVING PLAN
DRIVER STATISTICS
DRIVER TESTS
DRIVER TRAINING
ELEVATED HIGHWAYS
ENFORCEMENT
  Arrest forms
  Courts
  Police
  Violator's School
FIRST AID
GASOLINE DISCOUNT
GLASS
GRADE CROSSINGS
  Gates
  Signals and signs
GRADE SEPARATIONS
HEADLIGHTS
ICE CONTROL & SNOW REMOVAL

LAWS AND LEGISLATION
  City—Codes & Ordinances—Annual Appropriation Bill
  —Codes & Ordinances—Model
  —Codes & Ordinances—Right turn on red light
  Driver's license
  Federal Gas Tax
LIGHTING—Highway
MAINTENANCE—Highway
  Impact effect
MOTOR VEHICLES
  Operating costs
  Safety equipment
  Theft studies
PARKING
  Ordinance enforcement program
  Park-o-meter
  Statistics
PATROLS
  Awards
  Belts
  Legal responsibility
  Manuals
  Ponchos
PLAY STREETS
REGISTRATION FIGURES & FEES
  Wheel tax statement
SAFETY MATERIALS
SAFETY ZONES
SCHOOLS
  Driver training
  Elementary
  High
  Police
SIGNALS
SPEED
TAXES
  Diversion
  Gas
  License fees
    City
    State
  Special assessments
TIRES & SKIDDING
TRACK ELEVATION
TRACTIVE RESISTANCE
TRAFFIC CAPACITY
TRAFFIC CONTROL
  Air races
  One way streets
  Through streets
TRAFFIC COUNTS
WIDENING—Highway

Corporate Minutes.—An application of subject classification which is growing in importance is in indexing corporate minutes. The indexing of annual proceedings of trade associations and of their publications is another application. To go through minute books covering twenty-five or even fifty years to find what action has been taken on any topic, such as Pensions or the Branch in Minneapolis, is a time-consuming process without such an index. The indexing may carry enough detail including dates to give wanted information from the cards without actual reference to the minute books. The following sample might represent the indexing necessary for a subsidiary export company of a large corporation:

Export Company
    Proposal to supply a manager (date)   Vol 2 p 73; 118
    Commission appointed to perfect organization so
        that it can operate on a brokerage basis—5% net
        of foreign sales of each factory (date)   Vol 2 p 460
    Proposal to build a special machine for export
        trade (date)   Vol 2 p 570–1
    Precedence given export shipments from factories
        (date)   Vol 3 p 231
    Lumber and direct labor charges to determine costs
        of export boxing (date)   Vol 3 p 260
    Anticipated 50% business loss due to crop failure
        in Argentina (date)   Vol 3 p 641
    Appointment of company agent and attorney in
        France (date)   Vol 3 p 1516

Chapter 12

DUPLEX AND DECIMAL SUBJECT FILES

Duplex Numeric System.—There are times when the alphabetic arrangement of subject matter is not entirely an ideal method. This may be true where there are large subjects that may need to be further subdivided in the future. It may be true where it is desirable to group together related subjects.

In the architect's index, which is shown on page 141, the 40 main classifications follow the logical sequence of the erection of a building from the preparation of the site through the various processes of building, to laws and regulations. In other words, the file develops with the building. The arrangement of the main subjects in alphabetical order would not be practical.

In such a duplex subject file the main subjects are numbered consecutively, giving each number unlimited expansion, and the secondary subdivisions under each number are also numbered consecutively giving unlimited expansion, and so on under each subsequent subdivision. Each division of numbers must be separated from its subdivision number by a colon, a dash, a period, or some other distinguishing symbol. Sometimes a letter is used for small divisions which will not number more than 26.

1	PREPARATION OF SITE	
1a	Demolition of Structures	
2	EXCAVATION	(main division)
2a	Tests of Subsoil	(first subdivision)
2a1	Pits	(second subdivision)
2a2	Borings	
2b	Excavated Material, disposal of	

Letters of the alphabet are not as easily handled as numbers unless they have some mnemonic (memory) feature attached such as having the letter stand for the initial letter of the subject. In this type of file no regularity of subdivisions is required, because each number remains independent in its expansion. Numbers should be evaluated from left to right.

In the alphabetic index main subjects as well as subdivision subjects must be listed as they develop with proper numbers assigned. It is often wise, in addition, to type a list of the main classifications with the numbers on sheets for the use of those who have occasion to consult the files. A suggested form for the index follows:

2A2–2	Wash Borings

Fig. 41.—Index Card—Duplex Numeric System

The cross references may be kept in the index on differently colored cards or, if the file itself is small, colored sheets may be used in the file. Since the index is so frequently made up on 3″ x 5″ cards, an ordinary alphabetic arrangement of guides will be all that is required. For use with a loose-leaf book A–Z index tabs will be necessary.

The guiding for the material itself should have insert tabs, metal or celluloid. The inserts should carry both the subject heading and its number. The main classifications, the first subdivisions, and the second subdivisions should be clearly distinguished from one another by means of position and color; the main divisions might be a 4″ tab guide in center position with white celluloid; the first subdivision might be a 2½″ guide in first position with yellow celluloid; second subdivision in the second position with salmon. For every guide there should be at least one folder with label corresponding in color with its guide. No provision is made for miscellany.

Portion of a Filing System for Architects' Offices

The Standard Construction Classification

Adopted by the American Institute of Architects—Revised 1922

Main Classifications

1. Preparation of Site and Preliminary Work
2. Excavation
3. Masonry Material
4. Concrete and Concrete Work
5. Brick Work
6. Foundations
7. Waterproofing and Dampproofing
8. Stone Work
9. Architectural Terra Cotta
10. Block Construction
11. Paving
12. Roofing, Sheet Metal and Skylights
13. Structural Steel and Iron, etc.

(Through 40 main classifications)

Main Classifications with Subdivisions

1. PREPARATION OF SITE
    1A Demolition of Structures
        1A1 Ownership of Material
        1A2 Storage of Salvaged Material
    1B Protection of Trees, Shrubs, etc.
    1C Top Soil Removal and Storage
    1D Inspection and Testing
    1E Surveys and Photographs
2. EXCAVATION
    2A Tests of Subsoil

2A1 Pits
2A2 Borings
2A3 Loading
2A4 Test Piles
2B Excavated Material, Disposal of
2C Blasting
2D (For Caissons, see 6-B)
2E Shoring
2F Sheet Piling
    2F1 Wood
    2F2 Metal
    2F3 Concrete
2G Rock Dressing
2H Tunneling
2I Underpinning
2J Back-filling
2K Dredging
3. MASONRY MATERIALS
    3A Cement
        3A1 Portland
        3A2 White Portland
        3A3 High Early Strength
        3A4 Natural
        3A5 Keenes
    3B Integral Compounds and Floor Treatments
        3B1 Set Accelerating
        3B2 Hardening and Dustproofing
        3B3 Acidproofing
        3B4 Waterproofing See also 7-A
    3C Lime
        3C1 Lump
        3C2 Hydraulic
        3C3 Hydrated
        3C4 Specials
    3D Aggregates, etc.

Every paper prepared for file should be marked with subject heading and number in the upper right-hand corner. Cross references should be indicated at the time that the papers are marked. The sorter guides should be set up by *number*, a guide for each main classification being sufficient. In loaning material from a subject numeric file, it is necessary to record the subject headings and number on the top line, following with the usual information as to borrower's name, date borrowed, etc. Instead of being transferred at regular intervals, such a file should be kept weeded out, or as

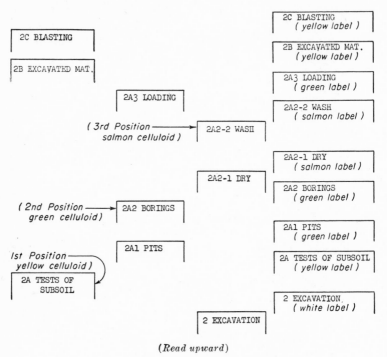

(*Read upward*)

Fig. 42.—Duplex Numeric Subject File

in the case of the architect's file, be transferred upon completion of building.

Dewey Decimal Classification.—The Decimal method of filing, like the Duplex Numeric, is a classed arrangement of a few main subjects, divided and subdivided many times, with a system of numbering or lettering the subjects and their various divisions to facilitate the handling of the material. In the Decimal system, the main groupings, usually

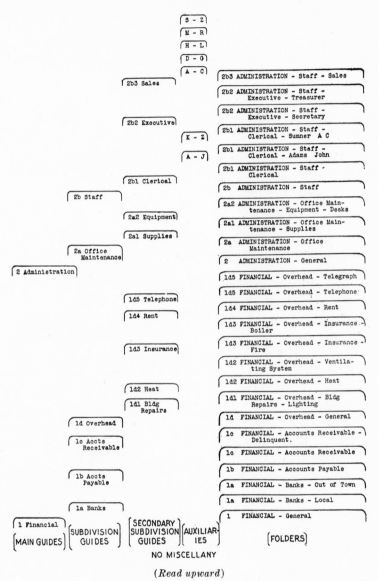

(*Read upward*)

Fig. 43.—Duplex Numeric Subject Setup

fewer in number than in the two schemes previously described, have been developed in some logical sequence, as from smaller to larger, historically from the oldest to the most modern, geographically, or in any one of a number of ways.

The first Decimal system was worked out by Dr. Melvil Dewey in the 1870's for the classification of library books. He conceived the idea of grouping all human knowledge into ten main divisions. Theoretically it seems absurd to divide all knowledge into but ten classes, but practically it has worked out very well. Each of these ten main groups he divided again into ten, subdivided each of these 100 divisions again into tens, making 1000 divisions, at which place he introduced the decimal point and then allowed each number expansion as needed. Decimal comes from the Greek word meaning ten. Thus the system became known as the Dewey Decimal system. The first summary or ten main divisions are given below. Note the phonetic spelling.

Dewey Decimal Classification

First Summary

000 General Works
100 Philosofy
200 Religion
300 Sociology
400 Philology

500 Natural Science
600 Useful Arts
700 Fine Arts
800 Literature
900 History

Second Summary

000 GENERAL WORKS
010   Bibliografy
020   Library economy
030   General cyclopedias
040   General collections
050   General periodicals
060   General societies   Museums
070   Journalism   Newspapers
080   Special libraries   Polygrafy
090   Book rarities

100 PHILOSOFY
110   Metaphysics
120   Special metaphysical topics
130   Mind and body

140   Philosofic systems
150   Mental faculties   Psychology
160   Logic   Dialectics
170   Ethics
180   Ancient philosofers
190   Modern philosofers

200 RELIGION
210   Natural theology
220   Bible
230   Doctrinal Dogmatics Theology
240   Devotional   Practical
250   Homiletic Pastoral Parochial
260   Church Institutions Work
270   Religious history

Dewey Decimal Classification (*Cont'd.*)

280 Christian churches and sects
290 Ethnic Nonchristian

300 SOCIOLOGY
310 Statistics
320 Political science
330 Political economy
340 Law
350 Administration
360 Associations and Institutions
370 Education
380 Commerce Communication
390 Customs Costumes Folklore

400 PHILOLOGY
410 Comparativ
420 English
430 German
440 French
450 Italian
460 Spanish
470 Latin
480 Greek
490 Minor languages

500 NATURAL SCIENCE
510 Mathematics
520 Astronòmy
530 Physics
540 Chemistry
550 Geology
560 Paleontology
570 Biology
580 Botany
590 Zoology

600 USEFUL ARTS
610 Medicin
620 Engineering
630 Agriculture

640 Domestic economy
650 Communication Commerce
660 Chemic technology
670 Manufactures
680 Mechanic trades
690 Bilding

700 FINE ARTS
710 Landscape gardening
720 Architecture
730 Sculpture
740 Drawing Decoration Design
750 Painting
760 Engraving
770 Photografy
780 Music
790 Amusements

800 LITERATURE
810 American
820 English
830 German
840 French
850 Italian
860 Spanish
870 Latin
880 Greek
890 Minor languages

900 HISTORY
910 Geografy and travels
920 Biografy
930 Ancient history
940 M   ⎧Europe
950 o   ⎪Asia
960 d   ⎪Africa
970 e   ⎨North America
980 r   ⎪South America
990 n   ⎩Oceanica and Polar
         regions

The division of the second summary again into ten divisions comprises the third summary. Many subjects are not divided further, some are carried out to four and five digits beyond the decimal point.

It is necessary to have the complete classification in order to assign a number but the following example gives an idea of how it is done:

```
300 Sociology
 330    "        –Economics
  331    "      –    "     –Labor & laborers
  331.1 "     –    "    –   "        "    –Rel. of capital to labor
   331.11 "   –    "    –   "        "    –  "    "     "     "   "  –Employment
    331.116 " –    "    –   "        "    –  "    "     "     "   "   –     "   Engaging Workers
     331.1163 –    "    –   "        "    –  "    "     "     "   "   –     "        "       "
                                                                Collective bargaining
```

Mnemonic Features Applied to Decimal System.—Dr.

Dewey has very ingeniously given mnemonic features to certain numbers which permit the user to carry in his mind many hundreds of combinations by simply learning a few of the key divisions of ten subjects and numbers assigned to them and how these are used in relation to each other. Certain numbers are assigned to certain subjects and whenever there is a repetition of those subjects or form divisions, they are given in the same order.

Literature divisions	*Geographic divisions*	*European divisions*
1. Poetry	Continents	1. Scotland & Ireland
2. Drama		2. England & Wales
3. Fiction		3. Germany & Austria
4. Essays	4. Europe	4. France
5. Oratory	5. Asia	5. Italy
6. Letters	6. Africa	6. Spain & Portugal
7. Satire and Humor	7. North America	7. Russia
8. Miscellany	8. South America	8. Norway, Sweden,
9. Minor literature of	9. Oceanica and the	Denmark
the group	Polar regions	9. Minor countries

It will be seen that not every 5 means Italy but that 5 in certain combinations does mean Italy:

> 900 History
> 940 European history
> 945 History of Italy
> 914.5 Travel in Italy
> 850 Italian literature
> 851 Italian poetry
> 853 Italian fiction

Planning a Decimal Subject Classification.—The Dewey

Decimal Classification is a more formal type of classification than any so far considered, with a wide range for expansion both in subject matter and in volume. In an alphabetic subject arrangement, entirely new subjects can be added any time in their proper alphabetic sequence; in a decimal classification, each new subject must be fitted into the proper place under the printed classes and their subdivisions. The divisions in the decimal follow each other in a logical sequence, bringing material on the same subject together. Thus it is obvious that a full alphabetic index is a necessity for use with the decimal classification.

The wide range of subjects covered in the Dewey Decimal Classification makes it impractical for a correspondence file. However, it has been used as a basis for various other classifications. Some lines of business, such as railroads, in the Williams' *Railroad Correspondence File,* have worked out suitable classifications but none of them is widely known. Usually each firm plans its own classification based on the Dewey.

The error most usually made in working out an individual decimal classification is that the divisions are most haphazardly planned. A new classification should be attempted only by an experienced clerk in cooperation with the heads of the departments of the organization. A bird's-eye view of the entire subject is necessary to discern the fundamental relations of the divisions of the subject matter and to decide on the ten main classifications and their subdivisions. The whole field of activity in question and its allied lines of development should be surveyed.

The same basis should be used for subdividing all divisions of equal rank. In other words, the same viewpoint should always be kept when classifying. The expansion of subjects and the interpolation of new subjects without destroying the basic plan should both be provided for. In the War Department Classification following, the whole of the 900 group, from 170 through 190 in the 100 group, 270 and 280 in the 200 group, etc., were left unused for future expansion. If a decimal classification is used for correspondence, the secondary arrangement within each group may be by date of the letter or alphabetically by the correspondent's name or by geographical location. Too many subdivisions should be avoided. The classifier should guard against becoming too much interested in the development of a complete classification at the expense of one that works with accuracy and speed. The service the classification renders is a good check against overclassifying or not having enough subdivisions.

In handling a decimal file it must be remembered that as time goes on there is bound to be a shift in emphasis on a given subject with the necessity for reclassification. The subject of Liquor was originally classified by Dewey under Temperance which rightfully falls under the heading of Ethics 170. Later the emphasis was placed on the medicinal value of liquor and it was put under Medicine, 610. Still later it became a political issue and was thrown under the heading of Law Enforcement 340. After the repeal of prohibition there developed the aspect of the control of the sale of liquor.

Alphabetic Index Required.—A full alphabetic index of the subjects, which serves as a key to the classification, should be made. It is often advisable when developing a subject classification to start by placing each subject on a card and then to sort the cards into the various main groups in order to check on the brevity, clarity, exactness, and uniformity of the subject headings chosen.

Dr. Dewey says that this index contains "all the heads of the tables, with the class number of each, as far as have been found; all the synonyms or alternative names for the heads; and many other entries that seemed likely to help the reader find readily the subject sought. Though the user knows just where to turn to his subject in the tables, by first consulting the index, he may be sent to . . . allied subjects, where he will find valuable matter which he would otherwise overlook." Cross references are found in the index as well as in the body of the classification.

Folders and Guides for Decimal System.—The setup of a decimal file is similar to that described for the duplex earlier in the chapter: a 4″ tab guide in center position for main classifications with smaller tab guides in first and second positions for subdivisions has proved satisfactory. The tabs should be of the insert type and should bear the decimal number and the subject. Differently colored inserts may be used to distinguish the main classifications from the secondary, the secondary from the tertiary. Another method is to have main classification guides in the first position with secondary division guides in the second position.

Since a subject file is of more or less permanent nature, cheap folders are an extravagance. Gummed labels may be used with heavy manila folders, when the papers filed are not heavy or bulky; but usually the weight of the material requires pressboard folders with metal tabs and insert labels. When the guide tabs come at the left of the drawer, folders with right-hand tabs are preferable. The folders should carry the decimal number first and then the subject. Folders are arranged in the file in numeric order. If a color scheme is used for the guides, it may be carried out on the folders as well: the folder for a main classification should have the same color label as a main classification guide, etc.

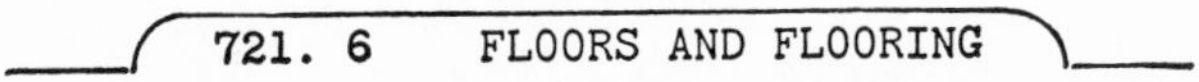

721. 6   FLOORS AND FLOORING

FIG. 44.—Folder Tab for Decimal File

Filing Routines.—In preparing the material for file the decimal number and sometimes the subject heading are penciled in the upper right corner of the paper. If cross-reference cards need to be made out they should be indicated as the paper is being scanned. If it is urgent that the bulk of mail get to the filing cabinets promptly, these papers requiring cross references can be laid aside for later action.

The charge record may be filed in the folder from which the paper is taken or may be kept on the clerk's desk arranged in numeric order in a box provided for the purpose.

As in the other methods of subject arrangement, files should be reviewed every three to five years so that all papers not useful in the transaction of current business or having no permanent value will be destroyed. Executive authority may be desirable for this destruction. The index cards should be checked at the same time that the papers are removed from file in order that no dead entries are left in the index.

Final Decision on System to be Used.—With the presentation of these several types of subject files, it remains to comment on the fact that commercial lines of business, and even technical, highly specialized, and professional lines are not as fixedly established as is sometimes thought. The users of their files approach the material from many different and often rapidly changing angles. Rarely is the logical sequence in handling material maintained as anticipated. In actual practice a bit of information is taken from here and another bit from there to construct something new or to present a new point of view. The constancy of the angle of approach varies greatly. Thus it is that subject files are constantly undergoing changes.

Of the three methods of subject filing described, the most common by far is the alphabetic dictionary arrangement. The method of classification chosen should be the one which will give the most complete service.

Even before a decision is made as to the type of subject file to be used, there should be a careful analysis as to whether a subject file is actually needed. Oftentimes the amount of subject material in a given firm is proportionately so small that it can easily be grouped in the alphabetic name or location file without an index, or can be brought to attention by means of a card index arranged by subject.

War Department Classification

First Summary

000 General
100 Finance and Accounting
200 Personnel
300 Administration
400 Supplies, Equipment and
     Services

500 Transportation
600 Buildings and Grounds
700 Medicine, Hygiene and Sanita-
     tion
800 Rivers and Harbors
900

Second Summary

000 GENERAL
010 Laws and Legal Matters
020 War Department (Powers,
     Functions, etc.)
030 President and Congress of the
     United States
040 Executive Departments of the
     United States
050 Statistics
060 Maps, Charts, and Tables
070 Inventions
080 Societies and Associations
090 Local Affairs

100 FINANCE AND ACCOUNTING
110 Appropriations
120 Funds, Disbursement
130 Accounting for Funds (Money)
140 Accounting for Property, Sup-
     lies, etc.
150 Claims and Accounts
160 Contracts
170
180
190

200 PERSONNEL
210 Commissioned
220 Enlisted
230 Civilian Employees
240 Pay and Allowances
250 Discipline
260 Pensions
270
280
290 Miscellaneous

300 ADMINISTRATION
310 Business Methods and Proce-
     dure

320 Organization of the Army
330 Military Control
340 Recruitment
350 Education
360 Aviation and Aeronautics
370 Employment, Use, and Move-
     ment of Troops
380 War and Peace
390

400 SUPPLIES, EQUIPMENT, AND
     SERVICES
410 Building Material, Machines
     and Hardware
420 Clothing, Equipage, and Toilet
     Articles
430 Subsistence Stores
440 Medical, Surgical, Dental, Vet-
     erinary Supplies, Equipment,
     and Instruments
450 Supplies for Transportation,
     Animals and Packing Sup-
     plies
460 Other Supplies
470 Armament and Ammunition
480 Services, Other than Personal
490

500 TRANSPORTATION
510 Transportation of Persons
520 Transportation of Supplies
530 Transportation by Land
540 Transportation by Water
550 Transportation Rates, Tariffs,
     Accounts, Contracts, Tickets
560 Harbor Boats and Vessels
570 Transports and Army Trans-
     port Service
580
590

Williams Railroad Classification

A Decimal Classification for Indexing Railway Correspondence and Records

0	General	500	Transportation and Storage
1	Executive and Legal	510	Track and Terminals—Working
2	Finance and Accounts	520	Trains
3	Roadway and Structures	530	Locomotives—Utilization of
4	Equipment and Shops	540	Cars—Utilization of
5	Transportation and Storage	550	
6	Traffic, Rates	560	Safety Measures—Signals
7		570	Telegraph and Telephones
8		580	Accidents
9	Local Facilities and Affairs		

500   Transportation and Storage—General
   500.1   Statistics
   500.2   Associations
    500.21   International
    500.211 International Railway Congress
    500.22   National
    500.221 American Railway Association
    500.222 Association of Railroad Superintendents
    500.223 Association of Superintendents of Telegraph
    500.224 Train Despatchers Association
    500.225 Eastern Railway Association
    500.226 General Managers Association
    500.23   Association Formed by Company for Advancement of Employees
    500.231 Association of Transportation Officers
    500.24   Car Service Association
    500.25   Travellers' Aid Societies

510   Tracks and Terminals—Working
   510.3   Trackage Rights
   510.4   Lease of
   510.5   Joint Use of

511   Tracks—Working
   511.1   Operation of Single Track Line, Capacity, etc.
   511.2   Operation of Two or More Tracks, Capacity, etc.

512   Yards—Working
   512.01   Rules of Operation of
   512.1   Condition of
   512.2   Cost of Handling Cars in
   512.3   Switching Service (for Rates, etc., see 620.151)
   512.4   Lighting Yards

513   Stations—Working
   513.01   Station Names
   513.011 List of Stations
   513.02   Receipts and Expenditures
   513.03   Bureau of Information
   513.04   Station, Hours for Opening and Closing
   513.05   Station Cleaning and Sanitation
   513.06   Non-Agency Stations

513.1   PASSENGER STATIONS—WORKING
  513.101 Carriages, Omnibus, Cabs, and Taxicabs
  513.102 Hotels, Restaurants, and Dining Rooms
  513.103 Barber Shops and Shoe Shining Stands
  513.104 Station Privileges

Chapter 13

FILING PRINTED MATERIAL

Library Material in the File Room.—Often it falls to the lot of the file clerk to care for printed matter, such as clippings and periodicals. These rightfully belong in a library but since most firms do not have libraries, the file department is the logical place for such material. The file clerk should never attempt to be a librarian without proper training, but it is entirely possible to care for the printed material that comes into the firm in a simple, efficient way until the time is ripe for library service. That the two services should not be confused is demonstrated by the fact that the essentials of filing service are accuracy and speed while the nature of the librarian's problems does not usually permit such accuracy or speed. While some definite information is asked for from the librarian, often *trends* are of greater importance and both may require long research to obtain. Yet at certain points, such as in the handling of printed material, the work of the two vocations overlap.

Practically every type of business where the technical, financial, or managerial phases are important requires reliable, up-to-date information continuously at its command. Clippings are of particular value to such firms in that they often give pertinent facts long before they appear in more permanent book form. They may be used for securing new customers, for technical information on new products and new methods, for checking on advertising of their own and of their competitors. The sources of clippings are newspapers, magazines, national commercial organizations, banks and investment houses, federal and state governments, chambers of commerce, and clipping bureaus.

Every clipping should be marked with the source, date of publication, and subject heading, as well as notation if a numbering system is used. The title of an article does not always indicate its precise subject, especially if a catch title

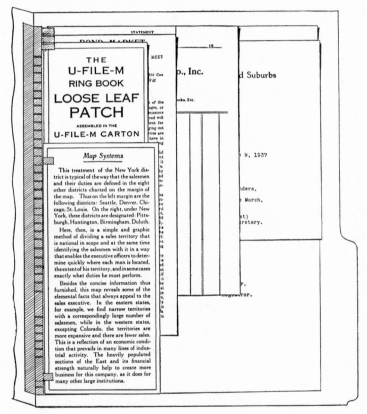

FIG. 45.—U-File-M Folder

has been used. Oftentimes the subject is ringed in the article instead of being written out.

Clippings as Part of Data File.—Clippings are filed by subject matter and may be part of a data file containing pamphlets, government reports, and statistical data in various forms, or they may be filed separately. As part of a data file they may be either unmounted or mounted. If unmounted use heavy manila envelopes of the same size as folders, and file immediately behind the pamphlet folder on the same subject. Regular folders may be used when the sides have been fastened with a stapling machine to make a pocket. Indicate the source, date, and subject at the top of the clipping or at the back. If mounted use stiff sheets of manila, kraft, or bond paper, bind with manuscript cover, indicating source, etc., on the cover, and fasten into folders with binder strips, or fasteners. The U-File-M fastener is a strip of gummed paper that is glued into the folder and has little tabs that project and are glued to the papers to be inserted, permitting clippings to be turned as pages in a book. Several rows of newspaper clippings may be pasted to a folder side through the use of these binder strips. For mounting clippings trim evenly and closely, leaving space at the top for needed information. If two or more sheets are needed for a long article, fasten along the left margin.

Separate Clipping File.—Where clippings form a separate file, they may be handled in several different ways. If the items are short, paste on one of the standard-sized cards and file in an index. If they are long, or mixed long and short, fold and put into envelopes properly labeled; mount unfolded on letter or legal-sized sheets and file in vertical folders; or if the mount is stiff, omit folders, but fasten into pressboard pamphlet binders with fasteners or strips. If magazine page size, file loosely in letter-sized folders closed at the sides; or paste into scrapbooks with glue, paste, or rubber cement. Or if unmounted and on the same subject, fasten clippings together and file in an envelope; or mount on punched sheets and lace together. The folding of clippings is not desirable as the paper breaks at the fold.

When clippings are kept in filing cabinets, the folders should be the same size as those used for correspondence. The labels should be typed as for any other subject file with the main classification on the top line, with secondary classifications continued on the top line or on the second line. Small subject files are often seen without guides but with folder labels carefully marked. Guides may be of the alphabetic combination type or of the insert type with the main subject headings indicated. Clippings should be charged out as are papers from any other file. The subject heading is of prime importance and should be written on the top line of the charge card together with the source and date of publication, borrower's name and department, and the date borrowed.

It is advisable to go through a clipping file once a year to weed out material no longer of value. Often the discarding depends upon other resources, such as the public library. If a clipping file is of transitory value, the clippings may be kept unmounted for a determined period, then valueless or duplicate clippings weeded out, and the balance which are of permanent value mounted and kept in the data file. There is great expense involved in the care of clippings, so they should be selected with discretion.

Procedure for Routing Current Periodicals.—Periodicals or business journals enable a business man to keep abreast of the times in his own line. Every industry and profession has its journals. The N. W. Ayer & Sons directory in the public library gives the titles of such periodicals, frequency of issue, subscription price, etc., as may be of interest to any one type of business.

The pages of periodicals of particular interest to the business man contain the leading articles, reports of meetings found in the notes, and the classified lists found among the advertisers' pages.

Periodicals often go unopened to the executives and often continue to remain unopened because of press of duties. It is preferable, therefore, that periodicals be sent upon receipt to the filing department if there is no library. The file clerk should learn to do the preliminary reading and to mark articles of interest to the executives. This is often a matter of being thoroughly familiar with the business and of having sufficient vision to recognize new trends in that business. Upon receipt periodicals should be stamped with the word "Files" and the name of the organization. One record card, 3″ x 5″, for each periodical, filed alphabetically, should have spaces for the recording of all copies to date and on the back a record of expirations, source, publishers, and renewals, also names of persons to whom periodical is to be sent and its disposition, whether to be clipped, bound, or destroyed. This is called a check-list. A new card should be started at the beginning of each new volume and kept behind a current guide. There are different methods of checking the non-receipt of periodicals:

1. Colored clips attached to cards indicate when the magazine is due. The clips are moved to a new position when an issue is received, thus showing up overdue issues.
2. A separate follow-up gives the title of the periodical and is filed under the due date.

There are different methods of routing a magazine: attach to each issue as it comes a slip bearing the names of the persons who are to see the periodical, in the order in which they are to be circulated.

Another method is to send the periodical to one person at a time with a clip on the cover calling attention to the article of special interest. When this is returned to the file room, send it to the second person, and so on. Two days should be the time limit of loan to a person. A 3″ x 5″ loan record kept under the name of the periodical will enable the file department to know instantly where each magazine is.

Disposition of Periodicals.—A definite decision should be made on the disposition of periodicals, whether the important articles should be clipped and filed and the balance of the magazine discarded; whether the magazine should be kept intact for six months and then discarded; or whether it should be bound for permanent reference. Many magazines are not worth binding as they contain facts of current interest only. When a particular article seems worth indexing and clipping, indicate on the outside cover of the periodical the page number. As magazines are being discarded watch for

---

DON'T LOSE THIS MAGAZINE

When you have finished reading it, see that it is passed on promptly to the next man checked. Any failure to follow strictly this request robs another of the opportunity to get information valuable to his work and to the company.

Date rec'd   Put initials after
                                        your name when rec'd

_____J. A. Caselton_____
_____G. C. Taussig _____
_____G. A. Grisham _____
_____B. C. Sweet   _____

Remarks_____

Last name checked will please return to Files.

FIG. 46.—Magazine Route Slip

---

these page numbers in order not to miss the wanted article. Use special colored cards in the subject index to flag the material to be found in the periodicals. Since most of this periodical material is ephemeral, weed out the index of these colored cards at frequent intervals. When an article clipped has another article on the back which is worth keeping, copy such article, cross reference it, or have it photostated. The H. W. Wilson Company, New York, furnishes back numbers of periodicals which contain articles desired.

Periodicals may be housed in pamphlet boxes and put on shelves. Such boxes may be secured from any library supply house. Often current issues are put flat in drawers with the latest issue in a binder on shelves or standing upright on a magazine rack. If of permanent value they should be bound.

Sources of Information.—The various departments and commissions of the Federal Government publish in pamphlet form or on mimeographed sheets information invaluable to the business man. The Superintendent of Documents, Washington, D. C., issues a monthly catalog entitled "Monthly Catalog of United States Public Documents." This catalog lists all Government publications, giving prices of all available for sale, with an annual index issued separately. "Vertical File Service Catalog," published by the H. W. Wilson Company, is also a valuable source of information on pamphlets.

The Library of Congress, Washington, D. C., publishes the "Monthly Check List of State Publications," which lists the information issued by the state government departments.

The Public Affairs Information Service, New York City, issued weekly; and the Industrial Arts Index and the Agricultural Index, issued monthly by the H. W. Wilson Company, New York, index under subjects articles to be found in a large number of periodicals including reports issued by the government and by individual organizations.

Trade Catalogs.—Trade catalogs contain printed information which, while not of direct interest to executives, are nevertheless important to purchasing and sales departments. The problem involved with catalogs is that of the method of indexing. A catalog may be called for by the name of the firm; all catalogs listing a certain item may be wanted; the latest catalog issued by a firm is usually the one most needed. They must be arranged alphabetically by name of vendor; alphabetically by type of items supplied; as received with date of receipt stamped on the catalog.

If arranged by name of firm, a card index by items is necessary. The main card under the firm name gives the title of the catalog and the date issued, also date received. All items indexed are listed on this card. When a new catalog for a given firm is received, it must be carefully compared with the main card to see that it contains the same items or the card must be revised. The old edition is usually destroyed or filed in a storeroom.

If catalogs are arranged alphabetically by item an index by firm name is needed, and doubtless some analytic work for important individual items. To keep catalogs thus arranged up to date, a signal is used on the main card, or the card index is examined once a year for dates. If the main card is of distinctive color, the record may be quickly revised.

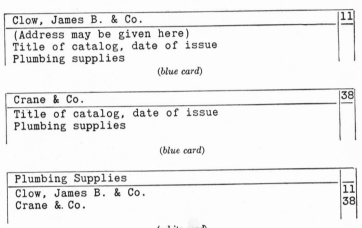

(blue card)

(blue card)

(white card)
(Names of company may be omitted and reference made by number only.)

FIG. 47.—Index Cards to Catalog File

If catalogs are arranged as received, they are numbered consecutively, the last one received having the highest number. A card index by items and by vendor's name as described above is required. The catalog number must also be given on the index cards. For instance, if James B. Clow and Company issues a catalog on plumbing supplies which has received number 11, and later a catalog is received on plumbing supplies from Crane and Company which is numbered 38, the cards should read as given in Figure 47.

Catalogs may be arranged like volumes in a bookcase or they may be filed in legal size cabinets, with guiding similar to that of correspondence files, attention being given to the strength of guides and folders, as the catalogs are heavier than papers. Catalogs stand upright in the files without difficulty (bound back up), but supplementary sheets must be placed in folders for protection and to keep them grouped together.

Value of Printed Matter File.—The type of material described in this chapter is the kind of information often found hidden in executive desks. It is the kind of paper most generally neglected by file departments. Often executives do not realize what they are lacking in their offices because they have never had the printed matter cared for and presented to them in systematic form. It is to be remembered, however, that it is not the amount of material collected which is important, but the discretion used in selecting the material to be retained and the care given to weeding out obsolete matter.

Chapter 14

SOME DEPARTMENT RECORDS; GOVERNMENT FILES

Certain kinds of records, such as invoices, vouchers, checks, credit memoranda, and correspondence, are so common to every office large or small that methods of filing them are fairly well known. Other papers not as common and usually not found in volume in any business office are frequently neglected. Because they occasionally present a definite filing problem, they are here given special consideration.

Accident Records.—By name of person to whom accident occurred, or by state in which accident occurred.

Applications for Positions.—Usually a form is used for this purpose, a card or letter-sized paper. These are filed by type of position the applicant is applying for, as vampers, lasters, eyeleters, heelers in a shoe concern. Under each subdivision the applications are arranged alphabetically by name. It is a simple matter under this arrangement to run through the cards for the most likely candidate of a certain class. If filed by name applications are lost in the file as the name is apt to be forgotten. An applications file should be weeded out frequently so as to eliminate applications more than a few months old.

Bills of Lading.—The Freight Classifications filed with the Interstate Commerce Commission require three copies of the bill of lading for each shipment. These conform to classification requirements, although companies often have their own bill of lading forms which must have contract terms and conditions shown thereon. These three copies are called "original," "shipping order," and "memorandum." The duplicate or shipping order copy is retained by the transportation company; the shipper sends the original to the consignee and retains the memorandum copy, filing it by name of consignee. The usual size of a bill of lading is $8\frac{1}{2}'' \times 7''$ or $8\frac{1}{2}'' \times 11''$. They are filed in correspondence size cabinets. Sometimes bills of lading are kept in the traffic department, but more frequently they are sent to central file.

Canceled Checks.—In a home office having branches, canceled checks are usually filed first by location of branch and then by name of bank in that city, and then by months, which brings them practically in order according to check number. Monthly bank statements are often filed with the checks after they have been reconciled.

Cuts.—Are bulky and difficult to house because the metal plate must not be scratched. The most convenient housing for cuts has been found to be shallow drawers or shelves. Cuts should be classified: all the cuts for one book or catalog should be kept together, or if a cut is used for many different purposes the collection should be classified in some such method as:

> Borders
> Cartoons
> Charts and graphs
> Letterhead designs
> Signatures
> Trademarks, etc.

Automobile manufacturers, for example, have a separate classification for the cuts illustrating each different model. They are placed in drawers or on shelves beginning with the first alphabetical classification. Each drawer is numbered and then each cut within the drawer numbered, always on the side of the block facing the drawer pull. The stamping is done with metal punches, or if unmounted the metal is scratched with a sharp point upon the back. If a cut is located in cabinet B, drawer 10, with its individual number

57, then B10–57 is stamped on the cut. Copies of cuts should be filed in vertical cabinets by classification number.

Freight Claims.—All original papers pertaining to claims are sent to the transportation company and the copies are filed together by number. Loss and damage claims require: (1) the original bill of lading, (2) destination freight bill, (3) certified copy or original invoice, (4) indemnity bond in lieu of any of the papers listed under 1–3. Overcharge in weight or rate claims require: (1) the destination freight bill, (2) statement showing how difference in weight or rate is figured. Other papers are necessary but vary with the nature of the claim, such as papers showing attempts to trace shipment. The necessary papers are taken out of regular file to make up the claim which is kept indefinitely.

Leases.—By location of property for which lease is held. In vault.

Mailing Lists.—The compilation of a prospect list is extremely important. Lists secured at random are almost valueless. Practical suggestions in printed form for selecting live mailing lists can be obtained. After securing a good list, the next most important point is to keep it up to date. It is a theory among business firms that a list is of value for six months only, after which time it is obsolete. Often the file department is held responsible for checking returned letters against this file; noting salesmen's calls; checking new lists as they appear against the old names and addresses. Credit ratings often affect a list and require removal of some names.

Minutes of Directors' Meetings.—Often kept in bound books by date. Companies having minute books covering a span of 25 or more years are often hard put to find the record of some special action which has been taken without doing a great deal of thumbing of pages. Here is an opportunity to be of direct service to the heads of the organization. The detailed indexing of these minutes will permit of immediate reference to any action taken over the years on any subject such as "pensions." See the sample of such indexing on page 138.

Patents.—The United States Patent Office consecutively numbers each patent which it approves. Printed pamphlets are issued on each patent, giving name of author or inventor, name of assignee, subject matter of patent, illustration of

Illinois Pump Mfg. Co.,
845 N. Main St.,
Champaign, Ill.

2 Via I. C. Freight.
F2-B #8819 6/24 G1-80 #3420 #3 6/24
#40 Black-Shifting frames-Alloy.
Reg. Follow copy for State abbreviations.

FIG. 48.—A Record Plate of Alloy or Zinc Which Can Be Graphotyped (Cut) in Firm's Own Office. Blank cards attached to the upper part of the plate bear the imprint of the plate and act as an index.

same, number assigned. These pamphlets and supporting papers on patents should be filed by patent office number or by an arbitrary number assigned in the office. Three index cards should be made out in detail for every patent and filed: (1) by name of author or inventor; (2) by name of person or firm to whom the patent is assigned (Theodore Bender while employed with the Conover Corporation invented a water-softening process which patent is assigned to the Conover Corporation); (3) by subject of patent.

Stencils and Plates.—When a record plate of alloy or zinc is used, blank cards in strips or cut to fit the plate and attached to the upper half of the plate bear the imprint of the plate and act as an index. These plates are filed in pressed steel drawers made for all styles of plates and are equipped with lock follower which holds the plates upright in the drawer. Several styles of address plates have twelve sockets at the top. Removable tabs inserted in these sockets indicate different classifications, such as banks, corporations, individuals, or customers, prospects, etc. By adjusting the machine properly any of the divisions can then be "run off"

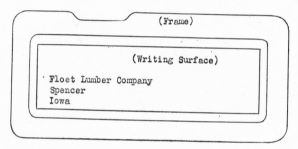

(Frame)

(Writing Surface)

Floet Lumber Company
Spencer
Iowa

Fig. 49.—Paper Stencil Cut on Typewriter

HEK   (guide)

(stencil)

(stencil)

HED   (guide)

(*Read upward*)
(*Further subdivisions are made by the color of the frame.*)
Fig. 50.—Discarded Stencils Utilized for Indexes

by itself, the machine printing only the desired stencils. Care must be taken not to allow the tabbing system to become too involved.

Stencils which can be cut on an ordinary typewriter are made of a heavy paper frame with a center portion of specially prepared paper. This stencil comes in eight different colored frames for purposes of classification. They are kept in removable trays.

Indexes can be made as needed by inverting discarded stencils and printing on the upper edge the alphabetic combinations, as shown in Figure 50.

Tariffs.—These are usually filed by the name of the railroad issuing the tariff and then under their number, as 5638K; if several railroads have their rates combined in one book, then under a committee issue, as Western Trunk Lines or Central Freight Association, followed by their number. Letter-sized drawers with heavy pressboard guides seem to furnish the best method of filing tariffs although flat shallow drawers are still much in use. If combination rates have to be figured often and shipments made frequently to a given customer, a card index may be set up to supplement the tariff file. This saves time of figuring rates each time a new shipment is to be made to the customer.

Tax Papers.—Because of penalties imposed for defaults, a dependable tax-paying schedule by means of a tickler system automatically brings up for attention all steps to be taken with respect to reports, assessments, payments so that there will be compliance with all provisions. For property and license tax records a card should be provided for each tax imposed. The top of the card can be divided into 12 sections in connection with which colored tabs are used to designate months for filing returns, presenting appeals, etc. During the current month the cards signaled for the following month are withdrawn and transferred to a 1–31 follow-up file. If few in number, copies of tax reports are filed by type: Federal, State, etc., and then by date.

For real estate the card form shows the date that the tax commences, the city, county, description of the premises, name of company conducting the local business, lease number, etc. The card may also indicate when taxes are due for city, county, and state, and the dates for filing of reports. In addition there should be a permanent calendar record preserving tax information with captions for year assessed, tax period, rate, kind, revision.

Virtually the same diary and record system is used by many companies for federal taxes and state corporation taxes. Card records indicating designation of taxes, to whom report is returned, due date, extension date, date filed, year ended, filing fee, date paid, and amount of tax, are filed by state and subindexed by subsidiary companies within the states. With this a complete tickler system covers all dates on which any action in respect to taxes must be taken.

Tear Sheets.—Are often large in size and have to be folded to fit in a correspondence size cabinet. Since they are proof of advertising they are often filed geographically according to the location of the newspaper. They may be mounted effectively in scrapbooks.

Trademarks.—This is always a special file under the heading of Trademarks and subdivided by name, as Bear Brand, Midas, Eveready, with a card cross reference by country. On the country card should be shown all the trademarks listed in that country. Or the file may be set up by country with the cross reference card by name in which case the name card shows all the countries in which that particular trademark is listed. In either of these cases the card must also indicate where the trademark has been registered, the expiration date, renewals, infringements, agreements, licenses, trademark number. Cards are also typed under the heading of Infringements so that those may be seen at a glance. Often a design is trademarked and then the description of that design is listed, as Arm and Hammer. An additional card file set up by years and months should show the expiration date of each trademark, for the purpose of prompt renewal if desired.

Traffic Department Data.—A list of subject headings suitable for traffic department material:

Advance charges
Applications for positions
Associations
Bills of lading
Bracing for car doors
Burlap
Canadian Railway Board
Car loadings
Car seals
Car service
Car supply
Cartage charges
Claims
Coal
Coke
Contracts
Custom house
Damaged goods
Delays
Demurrage
Embargoes
Export
Express
Fiber
Freight bills
Grain cargoes
Imports
Insurance
Interstate Commerce Commission
Lake traffic
Legislation
Lumber shipments
Meetings
Mixed C/L shipments

Ore shipments
Overs and shorts
Packing and loading machinery
Passenger traffic
Pig iron
Plant matters
Public relations
Rate adjustments
Reconsigning
Refuse
Reports
Returned shipments
Routing
Salaries
Sales to railways and express companies
Shipping Board
Spotting charges
State Commissions
Stopping in transit
Storage
Storage in transit
Subscriptions to publications
Switching
Tariff distribution
Taxes
Tonnage
Tracing
Trap car shipments
Twine
Vacations
Warehouses
Water shipments
Weights

Vouchers.—These are filed by name or number. The definition of a voucher is such papers or documents as prove the accuracy of a financial account. The firm sending out the voucher retains a carbon copy to which are attached all supporting papers, such as bills and correspondence pertaining to the bill. It used to be common practice to fold all papers connected with the voucher to document size and then file them on the short end. Reference to such folded papers is slow, and if they are tied with strings it requires even more time. Oftentimes, too, writing becomes blurred at the folds. A more modern method is to staple the voucher and its supporting papers together and to file them flat in folders. This method has been found to save filing costs and filing space; furthermore, it preserves the papers in better condition. See also page 120.

Government Material.—Because every business house has some dealings with the government, there is given below an outline of the federal departments together with their subdivisions. Departments are divided into Bureaus, and Bureaus into Divisions. Correspondence to and from the Weights and Measures Division, Washington, D. C., for example, would be filed in a folder labeled:

```
    UNITED STATES GOVERNMENT
      Commerce    Department of
        Bureau of Standards
        WEIGHTS AND MEASURES DIVISION
```

FIG. 51.—Folder Designation for Government Material

Major United States Government Departments as Listed by the Congressional Directory

AGRICULTURE   Department of
  Agricultural Economics   Bureau of
  Agricultural Research Administration
    Agricultural and Industrial Chemistry   Bureau of
    Agricultural Research Center
    Animal Industry   Bureau of
    Dairy Industry   Bureau of
    Entomology and Plant Quarantine   Bureau of
    Experiment Stations   Office of
    Human Nutrition and Home Economics   Bureau of
    Plant Industry Soils, and Agricultural Engineering   Bureau of
  Budget and Finance   Office of
  Commodity Credit Corporation
  Commodity Exchange Authority
  Extension Service
  Farm Credit Administration
  Farmers Home Administration
  Federal Crop Insurance Corporation
  Foreign Agricultural Relations   Office of
  Forest Service
  Hearing Examiners   Office of
  Information   Office of

AGRICULTURE   Department of
    (*Cont'd*)
    Personnel   Office of
    Plant and Operations   Office of
    Production and Marketing Administration
    Rural Electrification Administration
    Soil Conservation Service
    Solicitor   Office of the

COMMERCE   Department of
    Census   Bureau of the
    Civil Aeronautics Administration
    Coast and Geodetic Survey
    Federal Maritime Board
    Foreign and Domestic Commerce Bureau of
    Inland Waterways Corporation
    Maritime Administration
    National Bureau of Standards
    National Production Authority
    Patent Office
    Public Roads   Bureau of
    Technical Services   Office of
    Weather   Bureau of

DEFENSE   Department of
    Armed Forces Chaplains Board
    Armed Forces Policy Council
    Civilian Components Policy Board
    Guided Missiles   Office of
    Joint Chiefs of Staff
    Military Liaison Committee to the Atomic Energy Commission
    Munitions Board
    Personnel Policy Board
    Research and Development Board
    Weapons Systems Evaluation Group

    AIR FORCE   Department of
      Air Force Personnel Council
      Secretary of the
      General Counsel   Office of the
      Legislation and Liaison   Office of the Director of
      Public Relations   Office of the Director of
      United States Air Force Headquarters

    ARMY   Department of
      Army Boards, Exempted Stations, Military Missions and

      Commissions   Department of the
      Chief of Staff, United States Army
      Military District of Washington
      United States Military Academy

NAVY   Department of
    Aeronautics   Bureau of
    Judge Advocate General of the Navy   Office of
    Marine Corps
    Medicine and Surgery   Bureau of
    Military Sea Transportation Service
    National Naval Medical Center
    Naval Air Station
    Naval Dispensary
    Naval Gun Factory
    Naval Operations   Office of Chief of
    Naval Personnel   Bureau of
    Ordnance   Bureau of
    Ships   Bureau of
    Supplies and Accounts   Bureau of
    United States Naval Academy
    Yards and Docks   Bureau of

EMERGENCY AGENCIES
    Combined Shipping Adjustment Board   U. S. and Great Britain
    Defense Mobilization   Office of
    Defense Production Administration
    Economic Stabilization Agency
    Emergency Management   Office of
    Federal Civil Defense Administration
    Motor Carrier Claims Commission
    Philippine War Damage Commission
    Voluntary Foreign Aid   Advisory Committee on
    War Claims Commission
    War Contracts Price Adjustment Board

EXECUTIVE OFFICE OF THE PRESIDENT
    Budget   Bureau of
    Economic Advisers   Council of
    National Security Council
    National Security Resources Board

INTERIOR   Department of
Alaska Railroad
Alaska Road Commission
Alaska Rural Rehabilitation Cor-
poration
Bonneville Power Administration
Defense Fisheries Administration
Defense Minerals Administration
Defense Power Administration
Defense Solid Fuels Administra-
tion
Fish and Wildlife Service
Geographic Names   Board of
Geological Survey
Indian Affairs   Bureau of
Indian Arts and Crafts Board
Land Management   Bureau of
Mines   Bureau of
National Park Service
National Park Trust Fund Board
National Parks, Historic Sites,
Buildings and Monuments Ad-
visory Board on
National Power Policy Committee
Petroleum Administration for De-
fense
Puerto Rico Reconstruction Admin-
istration
Reclamation   Bureau of
Southeastern Power Administra-
tion
Southwestern Power Administra-
tion
Territories   Office of
Virgin Islands Corporation

INTERNATIONAL ORGANIZA-
TIONS
American States   Organization of
Food and Agriculture Organization
of the United Nations
Inter-American Defense Board
International Bank for Reconstruc-
tion and Development
International Labor Organization
International Monetary Fund
Pan American Sanitary Bureau
United Nations

JUSTICE   Department of
Alien Property Custodian
Federal Bureau of Investigation
Federal Prison Industries Incorpo-
rated
Immigration Appeals   Board of

Immigration and Naturalization
Service
Parole   Board of
Prisons   Board of

LABOR   Department of
Apprenticeship   Bureau of
Employees' Compensation Appeals
Board
Employees' Compensation   Bureau
of
Employment Security   Bureau of
Labor Standards   Bureau of
Labor Statistics   Bureau of
Veterans' Reemployment Rights
Wage and Hour and Public Con-
tracts Division
Women's Bureau

POST OFFICE DEPARTMENT
Accounts   Bureau of
Chief Inspector   Bureau of the

STATE   Department of
European Affairs   Bureau of
Far Eastern Affairs   Bureau of
German Affairs   Bureau of
Intelligence Activities
Inter-American Affairs
Near Eastern, South Asian and
African Affairs   Bureau of
United Nations Affairs   Bureau of
United States Mission to the
United Nations

TREASURY   Department of the
Coast Guard
Comptroller of the Currency
Customhouse
Customs   Bureau of
Engraving and Printing   Bureau
of
Fiscal Service
General Counsel for the Treasury
Office of
Internal Revenue   Bureau of
International Finance   Office of
Mint   Bureau of the
Narcotics   Bureau of
Office of the Treasurer of the
United States
United States Savings Bonds Divi-
sion
United States Secret Service

INDEPENDENT OFFICES AGENCIES AND ESTABLISHMENTS

Air Co-ordinating Committee
American National Red Cross
Atomic Energy Commission United States
Caribbean Commission
Civil Aeronautics Board
Civil Service Commission
Displaced Persons Commission
Economic Cooperation Administration
Export-Import Bank of Washington
Federal Communications Commission
Federal Deposit Insurance Corporation
Federal Mediation and Conciliation Service
Federal Power Commission
Federal Reserve System Board of Governors of the
Federal Security Agency
  Education Office of
  Food and Drug Administration
  Public Health Service
  Social Security Administration
  Vocational Rehabilitation Office of
Federal Trade Commission
Fine Arts Commission of
Foreign-Trade Zones Board
General Services Administration
  Contract Settlement
  Emergency Procurement Service
  Federal Fire Council
  Federal Supply Service
  National Archives and Records Service
  Public Buildings Service
Government Patents Board

Housing Expediter Office of the
Housing and Home Finance Agency
  Federal Housing Administration
  Home Loan Bank Board
  Public Housing Administration
Indian Claims Commission
International Boundary Commission United States, Alaska, and Canada
International Boundary and Water Commission United States and Mexico
International Fisheries Commission United States and Canada
International Joint Commission
International Pacific Salmon Fisheries Commission
Interstate Commerce Commission
National Academy of Sciences
National Advisory Committee for Aeronautics
National Capital Housing Authority
National Labor Relations Board
National Mediation Board
National Munitions Control Board
National Science Foundation
Panama Canal The
Permanent Joint Board on Defense
Railroad Retirement Board
Reconstruction Finance Corporation
Securities and Exchange Commission
Selective Service System
Smithsonian Institution
South Pacific Commission
Subversive Activities Control Board
Tariff Commission United States
Tennessee Valley Authority
Veterans' Administration

There are two methods of indexing government material:

1. The encyclopedic method of a setup by departments, subdivided by bureaus, subdivided again by divisions.

Main government guide is centered, departments and commissions independent of the cabinet departments at left, subdivisions centered, individual folders at right. Folders may be subdivided further by date, subject, or divisions of departments. If necessary, a set of 25 A–Z guides with miscellany to match can be inserted behind the United States Government guide for correspondence not voluminous enough to require individual guiding. For example, material from American National Red Cross could be filed in the A miscellany.

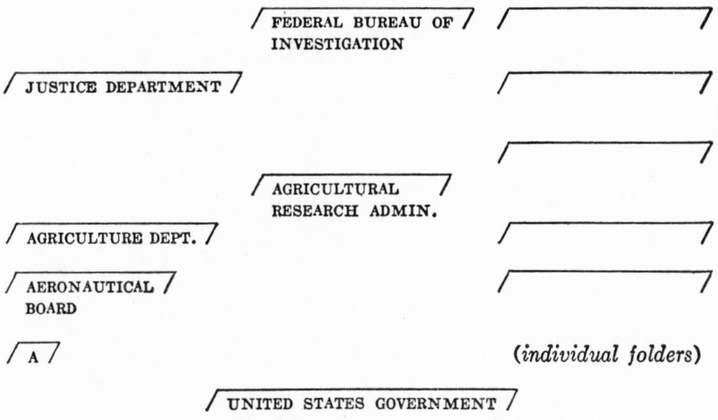

FIG. 52.—Encyclopedic Method of Indexing Government Material

2. The dictionary method of setting up government files in a strictly alphabetical arrangement is as shown in Figure 53, following.

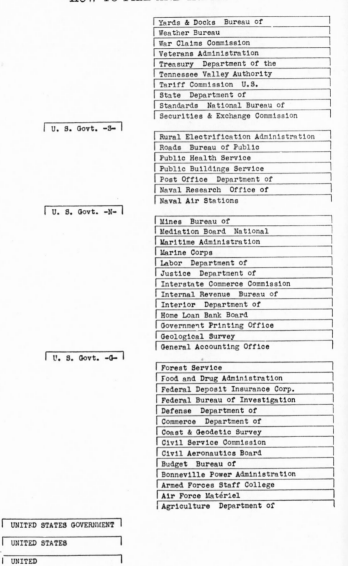

Yards & Docks Bureau of
Weather Bureau
War Claims Commission
Veterans Administration
Treasury Department of the
Tennessee Valley Authority
Tariff Commission U.S.
State Department of
Standards National Bureau of
Securities & Exchange Commission

U. S. Govt. -S-

Rural Electrification Administration
Roads Bureau of Public
Public Health Service
Public Buildings Service
Post Office Department of
Naval Research Office of
Naval Air Stations

U. S. Govt. -N-

Mines Bureau of
Mediation Board National
Maritime Administration
Marine Corps
Labor Department of
Justice Department of
Interstate Commerce Commission
Internal Revenue Bureau of
Interior Department of
Home Loan Bank Board
Government Printing Office
Geological Survey
General Accounting Office

U. S. Govt. -G-

Forest Service
Food and Drug Administration
Federal Deposit Insurance Corp.
Federal Bureau of Investigation
Defense Department of
Commerce Department of
Coast & Geodetic Survey
Civil Service Commission
Civil Aeronautics Board
Budget Bureau of
Bonneville Power Administration
Armed Forces Staff College
Air Force Matériel
Agriculture Department of

UNITED STATES GOVERNMENT

UNITED STATES

UNITED

UN

(Read upward)

Fig. 53.—Dictionary Method of Setting Up Government Files

Chapter 15

CENTRALIZED AND DEPARTMENTALIZED FILES; CENTRALIZED CONTROL

Departmental vs. Centralized Files.—Many companies start with departmental files, each executive having his own files beside his desk. One day the firm is inconvenienced by having one paper on a transaction in one file, further correspondence on the same subject in another file, a third angle of the matter handled by still another department and retained in that department's files. Not only is the material difficult to assemble under such an arrangement, but each department is apt to act independently of and often at cross purposes with the others. At this point a start is made at bringing records together. The centralized file may be defined as the centralized housing of such records as are of *general interest* in the organization. Orders and correspondence are often centralized first, being located near the department using these records the most frequently. This is done as advantageously in small concerns as in large. Centralization is not merely a matter of bringing the orders and correspondence in juxtaposition but of actually merging them under one index. Gradually other papers may be brought into this central file room even though they may be filed by number or by subject and cannot be merged with the original orders and correspondence. In other words, there may eventually be a series of different types of files located in one convenient spot.

It should be understood from the start that not every record in the house belongs in a central file. Only such records as are of general interest are included and these records are not always of the same type in different firms.

Generally, the following papers are included in this file:

General correspondence
Interoffice and branch correspondence
Orders
Invoices
Shipping tickets
Bills of lading
Vouchers
Estimates and quotations
Credit memos
Follow-up or tickler

Records which definitely belong in their departments are:

Confidential papers, such as payrolls, financial statements (usually), tax matters, legal correspondence, patent material.

Papers "in work," in the process of being acted upon, such as unfilled orders, unpaid bills.

Records of interest to one department only, as tariffs which are consulted only by the traffic department, sales analysis sheets in the sales department, price quotations in the purchasing department, electrotypes and cuts in the advertising department, blueprints and drawings in the engineering department.

The records of the following departments are least likely to lend themselves to a central file arrangement: employment, engineering, credit, advertising (general correspondence may be in the central file), purchasing (general correspondence may be in the central file), claim, legal, statistical, and traffic.

To decide what belongs in a central file is a matter of study in each firm. One kind of record which should be centralized in some firms (as a financial statement which is published and distributed) should not be centralized in others (as where the financial statement is confidential.) The physical location of a certain department at considerable distance from the central file room may make the centralization of its records not feasible even though ordinarily such records would be included in the centralized plan.

Advantages and Disadvantages of Centralized Filing.— The advantages of a centralized file are:

1. Elimination of duplication. In some sales organizations from 10 to 20 copies are made of each order, and the copies kept in as many different departments, if there is no centralized file. This means that 10 or more stenographers in various departments each file identical copies. The same is also true of financial statements, and various reports. By having the department which issues the paper send its original copy to the central file, the balance of the copies does not need to be retained unless one of the copies carries a penciled notation of information not found elsewhere, such as the shipping date on the shipping copy.

2. Better service given from the files, by placing responsibility for the care of the records upon one person designated for the duty. This makes for far more efficient filing than if every department stenographer does the filing for her department in her spare moments.

3. Uniformity of methods. Instead of each department head's files being set up according to his own theories, a simple system is set up throughout the house, making possible the wide use of filing resources.

4. Economy of time. There is only one place to send material for file, and one place to look for it. With separate files there is always a question as to who should hold papers of concern to several departments.

5. Economy in purchase of supplies because they are bought in quantities.

6. Economy in equipment and consequently in filing space because cabinets in a central file are not utilized for storage space.

7. Better executive control over departments.

8. Saving in delays because better routines are established.

9. Papers from other department files are not wrongly inserted in the files of the department where they are being consulted.

The disadvantages of a centralized file are:

1. Physical difficulties of not being near one's own files. A good distributing system is of help in this instance: tube or belt systems for the large organization; messenger service or dumb-waiters in the smaller houses.

2. Different departments have different needs which may call for different systems of arrangement. Whereas the central file may have correspondence set up by name, one department may desire information regarding customers by location. A card file arranged geographically can take care of such a requirement. Again, a department such as the traffic department may have penciled on their copy of an order certain notations to which they refer constantly and which they wish to keep filed in their department. Even where the departments retain their own files it is possible to have the file clerks go from department to department daily to do their filing, thus assuring centralized control if not the physical grouping of the files in one place.

3. Fear of publicity between departments. No one but the file clerk should be permitted access to the file.

Thus the advantages usually outweigh the disadvantages even in a small organization. The tendency today is for a new concern to start with centralized files so that there will be no general upheaval necessary later.

Planning the Classification.—Even though departments may be willing to allow their records to be taken from them and put in a central file room, they are rarely willing to allow their records to be merged in the same folders with the records of other departments. It means looking through too much material to find the particular paper wanted. Color may be used to distinguish one kind of paper from another. The primary classification of the papers is usually by correspondent's name; the secondary classification by department or by type, giving each correspondent several folders with the label bearing the correspondent's name and class of paper filed therein. For example, everything under John Smith Company will be together behind an Sm guide in the general file, but the material will be subdivided into four folders, as follows:

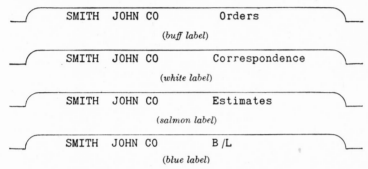

FIG. 54.—Subdivisions in General File—By Colors for Departments

Instead of dividing material according to type of paper handled by each department, the determining factor may be classes of matter:

ATLANTA GAS CO	Maps
ATLANTA GAS CO	Mains
ATLANTA GAS CO	Load Data
ATLANTA GAS CO	Lightning Arresters

(*Read upward*)

FIG. 55.—Subdivisions Arranged by Subjects

Points of Preliminary Consideration.—Unless the executives are thoroughly convinced that reorganization from department files to a central file is advisable for their organization, it is almost useless to try to install one. A file department depends upon the cooperation of other departments for its successful operation, and if the heads of the departments are opposed to a central file they can make a failure of it. The ground must be well prepared for a change of system.

Before centralization is begun the following points must be settled:

Will the floor stand the extra loading?

Will current and noncurrent material be in the same room?

What control is to be exercised over the files?

What protection is needed from fire? Thieves?

What equipment is needed for the clerks, such as sorters, tables?

What supplemental equipment is needed for reference to the files, as counters, dumb-waiters, messenger stations?

What departments will send the most material to the files and call most frequently for the records?

In what volume will the various papers come to file?

What provision will be made for expansion?

For what periods are clerks standing at the files?

See following chapter for layout of the central file room. The following requirements must be fulfilled before any centralized filing department can function successfully:

A manual of instruction must be adopted so that every one in the organization will know the limitations and scope of the file department and the duties of each clerk.

Regulations for the use of the files should be drawn up and posted.

The practice of retaining papers in desks must be discontinued because file clerks cannot be held responsible for papers not yet come to file.

The granting of personal files is not desirable in most cases.

Access to the files should ordinarily be confined to the file department.

Complete backing of the highest authority must be obtained.

Before consolidation can be effected, a preliminary analysis must be made to determine the names given to the various papers in the office routine, how they are asked for, why they are wanted. This information will help settle the problem of the method of filing to be used. To estimate the amount and nature of equipment and supplies needed for a central file and the personnel required, it must be determined how many papers of a given kind are received in a day (average); how many individuals must use the files; how their records are referred to: name, location, etc.; how many references there will be to the files daily (average).

Transition Carried Out.—Centralization should be undertaken one department at a time so that during the process of making the change service can be given from the files at all times. If the main file is to be an alphabetic name arrangement, the largest name file in the organization should be used as a basis. If it does not need revising for errors and the elimination of out-of-date material, the second largest department should be taken over and filed into the first alphabetic system. Each department should be taken over in the same way until centralization is complete.

If centralization involves the changing from one method of filing to another, as from a numeric to an alphabetic name file, one drawer of material from the numeric file should be thrown into the sorter alphabetically, filed into the central file, and then the second drawer started. In this way only one drawer is in confusion at a time, and it is still possible to give service from either the new alphabetic file or the old numeric system.

It is wise to make penciled notations on the tabs of the new folders, because often, especially in the case of subject files, it will be necessary to change the heading as further information about the matter comes to file. Toward the close of the centralization, the labels should be neatly typed according to the rules previously given.

Assignment of Work to File Clerks.—The allocation of work in a large filing department may follow one of two plans: each clerk may be given a certain section of files for which he is solely responsible, such as correspondence and orders from A to I. A second clerk may handle the same type of material from J to Z; a third clerk be responsible for the invoices, a fourth for the data, etc. Each clerk marks, sorts, files, and looks up the material in his own section of files. This method provides for mobility in the department. Each clerk knows each duty in the department and can be shifted around in case of a rush in one spot. For example, a certain department may have held back work and then suddenly dumped three days' material on one clerk. Since the file is expected to be immediately ready for reference extra help must be provided, even though permanent assistance is not necessary. Variety of work has the added advantage of eliminating monotony.

The second plan is to assign to each clerk some one process such as sorting or coding. For instance, a good way to start a beginner is by giving him the sorting to do. Such a division of work makes for great speed but care must be exercised to avoid monotony and to provide understudies for each worker.

Centralized Control.—In very large organizations one centralized filing department will not be feasible. In such cases files are centralized within each department, such as all accounting papers in a central accounting file, or all executive records centralized in one location. Supervision of all these departmental files must then be in the hands of someone who controls all the records in the organization in order to assure uniformity of filing methods, proper training of clerks, adequate routines in the department, as well as to maintain manuals of procedure, request supplies, and institute time and motion studies. Such a person, either a man or a woman, has the entire responsibility for the records from their inception to their destruction. This is known as centralized control with decentralized operation.

Chapter 16

LAYOUT OF A FILE ROOM

Location of File Room.—A central file should be located nearest to the departments which use it most frequently, for example, to the accounting and sales departments. On the other hand, the executives, the advertising and the traffic departments are not apt to refer to the files very often and so do not need to be next to the files. A flow chart of office activities will determine the most convenient spot for the files.

The central files may have:

> A room to themselves
> The cabinets themselves forming the walls
> Hallways or passageways
> Vaults

Vaults are to be discouraged because they lack light and ventilation and may be damp. If unusual protection is necessary, sectional cabinets provided with rollers can be used in a light space during the day and rolled into the vault when no longer needed. Where a vault must be used and there is apt to be a trace of dampness, a pail of slaked lime will prevent mildew.

Lighting.—Daylight usually penetrates 25 to 30 feet into a room, and since the filing personnel is reading constantly and therefore is one of the departments needing the best light, it is well to have this department placed fairly close to the windows. A north exposure is, of course, the most satisfactory. Where artificial lighting is required there is a choice of three different kinds:

1. Direct lighting where the light shines directly on the desk. There is a loss of eye efficiency from the glare of such lighting. Department files in very dark corners, where the wiring of the building does not allow for sufficient indirect

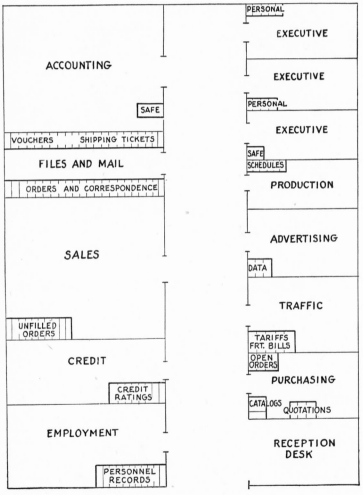

FIG. 56.—Planning Location of File Room in Relation to Other Departments. Notice departmental files

lighting, have been made usable by a long inverted trough being attached to the tops of the cabinets and extending out over the front edge of the cabinets an inch or two. Bulbs which throw bright light into the open drawers below are placed in this trough at regular intervals.

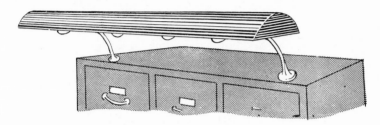

FIG. 57.—Direct Lighting

2. Semi-indirect lighting where a translucent bowl is placed under the lamp, projecting part of the light to the ceiling where it is diffused down again.

3. Totally indirect lighting, the best for file rooms because of absence of glare. An opaque reflector below the lamp throws all the light up to the ceiling which is colored in such a way that it throws a soft light down again. The following have been given by the National Office Management Association as the guide for lighting: 10 to 20 foot-candles for uniform work, 50 foot-candles for prolonged reading, 100 foot-candles for proofreading. Lamps should be changed periodically and kept clean.

Ventilation; Noise.—Authorities state that a range of from 65° to 72° Fahrenheit is the best working temperature with humidity 40%. Ventilation is also important, as "stuffiness" in a room tends toward causing drowsiness.

Special walls and ceilings with a high degree of absorption deaden the noise both from the street and from machines in the office. Although they are commonly used in stenographic rooms, such provision against noise makes for greater efficiency in any department of an office. Tests have shown that sound control increases efficiency from 10% to 25%. In the file room machines such as the typewriters should be kept as isolated as possible, with rubber or felt pads under the machines.

Arrangement of Cabinets.—Space for a file room may be oblong or square. Whatever the size allotted to the files, the space should be adequate for efficient operation. If the old transfer cabinets are kept in another building, there should be sufficient space in the file room to house at least one year's transfer. Space above cabinets may be used for shelving.

Cabinets may be placed against an unbroken wall, in a hollow square arrangement, or back to back. In a large room the placing of cabinets around the wall and additional ones back to back in the hollow center allows for the use of the greatest amount of space.

If files are placed back to back, they should not be parallel to the windows but at right angles to the windows in order that the light may penetrate into the aisles. In such a case, one aisle serves for two rows of cabinets. A long battery of files should be broken at intervals with an aisle.

Aisles between cabinets facing each other (illustration page 192) should preferably be 5 feet wide. Cabinets are usually 25″ to 28″ deep, and when a drawer is pulled out, at least 2 feet of aisle space is required. If a clerk is working in an opposite drawer, another 2 feet are used up. Then at least 1 foot should be allowed in order to pass between open drawers. However, the width of an aisle between rows depends upon the activity on both sides. Expansion should be provided by leaving the main aisle wider than needed. A main aisle 3 feet wide and other aisles 2½ feet will be found satisfactory. All aisles should be kept clear.

Where a filing room is part of an open office space, the 4- or 5-drawer-height filing cabinets may be arranged around an open square using 3-drawer height cabinets in at least a portion of the fourth side of the square. This arrangement

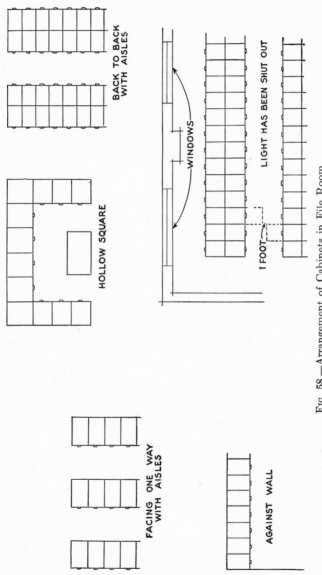

Fig. 58.—Arrangement of Cabinets in File Room

gives the proper protection to the files, while the counter height cabinets furnish a convenient space for file clerks to charge out materials and for patrons who need only quick reference to papers.

Transfer cabinets should be placed in the least desirable working space since they hold inactive records. Often these may be stacked 6 or 8 high to conserve space. Shelving over cabinets can be used for bound books, supplies, etc.

Arrangement of Clerks' Tables and Chairs.—Each clerk in the department should have a small table on which to

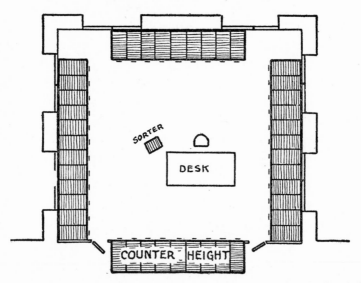

F̲ɪɢ. 59.—Square Arrangement of Files. In this arrangement the file clerk is equally distant from all his cabinets, and the counter-height cabinets in front make a good loan desk.

work. Desks are unnecessary, except for the supervisor, because they serve as too convenient a means of storing papers temporarily and then forgetting them. A sorter should be at the left-hand side, as one sorts into it with the right hand, except, of course, in the case of the large sorters on tracks which occupy a section of the room to themselves.

Clerks should not face each other across the same table or even from two adjacent ones. The temptation to converse is too great. Clerks should face in the same direction, their tables at least 30″ apart. The supervisor should sit so as to overlook the entire department, either behind them facing in the same direction as they, or in front facing them as a teacher in a schoolroom. Forty to 50 square feet of space is the usual allowance for a clerk; 75 to 100 for a supervisor. Chairs should be comfortable and adjustable to the height of the individual clerk. Each clerk should be located near the section of files for which he is responsible in order to save running back and forth.

The loan clerk should be near public access to the files for two reasons: to keep outsiders away from the files and to give instant service when someone comes for consultation. The supervisor, unless the only one in the file department, is not seated near the file room entrance. Material may be called out of the files for quick reference and need not in that case be taken out of the file room at all. For such cases, especially in a file room of good size, it is well to provide a small table and a couple of chairs or a bench for the use of those consulting the files. These pieces of furniture may be placed just inside the file room.

If a separate room is used for the files it is often found advisable to have a special door consisting of two parts—with the lower half locked so that no one can enter. The top of this half may act as a small shelf. The top half is also closed at night, but during working hours it is swung back so that a patron may be seen from the inside as he comes to the door. Or, a railing may be installed near the entrance to the files and the lookup clerk's desk placed near the railing to insure prompt service.

Arranging the Layout on a Floor Plan.—The expenditure of time and money in rearranging a poor layout is frequently far less than the cost of waste space and loss of energy with consequent reduction in output. A good way to

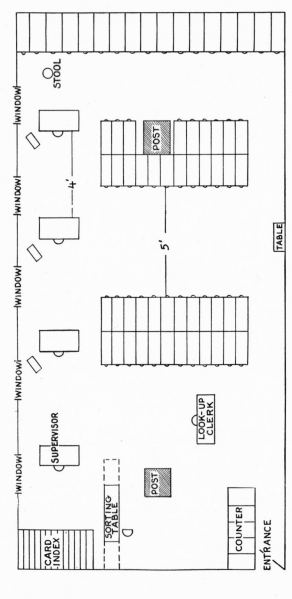

Fig. 60.—Layout of a File Room on a Floor Plan

judge the best and most compact arrangement of furniture is to make a drawing of the room to scale. A layout cannot be worked out satisfactorily in the mind's eye because a post, a 3-inch projection of a wall, or a radiator is too apt to be overlooked so that a table or battery of files will not fit into the space allotted. The entire plan will require revision.

Often the architect of the building will furnish a floor plan; if not, it is not difficult to draw one up roughly, showing partitions, doors (noting which way they swing), windows, posts, lavatories, lights, shelving. Common measurements are an eighth or a fourth of an inch to a foot. For instance, if the room is a rectangle measuring 32′ x 16′, the drawing would be 4″ x 2″, or 8″ x 4″. The drawing should be attached to a drafting board or a heavy cardboard so that pins will adhere readily.

Each piece of furniture and equipment in the file room should be carefully measured and drawn to the same scale on cardboard. Tables and chairs may be shown together. These diagrams, called templets, should then be cut out and shifted on the floor plan until the logical arrangement has been decided upon. Templets may be cut out of differently colored cardboard: one color to represent old equipment, another color, needed furniture, which is not yet purchased. Templets may be secured at some stationery stores. Plastic cutouts for drawing templets to scale and three-dimensional templets are also available. Ease of movement, expansion, proper lighting in aisles, and elimination of waste space are particularly to be watched for. When the best arrangement has been found, the templets should be fastened onto their space with a pin, or pasted.

To facilitate moving a file room to new quarters, every piece of furniture should be tagged and numbered. The templets should carry corresponding numbers. As the furniture is brought into the new room, a guide with the plan in hand should direct the exact placement of each piece so that as the last piece is brought in, the room is in order.

Chapter 17

PLANNING A CARD FORM; VISIBLE FILES; CARD EQUIPMENT

Purpose of Card Records.—To attempt to give an adequate idea of the current uses of card records would be to enumerate activities in almost every department of a business. Classifying cards in a broad way, they are used for two purposes: for indexing a collection of material already arranged in some systematic form, so as to make this material readily available from another point of view, and for recording desired facts and figures accumulated from various recorded, verbal, and observed sources.

Special lines of business, such as banks and insurance companies, have developed standardized forms, thus gaining uniformity and completeness. Other types of concerns need to plan their own forms because there is nothing on the market exactly suited to their needs. Business has profited much by the long, systematic, cooperative experimentation of librarians with card methods.

Sizes of Cards.—The first point to be taken into consideration when planning a card form is its size. The standard sizes for drawer filing are $2\frac{1}{4}'' \times 3''$, $3'' \times 5''$, $4'' \times 6''$, $5'' \times 8''$. The dimensions shown throughout this chapter are in the order of height and width. A $3'' \times 5''$ card means 3 inches high, 5 inches wide. The visible sizes cover a wider range than the drawer files, including $8'' \times 10''$, $10'' \times 10''$, $11'' \times 9''$, $12'' \times 6''$, $13'' \times 6''$. The standard card sizes are somewhat augmented by the fact that certain of them are ruled and printed so that they may be filed on the short edge. The size of the card to be adopted must be determined by the amount of information required; that is, a small card should not be made to serve through the device of printing the lines closely together when considerable information is desired from the card; or conversely, a large card used with the information spread through the use of widely spaced lines. The space between lines should be determined by the method of posting. If this is done by machine, typewriter space should be used; if by hand, much wider space is needed; if merely a check mark will suffice, the lines can be printed closely together.

Card Stock Required.—The use to which the card is to be put and the length of time the card must be retained should determine the card stock to be chosen. Card stock is known as index bristol by the paper trade, but few paper factories make it. There are many grades of card stock ranging from 100% clean hand-picked rags, through grades with sulphite mixture, to grades that are pure wood pulp. Those firms which do not maintain their own testing laboratories can usually get a test of sample cards made, free of charge, by a reliable paper house. A permanent card record requires 100% rag stock. Records that serve their purpose in a few weeks or months or are handled by only a few persons take an inexpensive grade such as is found in the wood pulp stock. A new type of card being tried by libraries in their public catalogs is 100% rag, designed for long service, and is resistant to moisture so that it may be cleaned by sponging.

TEARING TEST: Tear with and against the grain. Note strength and character of interlocking fibers:

           1. Hard and sharp—short fiber
           2. Soft and fuzzy—long fiber

Resistance to tearing shows toughness of paper.

LIGHT TEST: Cloudiness denotes imperfect mixture of fibers. Short fibers evenly distributed give an excellent surface, a clear color and a rigid card.

SNAP TEST: The sharper the ring the better the stock.

ERASURE TEST:

        1. A fine powder indicates well made card

        2. Fluffy flakes indicate poorly made card

A good card will stand considerable erasure.

ABSORPTION TEST: Ink from a pen or typewriter ribbon will not spread and blot on a high grade card. The ink feathers easily on a poorly made card.

FOLDING TEST: Long fibers will not break but generally will not stand hard usage unless very well made. Short fibers will break when folded but stand erasure and hard usage.

BURNING TEST: Apply a lighted match to a card, and the presence of clay or other fillers will be easily detected. Clay leaves a greasy ash which is identified when the ash is rubbed between the fingers. Pasted stock will show layers (stock used in guides, if genuine pressboard, will not show layers when subjected to burning test.)

CUTTING TEST: Cards should be rotary and not guillotine cut. Rotary cut gives a sharp, clear edge that does not fray with wear. Guillotine cut shows signs of fray from the start and wears badly.

Colors of Card Stock.—Paper manufacturers are attempting to reduce the number of colored papers for ordinary use to six distinct colors. So-called white cards range from a dirty white to a clear eggshell. While the largest percentage of cards used is white or buff in color, a secondary classification can be obtained through brighter colors, such as in a single alphabetic name list where the names of those native born are on white or buff, foreign born on blue. A color such as cherry should be used very sparingly because every reduction of the brightness contrast between printed matter and its background reduces visibility. Buff is the softest color to the eye. Buff cards with black printing and white cards with green printing are restful. Where the light is poor it is best to use white paper. Colored paper can be used where light is good. There are important factors in visibility and readability other than the color of the paper or the ink used. The quality of the paper used, the finish of the paper, the quality of the ink, the ability of the machine used to reproduce copy, and last but not least, the brightness of the diffusion of the light sources in the area where the clerks are working must also be taken into consideration. Paper should not have a glossy surface, and ink should also be nonglossy.

Arrangement of Information on Card.—The information placed on a form card should be carefully grouped, the word under which the card is to be filed standing first so as to reduce the possibility of mistakes in filing. Since the top edge of the card is first seen in drawer files, that is where the most important information should be placed. This may be the name on a signature card, the expiration date for an insurance card, the article for a stock record, or street address for the meter card of a utility concern. In visible files, the bottom line may be the most important. Like information should stand together and a sequence in subject matter should be followed.

The briefest terminology possible should be chosen so as to leave the most space for the information to be filled in. Abbreviations are often used. The type used should be concise, clear but small, and it is often advisable to use several different sizes of type to make the information stand out plainly. Sometimes different styles of type in two or more colors are desirable. In no case should the printed matter be confused with the typewritten fill-in. Blank cards or those with marginal rulings only are used when the record is entirely typed. Horizontal blue lines are provided for handwritten records.

DATE	ITEM	CHARGES	√	CREDITS	BALANCE	DATE	ITEM	CHARGES	√	CREDITS	BALANCE

FIG. 61.—A Card Form Showing the Shortness of Reading Line

The spacing of the information on the card is important. The length of the printed line should not exceed 4″, as the eye cannot travel farther than this without wavering. The 5″ x 8″ form shown above is divided into halves with the left-hand side filled in before the right-hand side is started.

Box design clearly defines the area for each entry. Place each descriptive item requesting information in the upper left corner of a boxed space.

Name	Address		
Telephone	Age	Marital Status ☐ Married ☐ Single	Nationality

In the lower left-hand corner of the card the name of the company, department, and form number are given. Forms should be listed and consecutively numbered as made so that they may easily be reordered.

Usually it is not considered good form to use the back of a card (tumbling a card as it is called) because of the necessity of referring constantly to the front side and thus wasting time, or of recopying the pertinent information on the back side of the card.

Tabs and Signals on Cards.—For flagging information a card may be tabbed with one or more projections of the same stock as the card itself. Sometimes a card has a number of tabs distributed evenly across the top, spaced according to some order. Such a "scalloped" card is called serrated. In the example shown in Figure 62 the second and fourth tabs would be left and the others cut off if suburban property is offered for sale. Sometimes tabs are concentrated in the

Fig. 62.—Serrated or "Scalloped" Card

middle with supporting shoulders on both ends, used much for stock records which have heavy wear. Cards on visible panels may also be tabbed.

Metal and celluloid signals may be used on straight-edged cards for flagging purposes. They are either immovable or movable. The immovable type is manufactured with the projection of colored celluloid and the bottom of gummed linen which is attached permanently to the top of a card. When signals are used to indicate changing conditions, such as in the progress of an order from one department to another, or in the expiration of subscriptions and insurance policies, or for the due date of unfilled orders, movable signals are required. They are made of steel with enameled tops, come in a number of sizes and a variety of colors,

Fig. 63.—Lateral Type Rolling Tray Equipment (Rol-dex Co.)

printed with numbers or months if desired, and should grip the card tightly at the lower edge if they are to be considered practical.

If cards are to be handled by many persons, it is well to consider the advisability of having them punched so that they can be locked into the cabinet with a rod.

Cabinet Card Files.—There are two methods of filing cards: on edge in drawers or trays built up in cabinet units or solid sections, and by visible methods. The card drawer units may be had in any one of the standard card sizes built up in horizontal or vertical cabinets to the desired size or may be built in combination with the paper-sized drawers. Drawers are made for a single row of cards and also for two or more rows within the same drawer. Standard size lift-out trays are also fitted into drawers. Card drawers are provided with angle blocks at the front to allow cards to fall into natural position. Very large card files are almost invariably housed in the drawer type of equipment because they are most economical to operate both from the angle of space required and of labor. Averaging 100 cards per inch, a 3" x 5" card cabinet of 12 double compartment drawers 28" in depth will take 4200 cards per drawer easily, or 50,000 cards per cabinet, allowing liberally for guides, follow-block, and the necessary freedom of action.

Trays of Card Files on Movable Tracks.—The operator sits beside movable trays of cards where there is a capacity of from 3000 to 60,000 records at her finger tips. All loss of time in traveling from desk to upright filing cabinet is eliminated. Since this method of handling cards does not require the operator to walk or stoop, it is less fatiguing than the cabinet method. This type of equipment requires more floor space than a vertical cabinet housing the same number of cards. (See Figure 63.)

Another version of this type of equipment is stationary with the operator's chair on tracks so that it can be rolled back and forth along the length of the desk-type files.

Visible Card Files.—The first real visible file (invented by a bank cashier) consisted of an ordinary ledger, the cover of which extended beyond the pages about 3 inches. On this extension sheets were tacked, bearing the names of the depositors of the bank. Little index tabs were pasted on the ledger sheets opposite the name on the cover.

FIG. 64.—Simplafind Card System Operated Electrically. (Wheeldex & Simpla Products, Inc.)

There are a variety of forms and panels devised for the purpose of making information visible, but the most common is that in which cards are attached to a rod or strip which is flexed into grooves or devices on either side of the face of a panel in such fashion as to expose one, two, or three lines at the top or bottom of the card. It is a reversion to the old flat method of filing. There is also a wide variety of containers for these panels: vertical drawers, housing

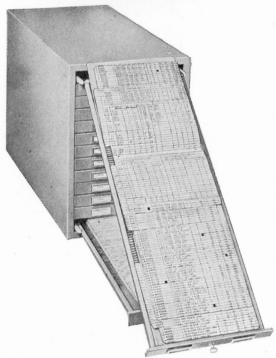

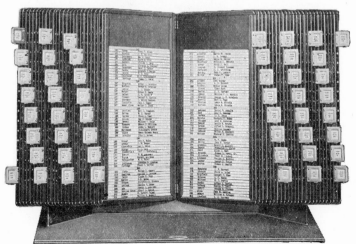

Visible Files (Post Index Co.)

Fig. 65*b*.—Another Type of Visible File (Post Index Co.)

Fig. 66.—Cabinet Style Visible File (Remington Rand Inc.)

especially constructed filing panels; shallow drawers, each containing one panel which lies horizontally and each hinged so that it can be pulled out; standards with rods on which panels are hinged so as to form upright leaves which can be swung back and forth; or a binder which may be opened like a book, containing panels as pages.

Occasionally a whole card of information is unnecessary if only a name and address or name and telephone number are needed. In such cases one- or two-line entries are typed on long bristol strips which are perforated and easily detached. The strip is flexed into grooves on a panel or put into a celluloid tube for protection and then flexed into grooves of the panel (see Figure 64).

Where slightly more information is required, it is possible to secure small cards which are interlocked by means of lugs at top and slots below. This is an inexpensive type of visible file.

Cabinet Style of Visible File.—The best known of the visible files is the cabinet form with shallow drawers, each containing one panel which lies horizontally and each hinged so that it can be pulled out. The frames and panels are usually steel throughout, including card hangers and hinges. One or two bottom lines of the card are visible. Both sides of the card are available. If more space is needed, an auxiliary sheet may be attached to the same hanger, giving four faces on which to transcribe so that the indexing information on both cards will be exposed. This doubling of cards reduces equipment requirements one half. Such doubling is only possible, however, where records undergo few changes. Sometimes the cards are inserted in pockets with the exposed bottom line or two of the card protected by means of transparent transoloid. When a tray is pulled out, the visible portion of every card is seen through a transparent covering which wards off dirt and moisture. The capacity of the trays varies with the size of the card and the manufacturer of the equipment. An average is about:

3" x 5" cards—71 to 94 in one tray, depending on manufacturer
4" x 6" cards—67 to 86 in one tray,   "   "   "
5" x 8" cards—63 to 80 in one tray,   "   "   "

The capacity of one cabinet is somewhat more than 1000 cards, depending on the number of trays.

A recent type of visible card equipment consists of a series of panels housed in a closed cabinet. The operator sits before a desk of proper height for posting and has in front of her a number of buttons, each one of which controls one of the 60 trays of cards. The trays within the cabinets are in tiers and out of sight until the key is pressed which closes the circuit and brings the desired tray out on the desk extension track. Pressing the button again returns the slide. A new one can then be brought to the desk top. Only one slide is available on the desk extension at one time. This is a way of obtaining the speed which comes from visible files with the saving in space which comes from cabinet filing.

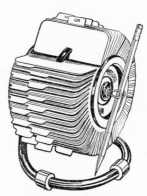

Fig. 67.—Desk Wheel File (Wheeldex Co.)

Modern card equipment includes the use of wheels. Cards are fitted into a tray or channel about the rim of the wheel. The wheel stands upright, revolving about a horizontal axle, and rolls toward the operator with cards filed in upright or ordinary reference position. The cards are held in place by a rod like the ordinary check-sorter rod. The cards are slot-

punched at the bottom and slip over this retaining rod so
that cards may be easily inserted or removed at any point.
They ride securely and can be inserted or removed easily.
The wheels are mounted in suitable desks or cabinets and

FIG. 68.—Robot Type Visible File (Remington Rand Inc.)

the file user brings any card before her by simply turning
the wheel. A recent development has been the motorization
of these wheels with a control switch which operates forward or reverse at the slightest touch.

There are two basic types of wheel files made to meet two
basic needs of card handling—posting and reference. Most
files comprise a combination of these two operations.

Another card device is electrically operated. Cards are put in a tray any way, no sequence being necessary. When the cards are needed, the tray is placed in a special machine in front of which is a keyboard. The name or number of the wanted card is typed, the operating bar is pressed and instantly the card is projected above the tray. With this device the labor of filing cards individually is saved and in order to *find*, no manual or visual searching is necessary.

FIG. 69.—Electrofile (Johnson Fare Box Co.)

Magnetism is being applied to record-keeping systems with a magnetic force exerting its influence to impel or repel. The channel of the card cabinet is permanently magnetized with either a positive or a negative charge. The cards to be placed within this cabinet have a small piece of iron about an inch square imbedded in the card on both the

FIG. 70.—Individual Cards Are Magnetized to Repel Each Other by a Permanent Magnet—Causing the Fanning-Out Action. (Business Efficiency Aids)

right and left sides, carrying the opposite charge from that of the file drawer itself. At a touch of the finger records move forward or backward fanlike; cards separate, exposing the top edges so that each one can be read as in a visible panel. No thumbing is required to separate the cards. Thus this device also combines the advantages of a visible file system with the economy and space saving of a vertical file.

Signals for Visible Files.—Visible card files make frequent use of signals. The visible tube files use a colored strip for a *permanent* secondary classification and insert colored celluloid for *temporary* signals. Steel signals may be attached directly on the bottom of a card. The celluloid type may be inserted in pockets. Signals come in different lengths so that various portions of the card may be covered. Other methods of signaling visible files are: pencil marks on extended portion of the card which may be erased; offsetting cards; use of differently colored cards or colored stripe on cards or coloring edge of card; clipping corner of card; punching card.

Accuracy of Typing.—The effect of a visible file can be ruined by improper typing. The choice of typewriter should be one with card attachments or one which permits the bottom line to be filled in without the card's slipping. Carbon copies may be made with light weight cards. The typing must be so exact that when the cards are in the panels the alignment of first letters is perfect:

Wade J H	139 Alice Avenue	Gas		
Wagner D W	2830 Plum Street		Oil	
Walters R S	1426 Clinton Avenue	Gas		Grease
Wyatt A B	20 Sheffield Street	Gas	Oil	Grease

Transferring Card Files.—Card files are not transferred periodically. Sometimes, when they act as an index to other records, they are never transferred. When transferring is done from visible records, the cards are placed in drawers or boxes. Ofttimes cards which are to be put into visible equipment have the pertinent information, such as the name and address, typed not only on the bottom line of the front side, but also on the top line of the back side. When the card is transferred to a drawer, all that needs to be done is to reverse the card.

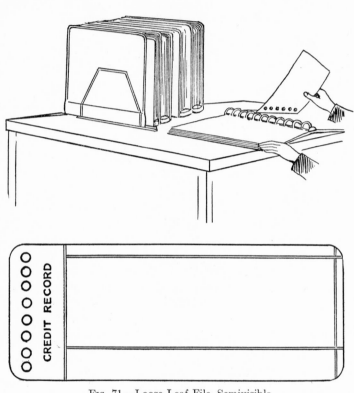

Fig. 71.—Loose-Leaf File, Semivisible

Loose-Leaf Records.—Half-way between drawer and vertical files come loose-leaf records. The various sizes of papers may be fastened in a binder so that they may readily be withdrawn or new sheets may be added at any point. These sheets are also arranged so that they overlap and expose several lines of a sheet. This is done by means of perforations at the left end of the sheet. A special shift enables the operator to insert extra sheets with little effort, thus providing for indefinite expansion. Each series of overlapping sheets is separated from the next by a tabbed "division sheet." These index tabs are alphabetical or numerical according to the kind of record. This loose-leaf equipment is often found in an accounting department.

Advantages and Disadvantages of Visible Files.—Visible records have two unique values over other types of card equipment: the visibility of the indexing information on each card reduces the time necessary to locate it; in other words, one looks *at* information instead of *for* it. Then this visibility furnishes a visible analysis of conditions controlled by the record, as interpreted by control signals. Thus visible records are said to serve business through reduced overhead. The visible equipment manufacturers claim that visible files accomplish 150% more than drawer files.

The present criticisms of the visible files are that the equipment is expensive. The frames are costly and they require a higher grade of card stock than is necessary for ordinary drawer use. Visible files take up more floor space than drawer files. The operation of inserting or removing cards in most visible files is not quite as simple as inserting or removing cards in a drawer file.

Chapter 18

EQUIPMENT AND SUPPLIES

Economies can be effected through the purchase of the proper equipment and supplies. The best filing departments are not necessarily those which have the most expensive equipment. Often makeshifts have worked out very satisfactorily, with the right type of personnel. Too rigid economy should not be practiced, however, because equipment and supplies are the tools with which the filing department works.

Selection of Card Equipment.—Before choosing card equipment a careful study should be made of the following points:

How many cards in the entire list.
If entries are to be posted on cards, how many.
Relative floor and cubic space required by each style of equipment.
How many cards must be readily accessible to one user at a time.
Speed necessary in consulting index.
Time required for making complete entry on a card in each case.
Rate of expansion of file.
Relative cost of each kind of equipment as to labor, original equipment, supplies.

Circumstances should alter the decision as to the equipment chosen. Each case should be individually studied. The most economical method as far as space and initial cost are concerned is to file cards in boxes placed two high on a table, but lifting boxes up and down makes such a method of filing almost prohibitive from the fatigue standpoint. Upright cabinets for housing cards conserve floor space, but require standing, walking, and stooping which increase filing time. Using the equipment on tracks which houses cards is rapid because records are brought *to* the operator and motion is practically unnecessary. However, this type of equipment requires more space than any other kind. Visible files are the most expensive and also require more space than do boxes or upright cabinets. Where speed of reference only is required, the visible files are advisable. The following comparison has been made between the time consumed in filing in a visible file and in a desk type of equipment.

OPERATIONS

Tray-type Visible File	Desk-type File
Select tray	Select cabinet
Pull rest tray	Select guide
Pull main tray	Finger cards to reach
Locate position of card	exact location
Release bottom lock	Insert card
Spread cards	
Take out empty card	
Insert card	
Spread for new card	
Insert card	
Interlock	
Turn down flaps	
Flap down metal	
Push in main tray	
Push in rest tray	

Filing Cabinets.—There are many grades of steel cabinets on the market, the cheapest of which is little better than a tin box. For a long life of uninterrupted service, modern business has found that the best first grade equipment is most economical. In order to gain the desired rigidity for the outer frame, a foundational frame is constructed of a channel formed of drawn 16-gauge steel. The outer shell is made of 20-gauge furniture steel. The whole is electrically welded together, often with over 500 spot welds and reinforced with steel angle braces.

The weight of a loaded letter drawer varies according to its construction, size, and contents, but it is usually from 60 to 70 pounds. A properly made first grade file drawer should operate easily with loads up to 100 pounds. The drawer should open or close easily without sticking or jamming, especially in active files or where speed is a factor and the quantity of work is so great that energy must be conserved. A progressive slide with telescoping members on each side operating on ball bearing rollers supports each drawer when fully extended and gives this ease of operation. Industrial engineers have tested drawer slides by attaching a spring scale to the handle of a loaded drawer and then checking the number of pounds' pull required to open that drawer. The difference in the weight multiplied by the number of times a day the drawer is opened gives the waste energy.

Fig. 72.—Four-Drawer File Cabinet with Drop Front (General Fireproofing Co.)

Follow-blocks made of steel, also called compressors, at the back of each drawer are used to keep the filed material in an upright position. They should move easily without sticking, hold the material securely when in the desired position, and not occupy more than one-half inch of space. Devices to replace the compressor have been invented, consisting of five or six metal drawer dividers which permit only a certain amount of material to be placed behind each one. They keep the drawer from being overcrowded and are especially useful when the drawer is filled with heavy papers, like documents.

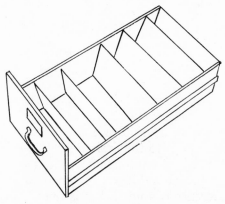

Fig. 73.—The Divide-a-File or the Wobble Block (Installed or moved without tools)

The file drawer is usually provided with a metal rod that runs from front to back in the middle of the bottom of the drawer. The guides, which have eyelets in the bottom, are strung on this rod so that they will not be lifted out by mistake when folders are withdrawn. Loose guides also "ride up" when the drawer is full, so that a sudden shutting of the drawer ruins the tops of the guides. Some cabinets are provided with a snap-out guide rod to lock the guides into place. To remove the guides all that is necessary is to press down the knob of the guide rod and pull out. Some five-drawer files have been built without rods in order to reduce height by conserving the space required by the groove into which the rod fits.

Each drawer is provided with a label holder which should

be large and well fastened to the drawer. Drawer pulls that can be readily clutched and wide enough for the hand to slip through easily are another essential feature.

A catch or drawer latch is a device that holds the drawer securely in the cabinet when closed and thus prevents unsightly, partly open drawers. Locks are provided for individual drawers or for units but must be ordered specially.

Bases vary considerably. A base raises the lower drawer to a better working height, but the top drawer must also be kept at a convenient working height. Bases are either solid or box construction; or there are leg bases of varying heights. A short leg base permits dirt to collect under the file while a higher leg permits easy cleaning. Glass and caster bases are also provided. Tops are a part of the construction in the solid file, but are removable in units that are built up. Tops of the three-drawer or counter height files are often covered with battleship linoleum which may be purchased in long strips and cut to the desired size to cover the whole row of cabinets. Linoleum tops sometimes have brass-bound edges to add to their durability and appearance.

Often a difference of four inches is found in the depth of the filing drawer. As 175 papers of ordinary weight can be filed to an inch, filing inches need to be counted with care. The manufacturers for the most part are agreed that a 28″ or a 28½″ depth should be considered the national standard. Thirty inches is too deep for ease in reaching to the back of the drawer.

Cabinets built in both letter and legal size and in two-, three-, four-, or five-drawer heights are designed so that with a pull of the handle (a) the front moves forward into a V-shaped expansion; (b) another model has a rigid front but an expanding back which permits the contents automatically to slope backward; and (c) still another model has a drop both front and back. Such cabinets actually give 4″ per drawer greater capacity than other models which are rigid. 4″ | There is full visibility and easy reference position | in each of the file drawers.

The inside dimensions of a file drawer should be enough larger than the papers filed therein to permit easy handling; in correspondence and larger sizes this is at least 1″ more in width and 2″ more in height, as papers tend to ride upward

FIG. 74.—Speed-File (Art Metal Construction Co.)

in the file. On the whole the paper sizes can be roughly classified as below. To this list are attached the drawer sizes required. The measurements of all manufacturers do not differ radically.

Vertical letter files may be purchased in one-, two-, three-, four-, and five-drawer units with various styles of bases and tops. The four-drawer height is the most practical for ordinary purposes; the three-drawer height permits a splendid counter top; the five-drawer is a space saver. The top drawer of a five-drawer cabinet is rather high for rapid

INSIDE MEASUREMENTS IN INCHES

Width	Height	Depth	Form and Form Size
10 5/16	4 5/16	Up to 26 13/16	Check or voucher
4 to 5 1/8	10 1/4 to 11 1/8	Up to 26 13/16	Document (folding is undesirable)
10 5/16	9 1/16	Up to 26 13/16	Invoice (7 x 8 1/2)
12 1/4	10 1/4 to 11 1/8	Up to 26 13/16	Letter (8 1/2 x 11)
15 1/2	10 1/4 to 11 1/8	Up to 26 13/16	Legal or Cap
10 5/16	12 7/8	Up to 26 13/16	Ledger (sizes vary greatly)

filing, although a three-inch platform modifies this difficulty. The one- and two-drawer heights are mainly used in executive offices and where there are but few papers to file. When

FIG. 75.—Counter-Height File Cabinet (Remington Rand Inc.)

filing cabinets are set alongside of each other in a row of uniform height, they are called a battery.

For standard commercial uses, wood filing equipment has been almost entirely replaced by steel in a variety of solid colors and grained finishes. Grained finishes are now giving way to light shades of gray, although the green enameled finishes are still widely used. The olive green and gray of the different manufacturers are not uniform; in other words, the finish has not actually been standardized. If there is any advantage in wood files it is when they are used in the executive offices where the furniture matches the wainscoting. Steel filing cabinets are noiseless when supplied with progressive suspensions and unquestionably offer a certain amount of fire resistance in that the material from which they are built does not burn. Steel filing cabinets are more easily kept clean, are verminproof, and because of the inherent qualities of the material from which they are made—i.e., steel—are not dependent upon bulk for rigidity, thereby offering greater advantage in the saving of floor space. Cabinet width is shown in the accompanying table.

WIDTH OF WOOD AND STEEL CABINETS
(in Inches)

Number of cabinets	Steel	Wood
1	15	16
5	75	80
11	165	176

Side-Filing Principles.—A new type of filing equipment in all standard sizes—letter, legal, card, etc.—differs from the conventional filing cabinet in that the compartments open sideways. There is no possibility of the cabinet overbalancing, as the center of gravity remains well inside, thereby permitting all sections to be open at once. Folder indexes and guides are slid out sideways instead of being lifted. Advantages of this equipment are as follows: since an open compartment does not affect visibility and accessibility of compartments above and below, two or three drawers of the same cabinet can be worked in at the same time; considerably less space is occupied than in the conventional filing cabinets.

Fig. 76.—Rock-a-File (Yawman and Erbe Mfg. Co.)

Shelf Filing.—Open shelf files which replace cabinets entirely are claimed by some companies to cost approximately 50% of grade A filing cabinets, nor is there any upkeep cost. From the standpoint of efficiency, the advocates of shelf filing claim that there is no comparison between pulling and filing folders on shelves and pulling and filing folders in cabinets because the opening and shutting of drawers is eliminated. There is no dust problem because the natural movement of the folders keeps them free from dust. Folders are not pushed down at the top and thus they do not break down. Shelves are slotted at intervals for removable steel dividers to hold the folders upright. Advocates of this method of housing files claim that the saving in filing space over that of cabinets is considerable. An alphabetic arrangement of material does not lend itself too well to this type of equipment. It seems to be most satisfactory when used in connection with a numeric file.

Transfer Equipment.—Transfer cabinets with pull-out drawers of the same size as the drawer in which the current material is kept come in single units in steel, wood, or a combination of wood and pasteboard. Some of the inexpensive steel ones are not much more than tin boxes, while others may be obtained with follow-blocks and roller bearings. When stacked four, six, or eight high, they must be bolted together. No shelving is required when these transfer cabinets are used. Sometimes an inexpensive steel or wood four-drawer file is used for transfer purposes. Corrugated board boxes now come in drawer style. They are reinforced with steel, have metal handles, and some of them are collapsible.

It is not necessary to have as many transfer cases as there are drawers of current material to be transferred, because inactive papers may be more tightly packed. Often only two transfer cases are required for three drawers of current material.

Storage boxes made of heavy damp-resistant corrugated fiber board come in ninety sizes. They are collapsible, have an automatic locking device, a pull strap of heavy webbing attached to the bottom end of the file, are reinforced by steel along the top, and come with labels. Since they open from the top, it is not possible to stack them. Shelving must be provided to hold them.

The old-fashioned 4″ box in which papers are filed flat cannot be recommended for transferring. It requires six of these boxes to hold the papers from one vertical file drawer. These boxes also must be stacked on shelving.

There is on the market a system of mobile storage units invented to meet the need for additional storage facilities in limited areas. Units are so constructed that a clerk can easily move by hand several fully laden units. Space is gained by having no fixed aisles, but by shifting units right or left on tracks to make aisles where needed. (See Figure 33.)

Sorting Devices.—A sorter is as essential as a file cabinet. The most familiar sorter is an open tray with low sides, outfitted with strong guides. It may be set on a table, or placed on a caster base which is easily rolled from the desk to the files. A newer device is the flat sorter placed on the table at the clerk's left hand.

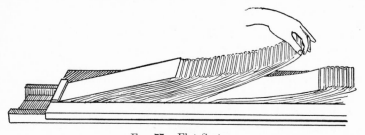

Fig. 77.—Flat Sorter

When a volume of material needs to be sorted, a fifty-division sorter may not suffice because the finer the break-downs of the sort, the fewer handlings are necessary. However, most sorters with more than fifty divisions cannot be handled on a stationary base because it requires too long a reach. Therefore, sorters are on the market which have a channel or track in which an easy-running carriage moves back and forth at a touch of the finger. This base unit is about 4″ x 26″. An interchangeable tab-unit rides on this carriage. Labeling is made up to fit special requirements.

These sorters come in 400, 500, up to 1000 divisions of the alphabet. (See Figure 7.)

It is claimed that the net result of sorting in these new devices is from 25% to 90% faster than in the tub sorter, as the basic principle of this flat sorting is fewer laying downs, fewer errors. Letter size papers can be sorted into these flat sorters at speeds from 1200 to 2000 and even up to 2500 pieces per hour, depending upon the readability of the names and experience of the operator. The average speeds in a large number of offices are from 1500 to 1800 per hour. Smaller size papers can be sorted even more rapidly than the speeds given above. Speeds of 2500, 3000, and even 3500 per hour have been attained.

Where material is of very short life it is accumulated in sorters and never transferred to filing cabinets.

If nothing else is at hand, it is always possible to utilize an empty cabinet drawer for a sorter. The second from the bottom is the most convenient if the clerk sits in front of it. A 25, or larger, division of the alphabet in letter size can be inserted and the compressor pushed up to the required distance.

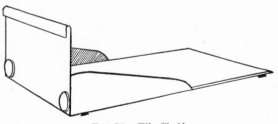

Fig. 78.—File Shelf

File Shelves.—A file shelf is very useful to the clerk when putting away papers or consulting them. It is hung on the drawer pull or on the side of the drawer. There should be some kind of hood or spring on the shelf to keep papers from falling off or being blown off. Pads on the back of the shelf keep it from scratching the drawer.

Stools.—Various styles of filing stools are on the market. The best for ordinary use is of steel, 14½″ high, with fiber or rubber casters. Some file departments have stools of three different heights.

Chairs.—Chairs in a file room should be given thought. If working at a tub desk, a typewriter, or where one is getting up and down frequently, a swivel chair without arms is advisable. Posture chairs are adjustable in height, fit the small of the back with great comfort, are light and easily rolled back and forth, and increase the speed and accuracy of the operator.

Guides.—The purpose of guides is to aid in filing and finding accurately; to aid in filing and finding quickly; to protect the folders from becoming torn and worn; and to help the folders stand upright in the file. They are manufactured for all standard drawer sizes. To overguide is as serious as to underguide, as it wastes space in the files and causes file clerks extra effort in handling. About 20 to 25 guides to a drawer is a good average. Guides should never be pulled forward by grasping the tabs but should be handled from the sides. With good care guides should be serviceable for eight or ten years, often longer.

The materials used in the body of a guide are pressboard, manila, or index bristol. Pressboard, which is a composition of cotton fiber and of pulp pressed together under high pressure and then highly surfaced, is the best guide stock. Much of the so-called pressboard on the market is not true pressboard but "stock" that is built up in layers, and therefore warps, bubbles, splits, and in other ways is undesirable. Pressboard may be tested by burning with a match to see if a clean ash is left. The grade of pressboard used varies, but it is usually from 20 to 35 points (a point in thickness is $\frac{1}{1000}$″). Gray and red are the colors most universally used.

Heavy manila stock is not durable enough to stand the strain of constant usage and is rarely seen now, even in the transfer. Index bristol, which is a heavy card stock in white or colors, is used for special guiding.

The body of a good guide should have rigidity or ability to stand up straight in file; durability, not deteriorating in strength or color within the desired length of service; pleasing and distinctive color so that it will clearly mark off groupings of folders; toughness so that it will not become brittle or tear easily. A guide should be no thicker or heavier than is necessary to meet the above requirements. Fractions of a centimeter soon accumulate into appreciable size, and space within a filing drawer is valuable. For most purposes, therefore, a medium weight guide is suitable.

A tab on a guide is the projection on the top edge which bears the index. They come in several styles: the tab itself of the same material as the guide with the index printed thereon; with a transparent celluloid covering to protect the printing and also to give added strength to the tab; and with insert or window tabs made by attaching a metal or celluloid device to the pressboard and inserting the label. An insert tab is preferable if the system is to grow more rapidly than can be provided for with the tabs permanently printed and supplemented by auxiliary guides. Metal or celluloid insert guides are more costly at the outset, but labels may be inserted to meet desired changes as long as the guide endures. The lastest type is of plastic with angle slant to permit ease of reading. The inserts may be printed or typed.

Tabs should be so constructed that they offer a smooth surface that will not scratch the hands. The method of covering the tab or fastening on an insert tab should be such that papers in the drawers will not catch in any way. The tab should be rigid, neither breaking nor bending above the body line, nor where attached. Tabs should have a surface that will not accumulate dirt and should be pleasing in appearance, as color can be used to great advantage in filing.

The tab receives very heavy wear; and if of the same material as the body of the guide. a stock should be chosen that meets every tab requirement. Metal tabs are attached to pressboard only. They may be vertical (straight up and down) or angled. (The latter are best in the lowest drawer.)

Fig. 79.—Magnifying Angle Tab on Guides (C. L. Barkley Co.)

Transparent celluloid slips, clear or in colors, are available to cover the inserted label. Celluloid tabs with insert labels may be vertical or angled and have sharp or rounded edges. Unless of high grade material, celluloid soon cracks, and unless properly attached to the pressboard it comes off easily.

Tabs come in varying lengths and the height may vary slightly also. The size of the metal tab does not always signify the label space. Standard cuts are one half, one third, one fourth and one fifth, but may also be had in other cuts on order—one tenth, one twelfth, etc. Tabs thus cut may be distributed across the top of the guides in first, second, center, fourth, or fifth position. A third cut tab on the extreme right is termed a third cut guide in the third position, while a third cut guide with tab at extreme left is termed a third cut guide in the first position. The standard cut and position of the tab describe accurately the guides wanted. Guide tabs distributed in all three positions equally are termed "third cut staggered," or "collated." Guides may be secured in staggered or collated positions, or all or part of a package of 100 guides may be had in any one position desired. Other positions and cuts may be provided on special order.

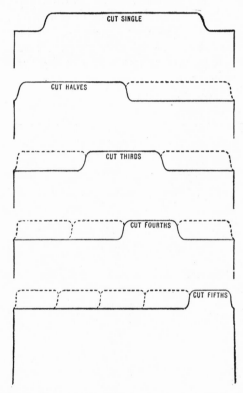

CUT SINGLE

CUT HALVES

CUT THIRDS

CUT FOURTHS

CUT FIFTHS

FIG. 80.—Relative Sizes of Tabs. The tabs are cut single, halves, thirds, fourths, and fifths.

Printed guide stock varies considerably but generally it is obtainable in sets of A-Z, also in names of months, names of days, and 1–31 for days of the month, names of states and U. S. possessions, and names of towns by population.

These notations are printed either directly on the guide stock or on labels to be inserted. Guides are signposts and lettering must be large and clear so that it can be accurately and quickly read.

In standard paper sizes all guides have a lug with a guard hole through which the rod of the cabinet passes to fasten the guides securely in the drawer, with the exception of some made especially for five-drawer cabinets. The guard holes should be reinforced so that they will not tear out easily and large enough not to bind on the rod. Some guides are made with three guard holes, one at the bottom and one on each side to facilitate the ease with which the guides slide back and forth over the rod.

FIG. 81.—Guard Hole on Guide

Guides may also be obtained without guard holes but with a steel roller bearing device which fits over the rod. While they are firmly held in place they have the added advantage of being removable without removing the rod. A slight twist of the hand releases them from the rod.

Folders.—Letters or other papers filed in vertical drawers are placed in containers, which are called folders, made of heavy paper folded once. The purpose of folders is to group papers belonging together, to keep papers upright in the file, to protect papers from becoming crumpled and torn, and to aid in quick and convenient reference.

Four main factors determine the material chosen for folders: the nature and quantity of the material to be filed, the amount of handling it will receive, and the length of service required. The most commonly used folder is of manila, in light, medium, and heavy weight, usually ranging from 7 to 11 points. For ordinary purposes a medium weight folder is suitable if the top is reinforced front and back with added strips (called triple top) to give strength where the greatest wear comes.

The grain of the paper should always run up and down the folder to give added strength and to prevent breaking where folded. Kraft folders are tough and darker in shade than manila so that they do not show soil easily. They, too, come in various grades. They have the additional advantage of being fairly inexpensive. Pressboard folders are used

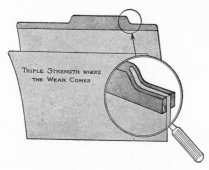

TRIPLE STRENGTH WHERE THE WEAR COMES

FIG. 82.—Triple-Top Folder (Filing Equipment Bureau)

for heavy, bulky material, for files which are not transferred frequently, such as credit papers. They usually are made in from 20- to 25-point stock. Leatheroid and fiber folders are also used for heavy materials. They run about the same thickness as pressboard and are usually made from hemp or jute fibers.

Folders are manufactured either with a straight edge or with a tab. The straight-edge or square-cut folders have a straight edge across both front and back flap. The latter is usually about ½″ higher than the front flap, providing a maximum space for labeling. It is called a straight-edge extension top folder. In a tab folder a portion of the tab has been cut away to give greater visibility in the file and to permit more definite emphasis upon the classification marked on the tab by means of its position. A medium weight folder with reinforcements at the top edge where the wear comes is often found to be as satisfactory as a heavier grade folder without requiring the same amount of space.

Folders are standardized in two heights. The guide height means that folder and guide tabs are the same height. They provide for greater visibility of tab. Body height means that the folder tab or straight edge of the back flap reaches only to the top edge of the body of the guide. Although the folder tabs are less visible, they receive less wear and tear.

Folder tabs come in styles and cuts similar to the guide tabs. The tab is most frequently of the material of the folder—the straight edge, extension top being cut away in halves, thirds, fourths, fifths, as the case may be. Folders may be purchased in any one of these positions—as, for instance, in fifth cut, right only—or staggered across the file. The tab may be covered with celluloid for protection (often done on printed tabs for miscellany) or may be an insertable tab of celluloid or metal either of which may be angled as in guides. Heavy tabs require a heavy material for the body of the folder.

It is a question whether folder tabs should be staggered as in second and third positions, or whether they should come in one position only. The argument advanced for the alternating positions is that the eye can read two names on two tabs in juxtaposition more quickly than it can read two names one behind the other. To keep order in alternate positions is easy enough when the file is first started, but when names are inserted one at a time, the tab sequence is at once disturbed and additional time is needed to find the correct position for the tab each time a folder is added. The argument advanced for the one-position tab is that the eye travels down one line more quickly than it does in a zigzag position.

Printed tab folders are most commonly sold for the alphabetic miscellany, for months, for days of the week, and for consecutive numbers.

A single scoring in the bottom of the front flap allows a $3/8''$ or larger expansion of folder. Some folders come with two, three, four, or more of these scorings. They should always be used when the volume is heavy because they offer a ledge on which the contents rest. This keeps the folder upright instead of slumping with the heavy weight to the bottom of the drawer. Pressboard folders have cloth hinges at the bottom which are also folded to allow for considerable expansion.

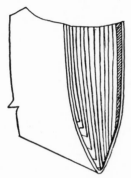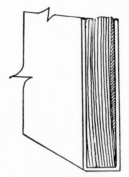

Manila folder. One fold at bottom. Papers riding up.

Score neatly folded so as to let papers down properly into folder.

FIG. 83.—Illustration of Non-Use and Use of Scoring on Folders

One type of folder is manufactured to hang on metal frames which fit over the sides of a file drawer. No follow block is needed and gravity keeps all papers and folders down, which eliminates need for jogging.

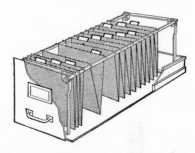

FIG. 84.—Hanging Folders (Oxford Filing Supply Co., Inc.)

Any heavy folder may be fitted with fasteners by which papers are bound into the folder. Cloth and paper hinges may also be used. As fasteners slow down the speed in operating a file, they should be used only when necessary to insure the safety of papers or when papers are to be kept in an unusual arrangement, as in legal cases or in various types of construction work where papers indicate a definite order of procedure. Many types of folders are manufactured for the more unusual materials which need to be filed or for unusual uses to be made of papers. Paper and cloth sides, folder for varying degrees of expansion, long and short flaps, and various kinds of fasteners and ties for the flap may be had.

Labels.—The label is a mechanical device to help save money in wear and tear on the supplies and equipment and reduce labor costs. Three types of labels should be given consideration: for drawers, for guides, and for folders. Each drawer content should be plainly indicated on the drawer label. Drawer labels are made of white or colored bristol board on which the simplest possible statement of content is lettered in clear bold fashion—typed in caps, hand-lettered with India ink, or made of cut-out letters pasted on a contrasting background. Transparent celluloid for covering the labels may be purchased in sheets and cut to the required size.

Labels for insert tabs on guides come in strips of the right height and width, perforated, ready for typing. However, it is always advisable to buy printed guide labels if possible.

Firms sometimes prefer to type directly on the tab of the folder, in which case a typewriter with a long platen or a billing machine is used. The folder tab should be plain and not printed with words and lines that rarely can be used to advantage. Gummed labels, about 4″ wide, may be purchased in manila and several distinctive colors, or with color bands on the manila. Color bands are preferred over solid colors, for the typing is more legible on the manila background. There are usually 10 labels in a perforated strip and 250 to 1000 labels in a package. A whole strip is typed at one time, then separated at the perforations and attached to the folder tab. Labels also come in rolls of 250. They lessen the time required for the typing because of obviating the necessity of inserting and removing the strips. Another type of label, called Kum-Kleen, is self-adhesive. It can be pulled off a backer and applied without moistening to any clean smooth surface by a mere finger touch.

The purpose of colored labels or color bands on labels is to make a secondary classification in a file. For example, in an A–Z file may be put orders, correspondence, and credit memos. To prevent the user of the file having to finger much correspondence before finding a certain order, each of these different types of papers is in a separate folder distinguished by a colored label.

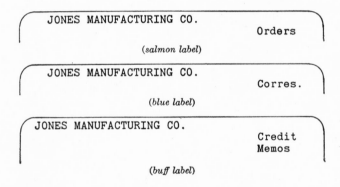

Fig. 85.—Contents of Folders Distinguished by Color of Label. Firms with a mailing list on stencils may apply these impressions on their folder labels directly.

New equipment and supplies for simplifying filing work are constantly appearing on the market—many with merit, others without. The current trade catalogs of the equipment and stationery houses will list these new items.

Chapter 19

ANALYZING FILES; STANDARDS OF ACCOMPLISHMENT

Purpose of Analyzing a Filing System.—One of the objects of analyzing a filing system is to determine its weak spots so as to reorganize it for greater efficiency. Just as there are certain fundamental principles in accounting, there are certain fundamental principles in filing. And just as every business has a bookkeeping system which is a bit different from that of another concern in the same line of business, so there are no two files which are exactly alike.

Analyzing a filing system involves a study of types and amounts of materials to be filed; routing of materials before they reach the file room; routines in the file room; methods of classifying and indexing the material; personnel; standards of accuracy and speed; equipment. Before starting an analysis the purpose of the survey must be clearly stated; in other words, what end is to be attained through such a study? Then in analyzing a filing system it is necessary to make an individual study of each kind of file: the correspondence, the vouchers, the data, the card index, etc. Upon the correctness of the study of each part depends all succeeding work. The collecting of facts is not sufficient; interpretation is the object of the study. Upon completing an investigation it is necessary to check the facts which have been secured against standards, and if such standards have not been attained, recommendations involving changes to be made are in order.

Causes of Trouble.—An analysis of a file which is not functioning as it should usually reveals several possible causes of trouble. Rarely is one alone answerable for filing difficulties; usually there is a combination of several causes:

A. Organization of the Record Department:
  1. An improper setup, such as a geographic system when a name file would be more suitable.
  2. Lack of controls:
      a) No systematic method of keeping track of material loaned from file.
      b) Transfer not made at regular intervals.
      c) Lack of a suitable follow-up system.
      d) No production records of work accomplished by each clerk.
  3. Lack of a manual:
      a) Describing the setup of the files and the daily routines so that (1) the work can be carried on smoothly, and (2) new clerks can be properly trained.
      b) Giving regulations for the users of the files.
  4. Work not organized properly so that clerks suffer from unnecessary fatigue.
  5. Improper correlation of departmental and central files so that there is duplication of material and labor.
  6. Improper location of file room in relation to departments using it most frequently.
  7. Storage files not properly organized and indexed for quick access to contents.
  8. Lack of an adequate retention program for removal of useless material.
B. Equipment, Supplies and Space:
  1. Drawers overcrowded.
  2. Poor system of guiding: guides not evenly distributed or too complicated in plan.
  3. Folders of such poor material that tabs break down.
  4. Folders overloaded.
  5. Name on folder not typed as it is to be filed; handwritten tabs.
  6. Transfer cases used instead of smoothly operating drawers for current material.
  7. Absence of a sorter, filing stool, or shelf.

     8. Poor lighting or ventilation.

     9. Insufficient aisle space.

   10. Improper arrangement of cabinets.

C. Staff:

    1. No competent supervisor if there are several clerks in the department.

    2. Clerks without proper qualifications assigned to the filing.

    3. An inadequate training program.

    4. Insufficient personnel.

D. The Paper Itself:

    1. Illegible signatures.

    2. Misspelling of names by stenographers.

    3. Customer signing different given name or initials.

    4. Customer writing on letterhead that is not his own and the letter being filed without having been carefully read.

    5. Executives pinning papers together for temporary use which get into file without being unpinned. The top paper is filed correctly and the others are misfiled.

    6. Use of clips.

E. Cooperation between the file room and other departments:

    1. Papers not properly initialed or marked before being sent to file.

    2. Executives keeping letters in their desk instead of sending them to file promptly after they are read and answered, and then borrowing them again when needed.

    3. Papers loaned from file being passed on to others by the borrower without being recharged.

    4. Flow of work into file department being slowed down by some "bottleneck" so that papers are requested from file before they reach the department.

    5. Office force other than the file department being allowed in the file room.

How to Gauge a File for Method of Arrangement and for Supplies Needed.—A filing system must follow the aim and the scope of the business. In order to determine what method of arrangement is best for a given file it is necessary to know how papers are called for. It may be that two different departments ask for the same paper in two different ways, such as customer's name and order number. Frequently two or more copies of an order are made up, one filed by name and one by number. To set up a sufficient number of files to meet every request is a satisfaction which it is often too expensive to indulge. If the secondary method of requesting a paper is infrequent, it is often necessary to set up the file in answer to the most frequent requests and ignore the others.

When analyzing a file from the standpoint of equipment needed, the notation on the guides must depend upon the usage of the papers, as explained in the previous chapter. The size of the system, whether a 500 or 1000 division of the alphabet, is influenced by four factors: the amount of current filing; the transfer dates; the annual rate of growth of the file; the amount of miscellany.

The amount of current filing can be determined by measuring the number of inches of papers in file, or if the drawers are uniformly filled, by counting the number of drawers. If the present system contains old material which needs to be weeded out an estimate must be made of how much of the material is current and how much old. This can be done by going through one drawer carefully and getting an average. If the total is ten full drawers of current material, and it is decided that 25 guides a drawer will be adequate, a 250 division of the alphabet will suffice. However, in buying a new system of guiding, which should last for eight or ten years, it is not enough to estimate present needs.

The rate of growth of a file is also a determining factor in deciding on the number of guides needed. While 20–25 guides per drawer are ample for a mature business, 40 guides per drawer in a new and rapidly growing file will permit of considerable expansion before outgrowing the guiding.

The length of time between transfers must be known; if a file is transferred twice a year, a division one half as large will be needed as would be the requirement if the papers accumulated for a whole year.

The amount of miscellany must be determined. If miscellany is unusually heavy, 40 guides per drawer with miscellaneous folders to match will be needed. On the other hand, if the business is a wholesale one with a few large customers, a small division of the alphabet with a large number of auxiliary guides (months, A–Z, and special names) will fit much better.

Measurements for Correspondence Files.

Cabinets: The inside depth of the cabinet which is to be used must be figured, then $\frac{1}{2}''$ subtracted for the follow block and at least $3''$ for free space so as to get the folders out and in between guides easily. (Exception: See page 216.)

Guides: Celluloid tab guides take approximately the following amounts of space:

25 medium weight guides	$\frac{5}{8}''$
25 heavy weight guides	$\frac{7}{8}''$
25 metal tab guides, heavy	$1\frac{1}{2}''$

Folders:

100 heavy weight folders	$3\frac{1}{4}''$
100 medium weight folders	$2\frac{1}{4}''$
100 light weight folders	$1\frac{1}{2}''$
25 miscellaneous folders medium weight	$\frac{1}{2}''$

The guides and folders furnished by various equipment houses vary somewhat in weight.

After subtracting from the inside measurement of the cabinet the amount of space which will be required by follow block, free space, guides, and folders, the remaining space will be left for papers, which average 150 to 200 an inch according to the proportion of letterheads and tissues. At best one cannot expect to file more than 3500 average papers in a drawer.

It is well to figure on the number of special name and other auxiliary guides which will be needed after the primary guides have been inserted. Then by inspecting each drawer it is a simple matter to pick out the spots where the folder bulk is too heavy and to insert auxiliaries.

Measurements for Card Files.

Cabinets: The inside filing space of the drawer to be used must be measured and $5/8''$ for the follow block subtracted. Also $1''$ for free space should be allowed, and a varying amount for guiding, depending upon whether the guides are light or heavy in weight.

Guides: A guide for every 25 cards is desirable. If there is little use of the file, one guide for every 50 or 100 cards is sufficient. Where there are many lookups some firms require a guide for every 8 or 10 cards. To make sure of an estimate the cards should be packed tightly together, one inch measured off with a ruler, and then the number of cards in that inch counted. The average is about 100 cards to an inch.

Time Savers in Operation of Files.—The analytic eye should also be turned upon the operation of filing. It may seem a trifling matter to train a new worker in the file department to fan a bunch of cards and handle them with rubber fingers on thumb and forefinger; but one minute saved out of twenty by utilizing this simple saving means three minutes an hour. Again, moving the hand from the drawer to the top of the cabinet which is utilized in the absence of a shelf may be accomplished in three seconds' time, but moving the hand from the drawer to the filing shelf hung on the handle of the next adjacent cabinet, a distance of about one foot, may be accomplished in two seconds' time. Seconds per motion multiplied by hundreds of motions will make quite a showing at the close of a week. Other savings can be effected through the elimination of duplicate effort. For example, a general alphabetical file containing orders, correspondence, credit memoranda, and shipping papers would have the preparatory sorting work done as a unit. The "A" drawer would be opened once with all the different types of papers filed therein. Contrast this to maintaining each of the four types of papers as a separate unit so that each type has to be sorted separately and four "A" drawers need to be opened in order to file the papers. These savings come as a result of close observation and careful training on the part of the personnel, and are entirely outside the results accomplished through the use of proper tools, through proper light and ventilation, or through the even flow of work into the file room.

It is entirely possible to set standards as to the amount of work to be done by each clerk. To determine these standards time and motion studies must be made of each operation. A time study is the analysis of time required to perform the units or elements of an operation. A motion study is the analysis of the motions performed. In making such time studies each activity is divided into "elements"; that is, the various steps in the performance of the job. Each element is rated separately. Studies are made of all elements at all times of day and on clerks of all degrees of efficiency so as to secure a fair average. Then certain standards of accomplishment are set. (See pages 242 and 244.)

Bonus Plans.—In some firms normal accomplishment in a file room is paid for by a definite weekly salary, with a reward in the form of a bonus for accomplishment over and above the normal production required. Several steps are necessary in applying a bonus plan. The standard should be scientifically set, not by amateurs unacquainted with the procedure, because a bonus plan which collapses because it was inadvisedly set up does much to ruin morale. Then the task should be set sufficiently high so that a full day's work may be secured from a first-class worker. There should be a rigid inspection of the completed task and the worker penalized for defective work in a reduction of bonus, not salary. Finally, the standard, if scientifically set, must be considered correct until the method is changed.

Where a bonus system is in force, all activities should be listed on a report which is conveniently arranged to permit a tally of output of activity performed by each individual. Output must be tallied by someone other than the worker and the sum of individual outputs checked periodically against what the total should be.

A wholesale hardware company has had a bonus system in effect for 25 years. Shortly after the installation of the plan, the cost of holding papers in file over a period of three years was reduced to one third and the personnel was reduced 50% without reduction of efficiency. In this company a unit of work consists of the time taken to sort one paper or to look up one paper or to file one paper, etc. If 50 units are produced in one hour's time, base pay only is earned. Additional units receive a bonus, the bonus rising strikingly as production increases.

> 50 units produced = base pay only
> 51 units produced = base pay plus $ .53
> 60 units produced = base pay plus $2.11
> 70 units produced = base pay plus $3.87

Approximately 430 4-drawer file cabinets are maintained in the department, averaging 36 4-drawer cabinets per file clerk. Personnel consists of 1 supervisor, 1 assistant, and 12 file clerks. Each file clerk averages 3910 units handled per 8 hours. Revised cost figures indicate .011¢ per sheet handled in the department. A detailed list of some of the standards for this type has been worked out as shown in the accompanying table.

One of the tested ways of securing accuracy in a filing department is by a continuous audit of the file. One insurance company reports that its misfiles have been reduced to less than ½% from an average of 3% by this one method alone. No clerk checks his own work. Detailed statistics are kept on the production and errors of each clerk. Errors are listed to indicate the kind. These sheets are excellent material for training new clerks.

FILING STANDARDS

Operation	Unit	Standard in Minutes per Unit	Units per hr. Required for Base Pay only	Units per hr. Required with a $2.11 Bonus
Major Sorting	Order or sheet	.067	746	895
Major Lookups	Per Lookup	1.650	30	36
File Orders in Large Flat Sorter	Per Sheet	.057	878	1050
Remove, Sort, Count from Large Flat Sorter	Per Sheet	.051	980	1175
Filing—Regular	Sheet	.155	322	386
Counter Calls—General	Requisition	2.77	18	22
Audit Folders	Folder	.580	86	104
Type Labels	Label	.299	167	200

Periodical Reports.—Office management engineers agree that it is essential in all but the smallest filing departments to maintain various reports. Such reports keep officers in touch with what is being accomplished; provide a comparison of the work accomplished this year with corresponding months of last year; give concrete evidence of the need for securing additional equipment and supplies, space, temporary help, or the reverse; and act as a check on individual clerks in the records department.

Useful reports include:

1. Volume Report. This should contain: the number of papers filed in a given period of time (each type of paper should be counted separately and not all papers totaled because it requires far more time to file 100 pieces of subject matter than it does to file 100 vouchers, which come to file in almost exact numeric sequence); the number of lookups in a given period of time; the number of lookups *not* found; the number of papers read and coded; the number of papers

31	to	12	11	10	9	8	7	6	5	4	3	2	1	
														Bills of lading
														Coding
														Checks
														Correspondence
														Credits
														Follow-ups
														Look-ups
														Messenger service
														Orders
														Reconstruction work
														Sorting
														Vouchers
														No. time TOTALS
														Incomplete work
														Month.......... Daily work record of.............. Filing Department

Fig. 86.—A Sample Production Chart

sorted; the amount of time spent in reconstruction work such as making up new folders or in auditing a file for errors; the amount of time spent in messenger service. When papers are fairly even in size and equal in weight they can be measured with a ruler and multiplied by the number of papers counted in a test inch. Or the number of papers per pound can be determined and the papers measured by weight. An actual piece-by-piece count goes very rapidly and is of course more accurate.

2. Production Report. It is estimated that the output of the average worker is but 50%. A production report is kept daily by each worker and turned in to the supervisor each day or week; a sample production chart is shown in Figure 86.

3. Audit Report: Spot check or a complete folder-by-folder check.

4. Personnel Reports.
   a) Attendance.
   b) Evaluation.

5. Reports of work done for other departments, such as sorting checks for the accounting department.

Standards of Accomplishment.—

To file cards in an alphabetic file	297 pieces per hour
To sort into a flat sorter	759 pieces per hour
To mark 8½" x 11" letters for a name file and to make the first A–Z sort	291 pieces per hour
To sort and file letters in an alphabetic file	176 pieces per hour
To file only papers in an alphabetic file	287 pieces per hour
To find papers in an alphabetic file	94 pieces per hour
To sort vouchers in a numeric file	512 pieces per hour
To file vouchers in a numeric file	451 pieces per hour
To file data by subject	147 pieces per hour

Chapter 20

PERSONNEL, TESTS, MANUALS, COSTS

Characteristics Necessary for an Efficient File Clerk.— Not every person is adapted to filing and records management. Of course, if the department is to be used as a training school for other departments it will be necessary to do the best possible with the material at hand. If, on the other hand, clerks are to be chosen with some idea of permanency in the records department several characteristics should be looked for in the applicant, the most important of which are orderliness and a liking for detail. Ability to work with others and a sense of wanting to give service follow closely behind. Desirable character traits are:

ABILITY TO HANDLE PEOPLE: Based on self-control.

ACCURACY: Filing papers and cards correctly according to a prescribed system; revising work carefully; transcribing information on cards or labels accurately.

ADAPTABILITY: Adjusting readily to new views; willingness to be shown a better way; meeting emergencies intelligently.

CONVICTION: Knowing the work thoroughly and then having confidence in one's self and in one's work even under criticism; presenting work to others so that they will maintain confidence; maintaining poise, calmness, dignity.

DEPENDABILITY: Keeping up an even high grade of work at all times without constant supervision.

EDUCATION AND BUSINESS ACUMEN: Knowing the aim and scope of the special type of business with which one is associated; keeping alive to changing business conditions by reading the best business periodicals and books.

ENTHUSIASM AND LOYALTY: To one's firm, to one's work.

HEALTH—based on vigor: Hearing distinctly; seeing clearly; no nervousness or excitement under pressure; relaxing quickly.

IMAGINATION: When marking papers for file keeping in mind the "finding" of them, months later; visualizing the borrower and his needs; classifying errors of those calling for papers and those filing so that clues may be followed when some paper is elusive.

INDUSTRIOUSNESS: Not being easily disturbed by interruptions; working steadily rather than in fits and starts.

INITIATIVE: Reporting desirable changes; solving minor problems without asking unnecessary questions; doing what is assigned to be done even if it is outside the usual scope of work.

INTELLIGENCE: Ability to grasp facts and apply them; ability to carry out instructions.

JUDGMENT: Noting relative importance of pieces of work and doing most important first; eliminating nonessentials.

KNOWLEDGE OF FILING SYSTEMS: Knowing the best that has been written on this subject; taking courses from time to time to add to one's technical knowledge.

MEMORY. Remembering papers as they are marked by keeping one's mind on the work; recalling rules without referring to them; knowing the exact location in the files of those accounts most frequently called for.

MENTAL CURIOSITY: Finding out the purport of transactions one is asked to handle rather than taking things for granted; knowing wherein the different types of records differ.

ORDERLINESS: Keeping every step in the handling of papers systematic, logical, proof against errors; keeping equipment in orderly condition; typing labels or cards uniformly; keeping papers in orderly condition within folders.

PATIENCE: Doing exacting work without being bored; working under strain without being annoyed.

SENSE OF HUMOR: Appreciating diverting incidents.

SPEED: Turning out work in reasonable time according to standards set; no waste motion in various processes; quickness in discerning irregularities in records.

TEAM WORK: Not only in cooperating with outside departments but within the department as well in carrying on the day's routine and meeting emergencies.

Tests of Ability.—It is often advisable to give tests to a prospective employee. This is not so necessary for a beginning clerk but one who claims to have had experience should have his measure taken. One simple test is to give 100 type-

written cards and a sorter to an applicant and have the filing
done then and there. If the cards are to be filed alphabetically by name, the task should be completed in ten minutes
without more than one error. Geographic filing takes somewhat longer. Exercises in alphabeting can be done on paper,
names chosen at random from a directory or from the company's own list of customers. The following is a sample:

Frank Adamek	Herbert Addie
Ada Furniture House	G. Samuel Addleman
Adamack & Co.	Adding Machine Co.
Adabelle Hat Shop	Albert Addison
A. C. Adam	Irene Addington
Annette Adair	Addis Grocery Store
Adairs Book Shop	Adkins, Young & Allen Co.
Adair Art Shop	George Ade
John Adair	George Adis
Adamson, Young & Ellis	Ade's Pharmacy
A. G. Adams & Co.	I. P. Adelman
William Adamson	Adel Hat Shop
A. Willard Adams	Isaac Adelman
Charles Adamson	L. P. Adee
Adams Adjustment Co.	Adelle Shop
Frank Adamski	Hyman Adelberg
Albert Adams	Add-a-unit Partition Co.
Hans Adamsen	Addison Cleaners
Adder Machine Co.	Admiral Hotel
Adapt Machinery Co.	Advance Lithographing Co.
Jane Addams	Advertising Poster Co.
Adaptive Printing Co.	John Adlis
Ad-craft Sales Co.	Adult Education Council
Adart Studios	Adelphia Apts.
E. E. Adcock	Adcraft Signs
Adco Dry Storage Co.	William T. Adams
C. H. Addy	Adolph's Gas Stations

If typewriting is required, have cards and labels typed.
Check for form as well as for accuracy and neatness. Civil
service examinations, federal or state, for file clerks or for
junior or senior clerical workers make excellent tests. Copies
of old examinations can be secured from the public library.
One such examination follows:

1. Write a brief note describing each of the following:
    a) Alphabetical filing.
    b) Numeric filing.
    c) Subject filing.
    d) Geographic filing.
2. Assume that you are permitted to select the filing system and equipment in an office, how would you file:
    a) Newspaper clippings.
    b) Booklets.
    c) Photographs.
    d) Reports.
    e) Unclaimed letters returned to the office.
3. What would you do in each of the following?
    a) An official requires a file for a considerable time and cannot release it; correspondence arrives on which immediate action should be taken by another official.
    b) The existence of a file has been overlooked and a new file formed.
4. Make a comparison of the relative advantages of loose-leaf and permanently bound books for records. State for what type of work each is best suited.
5. Suppose papers are loaned from your files to other clerks in the office. How would you arrange to locate immediately any paper needed?

Instruction of a New File Clerk.—A new worker should first of all be given a table, chair, and manual of instruction. The manual should be read and re-read until its contents are well known. Then some simple work should be demonstrated such as sorting. If she has had no filing experience, the new clerk should have each step of the new process clearly demonstrated so that wrong habits will not be acquired. Let the trainee watch a well trained person work. Let the trainee do the job and explain it to the instructor. Tell her something about the different customers so as to give a personal touch to the work. Check back on the work to see that it is being done accurately. Give responsibility and praise; the human relation aspects of supervision will make or break the efficiency level of a new worker.

Everything that is known about the files should not be taught to a new worker the first day. A step at a time until each is thoroughly mastered is a good rule to follow.

Firms vary in their opinions as to whether it is better to have each clerk do one type of routine, such as sorting, filing in cabinets, coding, lookups, etc.; or whether it is better to give each clerk complete charge of one section of the files— as from A to I in an alphabetic name file—and expect that clerk to do all the work for the section except the first rough sort. Although the first plan makes for great speed in operation, it also leads to unrest because of the monotony and has the additional disadvantage of having no understudies when some one is absent.

In a records department, as in any department of a business today, there is to be faced the problem of specialization with the attendant difficulties of coordinating these specialists into a smoothly functioning whole without stifling the initiative and development of the individual.

The war years have brought an acute shortage of clerical help in many localities. Standards have had to be lowered, apprentice training has had to be intensified. Renewed thought is being given to fatigue elements and general surroundings, so as to attract young people. Long hours of standing at file cabinets are not acceptable. The new worker must be taught how to do much of this work seated. Sorters, stools for working in the lower drawers, properly adjusted chairs and other labor and fatigue-saving devices are good investments for satisfaction with working conditions.

Manual of Regulations.—The manual is useful in any filing department, partly as a training medium, partly to set standards of performance, and partly to help others maintain the regular routines when key personnel are absent. Where there is but one clerk in the department, his absence may cause delays and annoyances throughout the office which a manual put in the hands of a substitute clerk can do much to mitigate. An office manual is usually divided into a brief history of the company and names of officers; rules of office procedure: hours of work, rest periods, overtime, absenteeism, vacations, grading of work for salary increases, requisitioning of supplies, care of furniture, fixtures, and machines. If there is no office manual the file manual may include these points and in addition the following:

A. An introduction, telling the purpose of the manual and the importance of keeping it up to date as conditions change. It may be well to list here all the files maintained in the firm, distinguishing between those in the central file room, those in the departments but maintained by the central file staff, and those in the departments maintained by secretaries, bookkeepers, etc.

B. The setup of each individual file in the central file room or in the departments, if serviced by the file department. The equipment and supplies used. Sample labels to show how they should be typed for each file.

C. Procedures: (Review Chapter 4)

1. Pickups—hours and from whose desks.

2. Inspection for file stamp or order number, removal of clips and pins, stapling, mending, and coding.

3. Cross references—kinds: visible, sheet or cards, half folder. Show samples. When used. *See* and *See also.*

4. Follow-ups; when made, how made, samples. How the file is used.

5. Sorting—what to sort, when sorting is to be done, importance of getting material into sorter at once.

6. Filing—how actually to put material into cabinets.

7. Charging—what information needs to be recorded on charge card. Show sample. Checking of old charges at regular intervals to insure return of papers.

8. Transfer—systematic removal of material of temporary value, as letters of transmittal, acknowledgments, reservations, requests for information. What transfer

equipment is to be ordered and when. If a retention schedule has been worked out, attach to report. Detailed description of what has been microfilmed. Labeling of transfer cases or rolls of film. Importance of cremation sheets.

9. Importance of not keeping papers in desks. An overnight cabinet if necessary.

10. Importance of keeping up to date. Checking miscellany to remove accumulations of five or more papers for a firm and preparing new folders.

11. How to keep a production record of the daily work done by the department or an occasional spot-check to determine if additional help is needed.

D. If there is a data file, a list of the subject headings should be included in the report. It may be necessary to describe what is included under each heading. This would be especially true in executive files.

E. Location and rearrangement of a file room—proposed or completed. A floor plan may be helpful.

F. Personnel—Duties of each person in the department. It may be necessary to describe how a new clerk shall be trained.

G. Rules for alphabeting. If there are any peculiar names or exceptions to the general rules, these must be noted. Rules for typing labels may be included at this point.

H. Samples of all forms may be assembled at the end.

I. A sheet index to the manual will be helpful if the report is long.

The *File User's Manual* is intended for those making use of the file room and should include:

A. How to mark material for file

B. Emphasis on promptness in sending material to file

C. How to ask for material in file (requisition, telephone) and how to identify a wanted paper

D. Length of time (3 days, 10 days) a paper may be kept out of file

E. How to mark papers wanted for future attention

F. Request for cooperation in keeping out of file department

G. If there is a data file in the department, an index of subject headings to aid in asking for material

H. A notation that the file department should have the final decision in selecting subject headings.

Checking for Errors.—It is a simple matter to catch errors made by a stenographer, typist, or bookkeeper, but often a file clerk's errors are not made manifest until something which is wanted cannot be found. Certainly every file clerk should have a check taken of his work at intervals. Some firms do this by having audits made of the files during spare time. On the other hand, some offices feel that checking, in itself, is no guarantee that all errors made by the first operator will be caught. The checker has to cover much perfect work in order to find a few mistakes. Where checking is done the clerk must not check what she herself has filed, since mistakes tend to repeat themselves, but should check another portion of the file. Some form of spot check will be all that is required to maintain high standards of clerical accuracy providing that the selection and training of the workers have been adequate.

In many offices 2% of errors (2 in 100) is considered unavoidable although this is very high. In well organized and managed file departments 0.1 of 1% (1 in 1000) has been the average. Studies covering all types of concerns have been made on the cost of errors. Figuring not only the cost of clerical hunting time, but intangibles such as executive waiting time and the loss of customer goodwill brings the cost per error to over $61.

Value of a Good Filing Department.—A great many firms look upon the filing department as merely an overhead expense and all monies spent upon it are spent grudgingly. It is true that on the debit side must be figured salaries, rental of floor space, equipment and supplies, and miscellaneous expenses such as light and heat. But there is a credit side which must be balanced against the upkeep:

1. The daily service from the records department rendered quickly and in complete form is of value to management in enabling them to make proper decisions
2. The files record the obligations of the company
3. The files are the history of the company
4. The files act as a safe deposit for valuable papers
5. Well kept records enable a company to give information to outsiders, such as the government or banks.

Costs.—It is estimated that every dictated letter costs at least $1. If the contents of a normal file drawer are 4000 papers, of which a fourth are dictated, the initial cost of setting up a 4-drawer cabinet has been $4000. The cost of maintenance of a file cabinet should include not only record clerks' and supervisors' salaries, but also the cost of the equipment amortized over the years of usage, supplies, overhead such as a proportion of rent and light based on the number of square feet in the records department. Of the total, salaries constitute by far the largest portion of cost. The figures given below vary in different localities but will serve as an approximation.

Cost of maintaining one current, letter size filing cabinet per year:

Space: cabinet and space to operate it, 6.7 sq. ft. at $3. per sq. ft.	$20.10	9%
Cost of cabinet amortized over 10 years	7.50	3.4%
Supplies at $5. per drawer	20.00	9%
Salary of clerk at $50., handling an average of 60 drawers	173.00	79%

Figuring 4000 papers per drawer, the cost of maintenance per year is $20. per M, because to the above figures must be added supervision, overhead, and carrying charges. It is because these figures are so high that management is more concerned today with its records than at any time in the past. If costs are excessive, it might be well to check the following:

1. Correct and time-saving habits of work on the part of the clerks with analysis of workers' motions to overcome slowness and unskillfulness.
2. Relief from monotony of work which increases fatigue
3. Setting standards of achievement
4. Incentive plans
5. Determination of the actual worth of papers filed
6. Straight-line flow of work in the department to save steps
7. Correlation with other departments so that work flows into the file department continuously
8. The simplest method of filing consistent with the use to which the records are put
9. Economical layout of the file room with the use of five-drawer cabinets where necessary
10. Labor-saving and time-cutting devices, such as proper sorters
11. Suitable equipment such as cabinets easy to operate, tables instead of desks, stools
12. Training of clerks in the proper use of supplies, salvage of used supplies
13. Suitable purchases of supplies with samples of supplies constantly tested and new products investigated
14. Audits of the department at unannounced times

Those firms which are up to date in the organization and management of their records have been willing to maintain high standards in the file room from year to year regardless of the economic climate. Some firms still lag behind in their thinking about their records and consider a record department merely as an expense. Record keeping has been one of the last activities in most offices to be standardized; yet when firms have taken the trouble to think through the filing problems to a logical conclusion, they realize that the benefits they secure from them can be translated not only into greater satisfaction, but into an actual saving of money. There are known cases of a 100% saving in file personnel through a reorganization of record-room procedures and proper training of clerks.

Chapter 21

FILING IN A LAWYER'S OFFICE

Numeric System Most Commonly Used.—Although the case files in a legal office may be kept by client's name, a numeric system is also effective although more indirect. Either every transaction for a particular client is given the next available number (as 182, 267, 432), or each client is given a number by which all business of the client is thereafter identified. The objection to using the straight numeric system is that matters pertaining to one client are scattered throughout the file because other cases have intervened. When each client is given one number, different matters handled for him are given secondary numbers:

$$432 - 1$$
$$432 - 2$$

The alphabetic index may be kept either on 3″ x 5″ cards in a vertical file or in a visible index. A manual of style should be followed for all cards so that name, numbers, symbols, and dates always appear in uniform position.

```
SMITH   JOHN                                      432

vs
Chicago Coal Company

Court         Town          Court No......
Municipal     Chicago

Claim for personal injuries resulting from fire

Action  4th Class tort $1000    Started........

Assigned to      JMB    Our docket 6 p 7092
```

FIG. 87.—Reference Card for Client

Versus or vs. is used to indicate a plaintiff and a defendant. If the action is brought against Chicago Coal Company, a card is also written for Chicago Coal Company and is given the client's (Smith's) number. Vs. and ads. are used

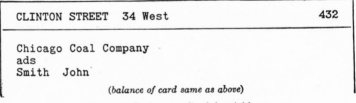

CHICAGO COAL COMPANY   432

ads
Smith   John

(balance of card same as above)

FIG. 88.—Reference Card for Defendant

on cards to distinguish the plaintiff from the defendant. A third card is written for the subject and a fourth card is written for the address.

FIRES   432

Chicago Coal Company
ads
Smith   John

(balance of card same as above)

FIG. 89.—Reference Card Filed by Subject

CLINTON STREET   34 West   432

Chicago Coal Company
ads
Smith   John

(balance of card same as above)

FIG. 90.—Reference Card for Address

Cross References.—There should be cross references under all peculiarities, all names appearing in the case, exceptions and doubts. In the lower right-hand corner of the client's card, for ease in disposing of the case later, the number of cards made out should be recorded; or in accordance with library practice, a list of these secondary cards noted on the back of the master card, four in connection with the case cited above.

Should John Smith be involved in another case the number assigned would be the next unused number, or a secondary number added to the original one:

$$432 - 2$$

A new card would then be written for Smith, John.

Often colored cards are used in the index, such as salmon to indicate court cases, white noncourt cases. For the case

```
┌─────────────────────────────────────────────────────┐
│  ILLINOIS COMMERCE COMMISSION              16302      │
├─────────────────────────────────────────────────────┤
│                                                       │
│  Cause No. 12237                                      │
│                                                       │
│  Illinois Natural Gas and Oil Company                 │
│      and                                              │
│  Waukegan Gas and Fuel Company                        │
│                                                       │
│  Petition for approval of purchase and sale of        │
│  certain property in Waukegan, Illinois,              │
│  And issuance and sale of certain securities          │
│                                                       │
│  19 -        JMB                                      │
└─────────────────────────────────────────────────────┘
```

FIG. 91.—White Card Made Out for Noncourt Case

in Figure 91 cards would be written for Illinois Commerce Commission, also Illinois Natural Gas and Oil Company, Waukegan Gas and Fuel Company, Waukegan (location), and Real Estate.

Guiding for Index.—Cards in the index are retained many years and therefore the stock should be durable and of good erasure surface. The index is divided into pending and disposed of cases, and both files should be well guided so that reference is speedy. A guide to every twenty-five cards is none too many.

Arrangement of the File.—Preparing a case for file requires first the assignment of a proper title. To assign the file number the clerk must refer to the card index to tell if the client is old or new. If old, a subdivision number may be added. If new, the accession book (numerical index of each case) shows the next unused number to be assigned. The necessary cards are then typed for the index, and the material is put into an expansion wallet on which is typed:

> Classification of case (number)
> Names of parties
> Nature of case
> Court number

Within the expansion wallet are placed manila folders so as to divide the material for quick reference. In some instances it may not be necessary to divide the papers pertaining to a case into more than two folders: correspondence and legal documents. For most cases the following classifications will suffice:

> Correspondence
> Pleadings, briefs, arguments
> Exhibits, evidence, instruments
> Memos of facts
> Memos of law, authorities for briefing

Fig. 92.—Expansion Wallet and Inner Folders

	Trustees
T	Traction ordinance
	Surveys
	Statistics
	Select committee to investigate real ·estate bondholders reorganizations
S	Securities and exchange commission
	Reorganization plans – consolidation of unification plan
R	Receivers
	Ordinance – comprehensive unified local transportation system
O	Opinion of counsel (extra copies)
M	Maps
L	Leases
H	Holdings
	Forms – drafts of letters to bondholders
	Foreclosures – bill of complaint
F	Foreclosures – acknowledgments of depositaries
	Committee – minutes of meetings
	Committee – financial reports of secretary
C	Committee – advisory
B	Bonds deposited
A	Agreement – amended bondholders deposit

(auxiliary guides)   *(folders)*

5112 CLINTON SURFACE LINES
(main guide appearing at center of drawer)

(Read upward)

Fig. 93.—File of a Traction Case

The inner folders must be low enough so as not to cover the information on the upper edge of the wallet. Straight edge or tabbed folders may be used. Five-drawer cabinets of legal size do not have the same inside measurements as four-drawer units so wallets must be measured to fit.

When a case grows to fill a drawer or more it may be necessary to eliminate expansion wallets and use only the manila folders, labeling the outside of the drawer with the name of the case. Suppose the case in question is a traction matter. Subdivisions might develop as shown in Figure 93.

Papers are grouped in chronological order within folders with the latest date on top. They may be fastened with flat-head paper fasteners, bending back the points after the papers have been impaled; perforator fasteners; pasting to a file back. Or they may be attached directly to the folder with a compression spring clip or with brass paper fasteners thrust through the folder.

FIG. 94.—Expansion Wallet (Quality Park Envelope Co.)

Some law firms like a recapitalization of the case on the front cover of the expansion wallet rather than only the number of case, names of parties, nature of case, and court number. In that event the wallets can be printed to order somewhat as shown in Figure 95.

The most satisfactory guides for legal files are of heavy pressboard with metal tabs, usually at the left side of the

FILE NO.

We represent _____ pltf
def

Opposing counsel _____

Address _____

Telephone _____

Ask for _____

Date	Correspondence	Conferences

Court _____ Action _____

Genl. No. _____

Returnable _____ Room _____

Assigned to judge _____

Name _____

Address _____

Telephone _____

VS

Name _____

Address _____

Telephone _____

Calendar No. _____

Answer filed _____

Set for trial _____ Room _____

Continued _____

FINAL DISPOSITION

Judgment on _____ For _____

Execution No. _____

Bailiff or sheriff No. _____

Date	Record of orders

Fig. 95.—Data Blank Printed on Expansion Wallet in Some Law Firms

drawer. The inserts should carry the number and the name of the case and be arranged by name if it is an alphabetic file, or consecutively, if a numeric file.

Inactive Cases.—The current file should contain only the active cases. At regular intervals, once or twice a year, a list of cases which have been inactive should be submitted for approval for transfer. Since these cases may be appealed to a higher court, they should be kept on the premises. The wallet should be stamped with the transfer date; the cards, also stamped with the date, should be withdrawn from the active index. Even a dead file which will never be reopened is not entirely destroyed. Some papers may be eliminated, such as duplicates and proofs of printed records; clients' own papers may be returned. These dead files may be kept in a warehouse.

In checking the files for inactive cases it is well to check also the active cases against the numerical index in order to discover misplaced files.

Collection Files.—In the case of collection files the folder must carry a recapitulation of details, such as dates of calls and correspondence, amounts collected, and disbursements. A card follow-up system with guides arranged by months and days of the month indicates each step of the procedure.

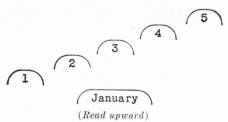

(*Read upward*)

Fig. 96.—Guides of Card Follow-Up System Arranged by Dates

Another method is to use signals on folders which bear a range of dates. The possibility of the signal being brushed off makes this method of follow-up not such a safe one as the card system.

Collection files are transferred when the collection is closed, some offices preserving only the letter of final settlement.

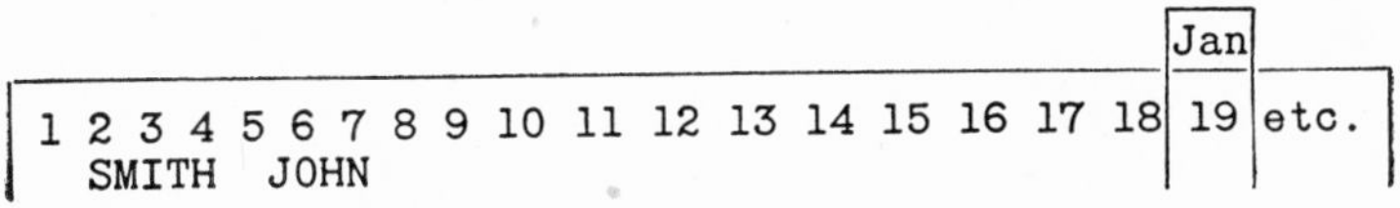

| Jan |
| 1 2 3 4 5 6 7 8 9 10 11 12 13 14 15 16 17 18 | 19 | etc. |
| SMITH   JOHN |

FIG. 97.—Follow-Up System Using Signals on Folders

In a small legal office the diary contains the record of services rendered a client and it is from these records that bills are computed. The diary may serve the double purpose of a tickler. It is better, however, to have a regular follow-up file with an extra card made up for that purpose at the time that a case is received. A card 3″ x 5″ in size is adequate. There should be a guide for each month and several sets of 1–31 guides as described above for the collection file. Indeed the two follow-ups may be combined under the one date index. If desired, guides may be inserted for succeeding years for cards showing future maturity of notes, etc. The advantage of such a card follow-up system over a diary is a saving of the writing of many entries because the cards can be moved forward to new dates and an assurance of greater accuracy because a card is not so easily overlooked as is an entry in a diary. To insure immediate attention, trials and hearings may be recorded on special, bright-colored cards.

In the larger law office daily report blanks headed with the attorney's name and giving in detail the work done on the different cases are filled out by those working on cases. A clerk posts these in the register, which is usually a loose-leaf book with sheets arranged alphabetically by client's name. This register summarizes the services rendered a client. From this register bills are figured.

Docket.—An attorney usually keeps a docket, showing every court order entered in every case in which he is interested. It is not necessary to use a printed form if one is not found which is flexible enough, although many printed forms are available which are quite satisfactory. These docket sheets give very complete information about the case, such as number, names of parties, addresses, telephone numbers and occupation, attorneys and their telephone numbers, nature of case, court number, date filed in court or opened, date closed (later). This docket sheet is ordinarily kept as a permanent independent record available for check if the file is stored. Frequently the file folder contains a duplicate of the docket sheet, especially if it is an active court case, such as a receivership. The printed file folder (Figure 95) eliminates the need for keeping a separate docket.

Miscellaneous File.—Since every legal office has correspondence of a miscellaneous nature (paid bills and other routine office matters) provision should be made for such papers by setting up a simple alphabetic file in a separate drawer with A-Z guides at the left of the drawer, the usual miscellaneous folders, and special folders for names or subjects running into some volume. These folder tabs should appear at the right-hand side of the drawer. This file is transferred annually.

Brief File.—When a special form of pleading, contract, etc., has been prepared or an opinion written, it is advisable to have an extra copy made to be put in what is called the Brief or Precedent file. Guide tabs at the left of the drawer should give the main subjects, as

Contracts
Torts
Real Property

with subdivisions in the center position:

(Read upward)

Fig. 98. Tabs for Brief or Precedent File

These cases are given numbers and filed in numerical sequence. Whenever a patient is re-admitted his original case record is called for and all subsequent data are entered upon it. Of the various methods used in filing records preference seems to be given to the folder type of equipment. This may be of bill or letter size, straight-edged or tabbed folder. At least the patient's name and number must appear on the folder, and often more detailed information is desirable. These folders may be thumb-indexed.

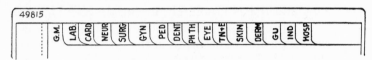

Fig. 104.—File of Patient's Case Record

In the clinics an "outpatient" record is made for each patient. These cases are sent to the record room each day at the close of each session of the clinics. These cases are likewise called for whenever the patients revisit the clinics. If a patient at the clinic is admitted to the hospital, his outpatient record is combined with his hospital record. In this way all data on any patient ever treated at a particular hospital are available in one place under the patient's file number. This is known as the "unit system." In many hospitals the hospital and outpatient records are filed together.

A good system of guiding with strong pressboard folders helps to keep the records upright and offers quick identification. A guide to every 20 folders is ample.

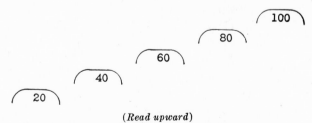

(*Read upward*)

Fig. 105.—Guides for Case Files

These case records must be properly cross-indexed. First comes the alphabetical registration card. An index by date of admission is often advisable. A summary card has been found helpful which covers significant facts in a case history otherwise not quickly available in the mass of detail. A geographical index is used by hospitals having patients from widely scattered locations.

Index of Diseases.—For the benefit of medical students an index of diseases or diagnoses according to a classification by systems affected is absolutely essential. Should a staff member be writing on pneumonia, for example, all the pneumonia cases which have occurred in the hospital will appear in the index including those with pneumonia as a secondary complication.

Each case history should be indexed by associated diseases or diagnoses; secondary conditions or complications; operations; causes of death. Several nomenclatures are on the market: Standard Nomenclature of Diseases, Massachusetts General Hospital, Bellevue, Dewey, Post, Clinical Index (Mercur). Some hospitals develop their own systems of indexing.

The Standard Classified Nomenclature of Disease compiled by the National Conference on Nomenclature of Disease is at the same time topographical and etiological; that is, each disease (including injury) is described and classified in terms of the tissue or organ where it is principally manifested, and in etiological terms: Tuberculosis of the Lungs and Fracture of the Femur illustrate the plan. For Poisoning it is necessary to refer to the Region or Organ affected.

The following classifications of diseases are used effectively by many hospitals.

TOPOGRAPHICAL CLASSIFICATION
MAIN DIVISIONS

0 Diseases of the body as a whole (including diseases of the psyche, and of the body generally); and those not affecting a particular system exclusively
1 Diseases of the integumentary system (including the subcutaneous areolar tissue, mucous membranes of orifices, and breast)
2 Diseases of the musculo-skeletal system
3 Diseases of the respiratory system
4 Diseases of the cardiovascular system
5 Diseases of the hemic and lymphatic systems
6 Diseases of the digestive system
7 Diseases of the urogenital system
8 Diseases of the endocrine system
9 Diseases of the nervous system
x Diseases of the organs of special sense

ETIOLOGICAL CLASSIFICATION

0 Diseases* due to prenatal influences
1 Diseases due to lower plant and animal parasites
2 Diseases due to higher plant and animal parasites
3 Diseases due to intoxication
4 Diseases due to trauma or physical agents
5.0 Diseases secondary to circulatory disturbances
5.5 Diseases secondary to disturbances of innervation or of psychic control
6 Diseases due to or consisting of static mechanical abnormality (obstruction; calculus; displacement and gross changes in form, etc.) due to unknown cause
7 Diseases due to disorders of metabolism, growth or nutrition
8 New growths
9 Diseases due to unknown or uncertain causes, the structural reaction (degenerative, infiltrative, inflammatory, proliferative, sclerotic, or reparative) to which is manifest; and hereditary and familial diseases of this nature
x Diseases due to unknown or uncertain causes, the functional reaction to which is alone manifest; hereditary and familial diseases of this nature
y Undiagnosed diseases

* In the sense of any considerable departure from the normal structure or function.

Subdivisions are indicated by additional numbers:

Topographical Classification

0 Diseases of the body as a whole
 02 Head and face
  020 Head and face, generally
  021 Head
  022 Forehead and frontal region
  023 Parietal region
  024 Occipital region
  025 Temporal region
  026 Scalp, generally
  027 Face, generally
  028 Cheek
  029 Chin

9 Diseases of the nervous system
 91 Coverings
  Meninges, cerebro-spinal
  910 Meninges, cerebral, combined
    regions
     Specify:
    Fronto-parietal
    Fronto-temporal
    Parieto-temporal
    Parieto-occipital
    Occipito-temporal
  910.1 Frontal
  910.2 Parietal
  910.3 Temporal
  910.4 Occipital
  910.5 Falx cerebri
  910.6 Falx cerebri, fronto-parietal
  910.7 Falx, cerebri, occipital
  910.8 Tentorium, upper surface
  910.9 Tentorium, lower surface
  910.10 Orbital
  910.11 Cerebellar
    etc.

Diseases of the Teeth and Gums

613 Teeth
614 Alveoli
615 Gums
  – 0 Diseases due to prenatal in-
    fluences
613 – 011 Absence of (unerupted)
    teeth
613 – 075 – Dentia praecox
613 – 031 Supernumerary tooth
613 – 077 Congenital fusion of teeth
613 – 1471 Hutchinson's teeth
  – 1 Diseases due to infection
    (lower forms)
613 – 100.0 Periodontal cyst;
    apical granuloma
613.1 – 190 Pericementitis
613.2 – 190 Pulpitis
614 – 100 Pyorrhoea Alveolaris
614 – 100.2 Alveolar abscess
615 – 100 Gingivitis
  – 1 – 4 Diseases due to trauma
    or physical agents
613 – 409 Avulsion or extraction of
    teeth, etc.

Excerpt from the Classification of Diseases as Adopted by the Massachusetts General Hospital and Other Hospitals

Main Classifications

1. Specific Infection Diseases. General Diseases
2. Diseases due to Animal Parasites
3. Diseases of Metabolism
4. Diseases Peculiar to Infancy
5. Diseases Due to Physical Agents
6. Poisonings. Intoxications
7. Tumors, Benign and Malignant
8. Congenital Malformations
9. Injuries
10. Special Skin Diseases
11. Diseases of the Circulatory System
12. Diseases of the Lymphatic System
13. Diseases of the Blood and Blood-Forming Organs
14. Diseases of the Ductless Glands
15. Diseases of the Nervous System
16. Diseases of the Bones, Joints, Muscles, Tendons, and Fascia
17. Diseases and Injuries of the Eye and Ear
18. Diseases of the Nose and Accessory Sinuses
19. Diseases of the Mouth, Lips, Cheeks, Pharynx, Tonsils, and Palate
20. Diseases of the Jaw, Teeth, and Gums
21. Diseases of the Tongue
22. Diseases of the Esophagus
23. Diseases of the Stomach
24. Diseases of the Intestines
25. Diseases of the Liver and Gall Ducts
26. Diseases of the Pancreas
27. Diseases of the Abdomen and Peritoneum in General
28. Diseases of the Rectum and Anus
29. Diseases of the Larynx
30. Diseases of the Trachea and Bronchi
    etc.

Main Divisions with Subdivisions

Section 6. Poisonings. Intoxications.

6-66	Absinthe poisoning
6-66	Alcohol poisoning
6-66	Alcoholism. State whether acute, or chronic
6-175	Botulism
6-175	Cheese poisoning
6-175	Creatoxismus (Meat poisoning)
6-66	Dipsomania
6-175	Fish poisoning
6-175	Fish venom poisoning
6-175	Ice cream poisoning
6-68	Lathyrism
6-175	Milk poisoning
6-175	Mushroom poisoning
	Poisoning, accidental, from inhalation of gases. State agent
6-181	Acetylene
6-181	Ammonia
6-181	Anesthetic (for operation)
6-181	Carbon dioxide
6-181	Carbon monoxide
6-181	Chloroform
6-181	Ether
6-181	Illuminating gas
6-181	Marsh gas
6-181	Nitrogen-oxides
6-181	Sewer gas
6-181	Sulphuretted hydrogen
6-181	War gases. State agent if known
6-181	Other accidental poisonings from gases. State agent
	Poisonings, acute. State agent
6-177	Acetanilide
6-177	Arsenic
6-177	Benzol
6-177	Cocaine
6-177	Cyanide
6-177	Fulminate of mercury
6-177	Lead
6-177	Magnesium sulphate
6-177	Mercury
6-177	Morphia
6-177	Opium etc.

X-Ray Files.—X-ray files present a problem because they are so heavy when filed in cabinets that equipment has to be doubly reinforced to stand up under the weight. Then the films come in different sizes which may require different-sized cabinets to house them without wasting space. The sizes range from 6½" x 3½" which fit into bill-sized cabinets to 14" x 17" which require specially constructed oversize cabinets. Films are filed by number. Index cards by the patient's name not only give the numbers of the films but may also carry a letter to signify the size cabinet in which the film is filed: 6½" x 8½" film numbers may all be preceded by the letter A while 14" x 17" films may be designated by letter F, etc.

Stout envelopes for protecting the films are essential. These may be designated merely by patient's name and number or may carry an elaborate description of patient and film.

Importance of Complete Hospital Records.—The value of hospital records lies in their accuracy, up-to-dateness, and completeness. Short cuts and superficial methods in filling out records destroy their purpose. And just because of their completeness they must be considered inviolable. A good record, therefore, requires the cooperation of the physician, the record clerk who is insistent on its completeness and responsible for its loan, and the record committee of the medical staff that reviews records frequently.

Some hospitals find it advantageous to keep the record room open day and night.

BIBLIOGRAPHY

American College of Surgeons, Case Records and Their Use, Mayo Clinic, Rochester, Minn.

Chapter 24

FILING IN AN ENGINEERING FIRM

Drawing Files.—Drawings, tracings, and usually blue-prints are separated from other types of papers first because of their use and also because of their size. Original drawings and tracings should not be folded, although blueprint copies may for convenience be folded to letter size and may be filed with correspondence and orders. The numeric method of arrangement is the most satisfactory for this type of record, the number being assigned from the job in a contractor's office or from the order in a manufacturing office. In an architect's or contractor's office each building "job" or piece of work is given a number or title and under each job the drawings are numbered consecutively. 72–18 means job 72 and the 18th drawing on that job. It is usually necessary to consult a drawing both from the standpoint of the specific job and from the standpoint of the particular type of drawing. Therefore, a card index is maintained by customer's name. There may also be a card index by type of drawing, as ovens, carrying customer name and file number. Until a contract has been formally signed, a job or project does not receive a number. Preliminary drawings are filed under a temporary file number preceded by the letter P for prospect. When the contract is signed the papers are transferred to the permanent file and given a permanent number.

Equipment for housing drawings, tracings, and blueprints are vertical cabinets, shallow drawers, racks, and frames. Up to size $12\frac{1}{4}''$ x $15\frac{7}{8}''$ such papers may be filed on edge in standard vertical cabinets. Larger blueprints may be folded and kept in cabinets; this is a convenient method of filing, although folding causes wear at the folds. Specially constructed mammoth vertical cabinets may be secured for drawings 48″ x 36″ or smaller. A compression system in each drawer increases the capacity for filing small drawings. A compression guide is made of pressboard, the springs of highly tempered spring wire. From one single sheet of tissue paper to 500 sheets of paper can be placed between two compression guides without becoming misplaced. These guides are especially useful in a drawer where the contents to be filed are thinner along one side of the drawer than the other, as in this case some of the springs in the guides compress more than the other and give equal compression even under these conditions.

FIG. 106.—Compression Guide for a Drawing File

Filing drawers may also be equipped with four folders per pocket and fourteen pockets to a drawer. 2800 tracings may be filed per drawer; 2100 blueprints per drawer; 1050 photographs mounted on cloth; 1680 photographs not mounted; 1400 architectural plates.

Flat shallow drawers come as large as 50 inches in depth and 72 inches wide. A hood at the back of the drawer under which the back edge of the paper slips and a hinged compressor at the front, which can be lifted at will, prevent the ends of large sheets from curling. Papers to be filed in these wide drawers should have the title and description matter placed at the bottom. This permits finding the needed sheet quickly and removing it from the drawer without pulling out the drawer farther than to lift up the compressor.

Sometimes drawings are rolled and thrust into racks provided for the purpose. Papers soil and wear much more quickly under this method of storage than when kept in cabinets. On each roll of drawings should be hung a tag wrapper of linen, on one side of which should be listed the drawings contained in the roll, on the reverse side the numbers of the drawings as they are taken out. This method of filing drawings and blueprints is the most economical.

Cabinets have been constructed for drawings with double wall construction and lined between inner and outer walls with asbestos to protect papers against loss or damage. The contents are entirely suspended in space. Such a cabinet holds 5400 tracings with space for 54 or more folders. Not over 200 tracings can be stored and conveniently handled in a flat drawer described above, so that a cabinet equals about 30 drawers. The folders which hold the tracings are double folded at top edge for extra strength and are scored for expansion. Drawings are filed with face toward the rear side of the folder which brings the index of the drawings in the upper right-hand corner and the drawing right side up. Index labels under the cover carry the serial numbers of the folder.

Obsolete drawings should have the date of obsolescence recorded on the back and the drawing number that supersedes it. The drawing should be removed to a special file.

Research Files.—The research or data file invariably found in an engineering office is arranged by subject. Instead of each engineer retaining his own data, all this material should be pooled and properly indexed. In addition to an index on cards it is a good plan for the indexer to have typed on sheets of paper the headings of the main subjects for quick reference by the engineers. Since such subject matter is highly technical, the indexing must be done with care so as to prevent overlapping.

Benches	Charging equipment	Conveyors
Buckets	Dump buckets	Cupolas
Car pullers	Wishbone	

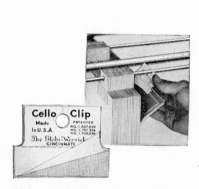

FIG. 107.—Maps and Plan Files Used in Engineering Firm (Globe-Wernicke Co. and Shaw-Walker Co.)

An alphabetical method of arrangement of subjects is the simplest, with blank insert guides for each of the main subjects, as shown above, at the left of the drawer and folder tabs at right.

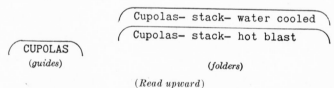

Cupolas– stack– water cooled

Cupolas– stack– hot blast

CUPOLAS
(guides)

(folders)

(Read upward)

FIG. 108.—Tabs for Alphabetic Data File

Engineers often maintain a file of catalogs. The handling of these has been described in detail in Chapter 13. They should be kept in bookcases, or in vertical filing cabinets, backs up. A satisfactory method of classifying is to number each one consecutively as it is received and to make out two cards for the index: one by vendor's name and the other by subject.

Shop Papers.—Blueprints and factory copies of orders are often illegible when passing through the factory because of the oil and dirt which have been accumulated on them. Cellophane envelopes open at one end and into which such papers can be slipped before being sent to the shop have been found an excellent means of protecting the contents while they remain visible. The envelopes can be used again and again.

Chapter 25

FILING IN AN ADVERTISING AGENCY

Clients' File—Alphabetic.—The most important file in an advertising office is that pertaining to the client. It is arranged alphabetically by name with important customers emphasized by means of special guides.

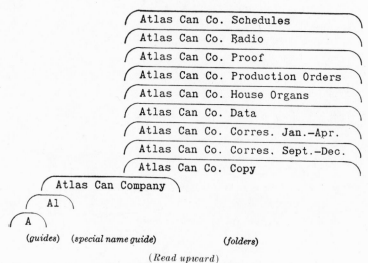

(guides)   *(special name guide)*   *(folders)*

(Read upward)

Fig. 109.—Tabs of Clients' File in Advertising Agency

In the moderate-sized advertising office each client's file contains a series of folders:

Copy.

Correspondence, memos, telegrams arranged in date order which if bulky may be divided by months.

Data including copy ideas and criticisms.

House organs.

Production orders filed by number of order. This is the history of advertising and refers to billing chiefly.

Proof.

Radio including correspondence with artists. Filed by date of program and subdivided further by:

> Script.
> Music.
> Timing.

Schedules.

Departmental Arrangement of Files.—In the larger offices it is preferable to segregate the production orders, proofs, copy, and radio material from the central file, and although continuing the arrangement by client's name, have them filed in the departments referring to them most frequently:

1. The Production Orders, used most frequently by the billing and service departments, should be filed conveniently near those departments. Often they are kept in binders.

2. The Proof file should be kept near the service, production, and creative (copy writers) departments. They should be filed by month. Sometimes each advertisement receives a proof number which is used for checking the billing. In that event the proofs are filed by client's name and then by number.

3. Since the Copy file is comprised of ideas provided by the agency to the copy writers the latter should have convenient access to these records.

4. The Radio and Television departments are usually highly specialized departments and thus often retain their files.

The Publication file is arranged by state, town, and name of papers. The home office address is used. The *Saturday Evening Post* correspondence is filed under Philadelphia even though originating in Chicago. This file contains correspondence, promotional and market data received from publishers. Sometimes rate cards, market studies, and circulation analyses are included. Occasionally rate cards are put in a separate card file and arranged geographically for quick reference.

The Insertion Order file is arranged by name of client, state, city, name of paper, dates of insertion. (Atlas Can Company, Alabama, Montgomery, Daily News, November 3, 5, 6, 7.)

The Acceptance slip is usually a duplicate copy of the Insertion order stamped "accepted" by the publication and filed geographically. Sometimes it is kept in a binder.

Miscellaneous File.—The Miscellaneous file contains all correspondence except that written to clients or to publications. It includes letters to and from banks, stationers, applications for positions, etc. It is set up by name with special folders for those names for which half a dozen or more papers have accumulated.

Picture File.—A Picture file assembled for the use of the artists is set up by subject in vertical cabinets. Like any other subject file it must be cross referenced in detail. The subjects may be arranged alphabetically but a decimal system has been found to have merit. An outline follows:

000　ADVERTISING CAMPAIGNS
　010
　020
　030
　040　　Proofs kept in conference room

100　ARTISTS AND THEIR WORKS
　110　　Individual artists and their works, including their portraits. Artist arranged alphabetically by surname. Includes artists of all times and all countries. All reproductions of their works.

200　PORTRAITS OF MEN, WOMEN, AND CHILDREN (alphabetically by name or order)
　210　　Gods, goddesses, and mythological characters
　220　　Biblical characters, religious orders
　230　　Noted men and women
　240　　Children
　250　　Special groups

260   Races
270   Fairies, monsters, giants, and legendary characters
280
290

>   For Indians see 970; for workers in various occupations, see
>   the occupations; for costumes see 640; for peoples of various
>   lands see 900.

300   HUMAN RELATIONS (SOCIOLOGY)
310   Religious
320   Family
330   Government
340   Political
350   Army, customs
360   Associations and institutions, insurance, charitable, etc.
370   Amusements
380   Holiday customs, Christmas, etc. (arrange alphabetically)
390   Customs, popular life

400

500   NATURAL SCIENCE
510   Mathematics and Astronomy
520
530   Physics
540   Chemistry
550   Physical features of the earth, etc. Not art views—coasts,
        glaciers, icebergs, mountains, plains, rocks, storms, etc. (arrange
        alphabetically by feature)

560
570
580   Plant life
590   Animal life

600   USEFUL ARTS
610   Materia Medica
620   Engineering
630   Agriculture
640   Domestic Economy
650   Commercial and Business Lines
660   Transportation
670   Manufactured Items and the process of manufacture both hand
        made and machine made of those items not already provided for

700   FINE ARTS
710   Landscape gardening, parks, lake fountains, arbors, etc.
720

730 Sculpture—for gods and goddesses see 210
740 Drawing, decoration
750 Painting
760 Engraving
770 Photography
780 Music—arrange all musical instruments alphabetically
790 Literature—books, manuscripts, etc.

800 ARCHITECTURE
810 Architectural construction. Foundations, walls, piers, columns, floors, ceilings, doors, windows, gates, grills, etc. (arrange alphabetically by name of part)
820 Business. Banks, garages, stores, factories, hotels, transportation and storage. (arrange alphabetically)
830 Ecclesiastic. Cathedrals, chapels, churches, monasteries, mosques, temples. (arrange alphabetically)
840 Education and scientific. Academies, galleries, laboratories, libraries, museums. (arrange alphabetically)
850 Hospitals, Asylums, Institutions. For children, insane, sick, prisons, etc. (arrange alphabetically)
860 Public Buildings. Capitals, city halls, engines house, police, post office. (arrange alphabetically)
870 Recreational and amusement. Baths, cafes, amusement, swimming, boat houses, theaters. (arrange alphabetically)
880 Residences
890 Outbuildings. Barns, greenhouses, porter's lodge

900 SCENES IN OTHER LANDS
910 Flags, coats of arms
920 Prehistoric and ancient countries. (arrange alphabetically by name of country; under name of country alphabetically by name of city). Ancient architecture under 810
930

Modern Countries

940 Europe. (Arrange countries alphabetically. Arrange cities under countries alphabetically)
950 Asia
960 Africa
970 North America
980 South America
990 Oceanica and Polar regions

When such a system is used each picture is numbered according to the decimal scheme. When a considerable number of pictures accumulate under any one number, a letter of the alphabet is added to the decimal number as an aid in sorting and in finding those needed. The decimal classification is so planned that whenever a given subject develops so that it is desirable to keep the pictures for that given subject together, a special number may be given them, and they will then be in the right relative location. The decimal plan thus provides for changing subject matter and for a collection growing in size. At any time undesirable pictures may be withdrawn without affecting the number scheme.

This decimal arrangement may be used without a card index. If many cross references are required or the pictures indexed under several subjects instead of one, a card index is essential. A cross reference will be necessary if there is a second picture on the reverse side of the original one. The cross reference may be a colored sheet placed in the file folder.

Folders will be needed for the larger groups of pictures. Smaller groups can be collected within these folders by placing them within a folded blank sheet secured by a clip with the number marked on the outside for quick reference. A clip on the lower edge of all folders will keep contents from falling out of the folders. The tab of the folder should give the decimal number and the subject.

210   Greek Gods – Zeus

FIG. 110.—Tab on Decimal Setup for a Picture File

Oftentimes not only pictures but finished drawings, paintings, bits of hand lettering, borders, and initials have to be kept in some kind of systematic order. These are difficult to classify because of the variety of ways in which they can be asked for. The customer's name and some such cryptic designation in a card index as "Man offering Camel to acquaintance in hotel lobby" might not always be sufficient. A camera has been the answer to such filing problems. Before any painting or drawing is filed, it is taken to the photographic bureau, placed under big carbon-arc lamps, and a small reduction picture is made of it. These thumbnail prints should be uniform, measuring perhaps $1\frac{3}{4}''$ over all and should be pasted to a card perhaps 11" wide and 9" deep, ruled on both sides. Each card might contain 24 blocks, $1\frac{3}{4}''$ square, under each of which is a horizontal panel, $\frac{3}{8}''$ wide. In the squares are pasted the miniature prints and under them the drawing number is written in ink. This number corresponds with the one shown in the rubber-stamped panel on the back of the drawing itself. At the top upper left is typed the name of the customer; at the top upper right, the month and year.

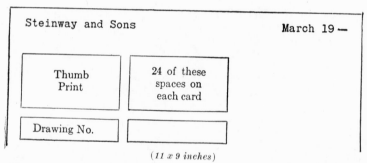

(11 x 9 inches)

Fig. 111.—Card Bearing Small Reproduction of Drawings in Advertising Agency.

A letter may precede the drawing-number to indicate divisions by size of drawing, for convenience in storing. For instance, some paintings may be on canvases as big as billboards, yet the little thumb-nail prints give perfect identification. Notations on the back of the card may indicate a more or less permanent disposition of a painting or drawing.

When a writer, production man, or layout man wants a drawing, he goes to the cabinet holding the cards required to catalog every drawing, and picks out the one he wants by number. It is then charged out to him.

INDEX